International Perspectives on Business Innovation and Disruption in the Creative Industries

Film, Video and Photography

Edited by

Robert DeFillippi

Professor of Strategy and International Business, Sawyer Business School, Suffolk University, USA

Patrik Wikström

Principal Research Fellow, ARC Centre of Excellence for Creative Industries and Innovation, Queensland University of Technology, Australia

Edward Elgar

Cheltenham, UK • Northampton, MA, USA

Published by
Edward Elgar Publishing Limited
The Lypiatts
15 Lansdown Road
Cheltenham
Glos GL50 2JA
UK

Edward Elgar Publishing, Inc.
William Pratt House
9 Dewey Court
Northampton
Massachusetts 01060
USA

A catalogue record for this book
is available from the British Library

Library of Congress Control Number: 2014937098

This book is available electronically in the ElgarOnline.com
Business Subject Collection, E-ISBN 978 1 78347 534 6

ISBN 978 1 78347 533 9

Typeset by Servis Filmsetting Ltd, Stockport, Cheshire
Printed and bound in Great Britain by T.J. International Ltd, Padstow

Contents

v

Contributors

Sophie De Vinck, iMinds-SMIT, Vrije Universiteit Brussel, Brussels, Belgium

Robert DeFillippi, Suffolk University, Boston, USA

Colette Dumas, Suffolk University, Boston, USA

Nadine Escoffier, UCLA Anderson School of Management and MCIS Agency, Los Angeles, USA

Natàlia Ferrer-Roca, Victoria University of Wellington, New Zealand

Angus Finney, MA course director, Exeter University and the London Film School, UK

Ken Hung, Suffolk University, Boston, USA

Pat Hunt, Suffolk University, Boston, USA

Rosemary Kimani, Global Business Director, eYeka, France

Axel Kwok, Independent documentary producer, Hong Kong and China

Tuen-Yu Lau, University of Southern California, Los Angeles, USA

Seppo Leminen, Laurea University of Applied Sciences, Espoo and Aalto University School of Business, Department of Marketing, Helsinki, Finland

Sven Lindmark, iMinds-SMIT, Vrije Universiteit Brussel, Brussels, Belgium

Mary Elizabeth Luka, Concordia University, Montreal, Canada

Bill McKelvey, UCLA Anderson School of Management, Los Angeles, USA and Kedge Business School, Marseilles, France

Lucia Naldi, Jönköping University, Sweden

Yannig Roth, Université Paris 1 Panthéon-Sorbonne, Paris, France

Pierre Roy, University of Montpellier, France

Laia Sánchez, Communication Sciences, Universitat Autonoma de Barcelona, Spain

Artur Serra, i2cat, Barcelona, Spain

Sergio Sparviero, University of Salzburg, Austria

M. Bjørn von Rimscha, University of Zurich, Switzerland

Naoki Wakabayashi, Kyoto University, Japan

Mika Westerlund, Carleton University, Sprott School of Business, Ottawa, Canada

Patrik Wikström, Queensland University of Technology, Brisbane, Australia

Jin-Ichiro Yamada, Osaka City University, Japan

Masaru Yamashita, Aoyama Gakuin University, Japan

Introduction

Robert DeFillippi and Patrik Wikström

The creative industries are particularly fecund empirical fields for investigating the processes of business innovation and disruption. The creative industries are some of the fastest growing sectors in many economies (European Commission, 2001; OECD, 2006; United States Census Bureau, 2010) and thus are worthy of study in their own right. Additionally, the study of the creative industries affords insights into how we understand the current economic transformation towards knowledge-based economies more broadly. The transformation toward knowledge-based economies has been foreshadowed by the transformation of creative industries such as publishing, film, video, photography, music and so on.

This volume focuses on industries associated with imagery, both moving and still images. Thus, this volume concerns those industries that are based on still imagery (Stock Photography) and moving imagery (Film, Video). Each of these image media technologies and associated industries has experienced a similar set of digital disruptions and related industry transformations, which we will briefly highlight in this introduction and which are detailed in the chapters of this volume.

DRIVERS OF DIGITAL DISRUPTION

Franklin (2012) characterizes digital disruption as the clash between exponential rates of technological change on the one hand, and incremental rates of change in society, economics, politics and law in the disrupted industries. Long-established firms in the video, film, photography and television industries have witnessed dramatic changes in how their imagery is captured, edited, aggregated and distributed. These technology-based disruptions have been accompanied by disruptions in traditional business models (including pricing and intellectual property monetization), cost structures and value propositions that matter to a digitally native audience of consumers. Each of these drivers of digital disruption will be briefly summarized below.

Hardware and Software for Image Capture, Editing and Distribution

During the past thirty years image capture hardware (photograph and moving image cameras) have evolved from analogue (physical film media) based to digital (electronic image sensor) devices, which have also evolved in the traditional hardware innovation trajectory of smaller, lighter, more mobile and easier to use devices. Associated with these hardware technology developments has been the improved visual quality and lower costs associated with employing portable cameras to shoot still or moving imagery. Consequently, cost and learning barriers to entry have fallen and more amateurs and independent professionals are able to shoot quality imagery at much lower costs than professional photographers, videographers and cinematographers were incurring a few years ago. The consequence of these developments is that digital production is faster and tends to be cheaper than analogue production (von Rimscha et al., 2014 in this volume).

The same technology trends for image-capturing hardware apply to the digital revolution in software for image editing. As a result, more amateur and independent visual artists are able to edit their own work and to prepare finished, post-production editions of their camera work without needing to outsource their work to an expensive editing service provider. Again this development speeds the post-production editing process while lowering costs of editing.

Lastly, the Internet enables content owners to deal directly with individual customers or groups at a significantly lower cost. Audiences can now access films at any time, any place, and on any device they want – both established ones (the cinema screen, the television screen) and new ones (the tablet, the smartphone). Additionally, the consumer no longer needs access to physical copies (whether they be home video tapes, DVDs, or Blu-ray discs) to access whatever film or video title is desired (De Vinck and Lindmark, 2014 in this volume). The unsettled question is the extent to which the Internet empowers content creators versus content aggregators in monetizing their owned content (see section on markets for hits and long tails below).

Evolution of Intellectual Property Regimes

As media-based industries have been digitized, the intellectual property regimes governing digital rights ownership have also evolved. For instance, new legislations such as the United States' Digital Millennium Copyright Act of 1998 have allowed Internet service providers across the world to avoid liability from posting copyrighted (pirated) works as long as they removed such materials when requested to do so by copyright owners of pirated materials. Some observers suggest that many online distribution companies have taken advantage of the allure of pirated material on their websites as a means to attract users and they view the marginal costs of take down notices trivial in relation to the advantages of posting content with or without copyright reimbursement to the content creators (Levine, 2011). More generally, Levine (2011) argues that the best industry profit sanctuaries or profit centres are migrating from the traditional content publishers (movie production studios, television production studios, photography studios) to these online content aggregators and distributors (e.g. Netflix, YouTube).

Another example of evolving intellectual property regimes is the Creative Commons licence, whereby the binary 'yes versus no' rights choices of traditional copyright are replaced by a continuum of rights to use copyrighted content. These new copyright regimes are inspiring new business models to capitalize on more freely available creative content. For example, Michael Gubbins (2012) discusses Jamie King's VODO service, launched in 2009 and billed as 'free-to-share films available through BitTorrent', which has seized on the potential of P2P (peer-to-peer) network file-sharing to distribute content for free while soliciting donations, hoping that even a small percentage of payments could make a significant difference if they originate from a large enough audience.

Participatory Culture

A major development in a growing number of creative industries is the rise of a participatory culture in which media content consumers are engaging with media products and services as content evaluators, content producers and content co-creators (Jenkins, 2006). A key consideration in participatory culture is the altered sensibilities of a new generation of media consumers who are digital natives and accustomed since childhood to actively participate in both the consumption and creation of their media experiences. Moreover, this is a generation that is accustomed to sharing their media creations and media experiences with others online.

Social media websites have created opportunities for specific media consumers to share their evaluations of media offerings with anyone who has access to the website. Indeed, some commercial websites (e.g. Amazon) incorporate consumer reviews and recommendations in their service offerings. However, the toolkit of digital media production and editing now empowers consumers to actively create and contribute their own content as alternatives or supplements to professionally produced media content. Again, websites have arisen to provide platforms for passionate amateur (and calculating professional) content creators to share their still imagery (e.g. Flickr) or moving imagery content offerings (e.g. YouTube). Lastly, a number of firms are now actively inviting audiences to co-create content with them (e.g. Amazon Studio). This type of co-production will be detailed further in the subsequent discussion of crowd-sourcing and co-creation.

INDUSTRY TRANSFORMATIONS

These external environmental shocks or disruptions are resulting in the corresponding industries undergoing transformations in a variety of practices as presented below.

The Rise of Crowd-Funding and Crowd-Sourcing

Crowd-funding is a new form of venture financing by creative industry entrepreneurs as an alternative or supplement to traditional (equity and debt based) forms of venture finance. Luka (2014 in this volume) defines crowd-funding as Internet- and digital-technology-based crowd-sourced funding activities which include the creation and growth of specific virtual social networks ('assemblages') of people who provide resources for cultural production. Typically, the cultural entrepreneur posts an Internet-based call for voluntary financial contributions on a crowd-funding web platform, which in turn links that entrepreneur funding seeker with potentially interested parties willing to pledge relatively small individual cash contributions to the crowd-funded project within the stipulated time period of the campaign. The fund seeker indicates in the call an overall financial fund-raising goal for the period of the campaign. Crowd-funding contributors typically receive some small gift or recognition but not equity ownership in the projects they fund.

The crowd-funding market has grown extremely quickly in its first five years (2008–13), with hundreds of websites offering platforms for crowd-funding projects. Two high-profile crowd-funding websites Kickstarter (www.Kickstarter.com) and IndieGoGo (www.IndieGoGo.com) are illustrative. Luka (2014) details in this volume the role of crowd-funding in supporting independent film projects.

A second related development in creative industries is crowd-sourcing, defined by Jeff Howe as 'the act of a company or institution taking a function once performed by employees and outsourcing it to an undefined (and generally large) network of people in the form of an open call' (Howe, 2006). Crowd-sourcing includes a process similar to crowd-funding: a company posts a problem online, a crowd of individuals offer solutions to the problem, the winning ideas are selected and awarded some form of financial (prize) and non-financial (invitation to work with company on implementing proposed solution) compensation, and the company uses the output for its own financial and non-financial gains (Brabham, 2008).

Technology advances in digital communication and web-based connectivity made it possible for any organization or individual to broadcast a call for content and to receive this content and assess, select and aggregate that content for subsequent dissemination to prospective users of the content. Crowd-sourcing has been employed in a range of creative industries to both access content and to edit that content. Examples found within this volume include video advertising (Roth and Kimani, 2014), film making (Escoffier and McKelvey, 2014 and Ferrer-Roca, 2014 in this volume), photography (DeFillippi et al., 2014 in this volume) and television (Leminen et al., 2014 in this volume).

Digital Platforms for Content Aggregation and Distribution

The Internet and its associated Web 2.0 tools for communications, connectivity (community) and commerce (Angus and Thelwall, 2010) are putting the aggregator (e.g. Google, Amazon) at the centre of content distribution. Moreover, the most web savvy aggregators are developing digital platforms that can collect and distribute a wide range of digital content from a variety of sources, both internal and external. These platforms are developing APIs (Application Programming Interfaces) that allow both digital content suppliers and buyers to conduct their respective transactions with the aggregator with ease.

An old nostrum of creative industries was that content was king. The evidence from a number of creative industries suggests that the possession of content is paramount but that there is no requirement that the aggregator create their own content. Moreover, digital customers are agnostic as to where they view their content (on TVs, computers, iPads or iPhones) and thus it is becoming increasingly important for content creators and content aggregators to distribute the content across multiple content consumption platforms. Recent research has identified an emerging and powerful set of globally focused online distributors of film and television, such as Google/YouTube, Apple, Amazon, Yahoo, Facebook, Netflix and Hulu who are also commissioning content in competition with film studios and television broadcasters (Cunningham and Silver, 2013).

Some independent content creators are attempting to deliver their content directly to these content consumption platforms without the services of the large digital content aggregators and distributors. This form of disintermediation is occurring to varying degrees in creative industries and bears closer examination in the industries covered in this volume (see Finney, 2014 in this volume).

Markets for Hits and Long Tails

Film making, video and other entertainment-based industries have often been characterized as markets for hits insofar as a relatively small percentage of all creative offerings make substantial profits and revenues in comparison to the paltry returns on the vast majority of creative offerings (Caves, 2002). This market structure has been employed to explain the blockbuster strategy of Hollywood film producers, and the frequent reliance upon well-known franchises based on earlier success in other genres, such as books, video games and comic books, upon which to appeal to the franchise's installed base of enthusiastic fans.

By contrast, Anderson (2006) argues that the proliferation of inexpensive digital technology for storing, accessing and disseminating digital media products significantly lowers the aggregate costs of capturing sales from many small markets (micro niches). This so-called *long tail* scenario argues that all creative projects can generate some market returns due to their ability to capture sales from very small and specialized appreciative audiences. A number of chapters in this volume will be exploring the opportunities for small independent creative content suppliers to succeed by developing more intimate, social media-based relationships with their audiences and to have these audiences and fan bases to participate both in the crowd-funding of their enterprises and in the co-creation of the creative offering. It is an open question whether such long tail innovations related to crowd-funding and crowd-sourcing can be a significant opportunity for independent content creators and producers serving smaller niche audiences and if such innovations will open up an alternative to the market for hits and blockbuster strategies of mainstream creative industry studios.

Collaborative Alliances

As the barriers previously separating various creative industry sectors collapse, it becomes challenging for creative firms to decide against whom to compete and with whom to collaborate. The digital convergence observed in so many media-based creative industries has challenged traditional industry analyses based upon well-defined industry boundaries and industry value chains (Porter, 1985). This volume examines some of the more dynamic forms of collaborative alliances and value chain restructuring underway within the film, video and photography industries.

Evidence from the Japanese film industry suggests the increasing use of film production consortia consisting of participating companies spanning multiple industries (Wakabayashi et al., 2014 in this volume). The prevalence and role of such strategic alliances and partnerships to collectively cope with the competitive challenges of diffuse creative industry boundaries is an area deserving further empirical examination.

CHAPTERS IN THIS VOLUME

The chapters in this volume provide a rich and diverse account of the transformation and disruption processes discussed above. The digital disruptions and industry transformations are examined in a wide range of country contexts, including Australia, Canada, China, Croatia, France, Germany, Ireland, Italy, Japan, New Zealand, Norway, Spain, Sweden, Switzerland, the United Kingdom and the USA. These country contexts are the focus of both country-specific studies and explicit comparative studies of the same practices across various subsets of the above country contexts.

Methodologically, our chapters include single industry case studies, comparative company case studies, and comparative industry case studies. The use of longitudinal case research in many of these chapters is supplemented by survey or interview research findings on specific practices of the participants in these studies. It is our perspective that longitudinal case studies are an exemplary mode of study for the emergence and evolution of industry transformations in response to digital disruptions to the industries and companies studied.

Theoretically, our chapters focus primarily on the phenomena of disruption (whether digital or otherwise) and how industry value chains, business models for value creation and modes of industry collaboration and competition are transformed. These types of transformations are the core focus of this volume and we are confident that the chapters to follow will make a substantial contribution to a deeper understanding of the drivers of these industry and firm transformations.

The 13 chapters have been structured into two parts: the first part consists of eight chapters that explore various aspects of the digital transformation of film industries in Asia Pacific, Europe and North America. The second part has a more narrow focus and consists of five chapters that all examine co-creation, crowd-sourcing and crowd-funding in the industries for film, video and photography.

Part I: Film Industry Disruption and Transformation

In the first chapter, Angus Finney explores the impact of digital technologies on the independent film industry's existing value chain. The chapter specifically delves into how, and in what ways the sector is being restructured as a result of these disruptive elements. In the next chapter, Natàlia Ferrer-Roca continues the examination of value chain transformation but she turns the focus to the film industry in New Zealand. By adopting Schumpeter's view of innovation and entrepreneurship she is able to demonstrate how new business opportunities can arise when technologies are used in an entrepreneurial and innovative way. The third chapter, by Tuen-Yu Lau and Axel Kwok, explores the transformation of the film industry in China during the first decade of this century. They show how China rapidly has become the world's second largest film market in a process driven both by regulatory and technological change. The fourth chapter remains in Asia and examines how film production consortia in Japan have been able to reignite and bring new life into the Japanese film industry. Naoki Wakabayashi, Jin-Ichiro Yamada and Masaru Yamashita discuss the unique features, competitive advantages, history and the roles of corporate producers in film production consortia.

The fifth chapter turns the focus from Asia to Europe. Bjørn von Rimscha, Patrik Wikström and Lucia Naldi present the findings from a study of how audio-visual production companies in eight European countries respond to disruptive change. The chapter concludes that many companies are reluctant to develop the new competences that are needed to cope with the digital transformation of their industries. Chapter 6 also uses Europe as its context and is specifically focused on the establishment of multiplex theatres in France during the 1990s. Pierre Roy explores a process that is particularly interesting since disruption is introduced by established firms and not by a challenger or an industry newcomer. The chapter discusses how a disruptive strategy actually can be a powerful way to reinforce leadership in a mature industry. The seventh chapter stays in the European film scene but explores how digital transformation of the film industries affects the ability of the European film industry to compete with the US-based industry. Sophie De Vinck and Sven Lindmark use a historical perspective and analyse how digital disruption has affected the position of the European film industry in the past. Sergio Sparviero applies a similar historical perspective in Chapter 8 in an analysis of the audio-visual media ecosystem in the US. Sparviero argues that institutional innovations have played an important role in forcing incumbent stakeholders to adapt and formulate new business strategies.

Part II: Co-Creation, Crowd-Funding and Crowd-Sourcing

Mary Elizabeth Luka opens the book's second part by exploring crowd-funding strategies among documentary film makers in Canada. Luka specifically examines the relationships among funders, creative producers and investors that can help or hinder the growth of crowd-funding as a financial and audience development strategy. In Chapter 10, Yannig Roth and Rosemary Kimani argue that the video advertising industry is under-going a fundamental change with the advent of a new set of intermediaries that they refer to as creative crowd-sourcing platforms. Based on a multiple case study methodology, they explain what role crowd-sourcing plays in the contemporary video advertising landscape.

Next, Nadine Escoffier and Bill McKelvey discuss the use of 'crowd-wisdom' as a way for film production companies to evaluate and generate new ideas. The chapter presents a case of how a film company has used the crowd to evaluate movies' market value before they are released to market. In Chapter 12, Robert DeFillippi, Pat Hunt, Colette Dumas and Ken Hung present the case of iStockphoto and Getty Images and how a series of digital technology advances in photography transformed the stock photography industry's value chain and the relationships between creative content contributors and microstock agencies. In the final chapter Seppo Leminen, Mika Westerlund, Laia Sánchez and Artur Serra report the findings from a study focused on users' roles in co-creating media content. The study shows that it is possible to open the culture of innovation to the general public by focusing on user-generated content and user-generated applications and services.

REFERENCES

Anderson, C. (2006). *The Long Tail: Why the Future of Business is Selling Less of More*. New York: Hyperion.

Angus, E. and Thelwall, M. (2010). 'Motivations for Image Publishing and Tagging on Flickr', in *Proceedings of the 14th International Conference on Electronic Publishing*, Hanken School of Economics, Helsinki, pp. 189–204.

Brabham, D.C. (2008). 'Moving the Crowd at iStockphoto: The Composition of the Crowd and Motivations for Participation in a Crowdsourcing Application', *First Monday* 13(6).

Caves, R. (2002). *Creative Industries: Contacts between Art and Commerce*. Cambridge: Harvard University Press.

Cunningham, S. and Silver, J. (2013). *Screen Distribution and the New King Kongs of the Online World*. London: Palgrave Macmillan.

DeFillippi, R., Hunt, P., Dumas, C. and Hung, K. (2014). 'Crowd Sourcing and the Evolution of the Microstock Photography Industry: The Case of iStockphoto and Getty Images', in DeFillippi, R. and Wikström, P. (eds), *International Perspectives on Business Innovation and Disruption in the Creative Industries: Film, Video and Photography*. Cheltenham, UK and Northampton, MA, USA: Edward Elgar.

De Vinck, S. and Lindmark, S. (2014). 'Innovation in the Film Sector: What Lessons from the Past Tell Us about Hollywood's Digital Future – and What That Means for Europe', in DeFillippi, R. and Wikström, P. (eds), *International Perspectives on Business Innovation and Disruption in the Creative Industries: Film, Video and Photography*. Cheltenham, UK and Northampton, MA, USA: Edward Elgar.

Escoffier, N. and McKelvey, W. (2014). 'Using "Crowd-Wisdom Strategy" to Co-create Market Value: Proof-of-Concept from the Movie Industry', in DeFillippi, R. and Wikström, P. (eds), *International Perspectives on Business Innovation and Disruption in the Creative Industries: Film, Video and Photography*. Cheltenham, UK and Northampton, MA, USA: Edward Elgar.

European Commission (2001). 'Employment Trends and Sectors of Growth in the Cultural Economy', Final report. European Commission DG Employment and Social Affairs.

Ferrer-Roca, N. (2014). 'Business Innovation in the Film Industry Value Chain: A New Zealand Case Study', in DeFillippi, R. and Wikström, P. (eds), *International Perspectives on Business Innovation and Disruption in the Creative Industries: Film, Video and Photography*. Cheltenham, UK and Northampton, MA, USA: Edward Elgar.

Finney, A. (2014). 'Value Chain Restructuring in the Film Industry: The Case of the Independent Feature Film Sector', in DeFillippi, R. and Wikström, P. (eds), *International Perspectives on Business Innovation and Disruption in the Creative Industries: Film, Video and Photography*. Cheltenham, UK and Northampton, MA, USA: Edward Elgar.

Franklin, M. (2012). 'Internet-enabled Dissemination: Managing Uncertainty in the Film Value Chain', in Iordanova, D. and Cunningham, S. (eds), *Digital Disruption: Cinema Moves On-line*. St Andrews: Dina Iordanova.

Gubbins, M. (2012). 'Digital Revolution: Active Audiences and Fragmented Consumption', in Iordanova, D. and Cunningham, S. (eds), *Digital Disruption: Cinema Moves On-line*. St Andrews: Dina Iordanova.

Howe, J. (2006). 'The Rise of Crowdsourcing', *Wired*, 14, available at: http://www.wired.com/wired/archive/14.06/crowds.html.

Jenkins, H. (2006). *Convergence Culture: Where Old and New Media Collide*. New York: New York University Press.

Leminen, S., Westerlund, M., Sánchez, L. and Serra, A. (2014). 'Users as Content Creators, Aggregators, and Distributors at Citilab Living Lab', in DeFillippi, R. and Wikström, P. (eds), *International Perspectives on Business Innovation and Disruption in the Creative Industries: Film, Video and Photography*. Cheltenham, UK and Northampton, MA, USA: Edward Elgar.

Levine, R. (2011). *Free Ride: How Digital Parasites are Destroying the Culture Business and How the Culture Business Can Fight Back*. New York: Doubleday Press.

Luka, M.E. (2014). 'Modes, Flows and Networks: The Promise of Crowdfunding in Documentary Filmmaking and Audience Development', in DeFillippi, R. and Wikström, P. (eds), *International Perspectives on Business Innovation and*

Disruption in the Creative Industries: Film, Video and Photography. Cheltenham, UK and Northampton, MA, USA: Edward Elgar.

OECD (2006). *International Measurement of the Economic and Social Importance of Culture*. Organization for Economic Co-operation and Development Statistics Directorate. Available at: http://www.oecd.org/std/na/37257281.pdf.

Porter, M. (1985). *Competitive Advantage: Creating and Sustaining Superior Performance*. New York: Free Press.

Roth, Y. and Kimani, R. (2014). 'Crowd-sourcing in the Production of Video Advertising: The Emerging Roles of Crowd-sourcing Platforms', in DeFillippi, R. and Wikström, P. (eds), *International Perspectives on Business Innovation and Disruption in the Creative Industries: Film, Video and Photography*. Cheltenham, UK and Northampton, MA, USA: Edward Elgar.

United States Census Bureau (2010). *United States Census Report 2010*. Available at: http://www.census.gov/2010census/.

Von Rimscha, B., Wikström, P. and Naldi, L. (2014). 'European Audio-Visual Production Companies Adapting to Strategic Challenges', in DeFillippi, R. and Wikström, P. (eds), *International Perspectives on Business Innovation and Disruption in the Creative Industries: Film, Video and Photography*. Cheltenham, UK and Northampton, MA, USA: Edward Elgar.

Wakabayashi, N., Yamada, J. and Yamashita, M. (2014). 'The Power of Japanese Film Production Consortia: The Evolution of Inter-firm Alliance Networks and Revival of the Japanese Film Industry', in DeFillippi, R. and Wikström, P. (eds), *International Perspectives on Business Innovation and Disruption in the Creative Industries: Film, Video and Photography*. Cheltenham, UK and Northampton, MA, USA: Edward Elgar.

PART I

Film industry disruption and transformation

1. Value chain restructuring in the film industry: the case of the independent feature film sector

Angus Finney

INTRODUCTION: THE CASE OF THE INDEPENDENT FILM SECTOR

Research and analysis using value chain models as they relate to the global film industry has predominantly focused on the American studio filmed entertainment system ('the Hollywood studios') rather than the independent[1] film sector (Bloore, 2009; Cave, 2000). An examination, however, of the impact that technological and social disruption is bringing to bear on the non-Hollywood film sector's value chain is timely and enlightening. The opportunity to develop both existing and new forms of content and distribution platforms is potentially transformational to many SME information businesses, entrepreneurs and creative individuals. This potential 'alternative sector' occupies a different yet connected space mapped out by the Hollywood studio system, with lessons for the creative economy gleaned through the examination of the independent film sector.

The global film industry's managers and players are currently grappling to understand how they fit into a restructuring marketplace and 'market space' (Rayport and Sviokla, 1996) that is increasingly complex and uncertain. Digital technological and social media change have given rise to a new landscape of changing formats, user-generated material, circulated via near-instant delivery systems available across multiple platforms. Whilst the traditional film format is anticipated to remain dominant at the cinema exhibition stage, creative skills and business entrepreneurs are currently adapting to a wider range of new media bases, platforms and delivery devices as the 'pull' digital entertainment economy increasingly commands both reach and economic scale.

The independent film sector's strength as a case site for research is due to a number of aspects. The independent film sector performs four key functions: (1) the sector is a key content provider for distribution, both to the six Hollywood studios and to independent distributors across more than 50 territories around the globe; (2) independent film accounts for a significant proportion of the sales and distribution market for English-language films (including the US independent production sector); (3) the sector dominates 'world cinema' and the production and distribution of local-language films, the popularity and profitability of which is growing in certain key territories and in particular Western Europe (Finney, 2010); (4) the talent base and entrepreneur-ecology, while fragmented and predominantly non-vertically structured, nevertheless offers considerable 'soft' skills, innovative trends and flexibility that could both cater for and inspire new digital entertainment markets if successfully tapped and stimulated through both private and public sector initiatives.

While these headlines set out a potential independent sector's counterweight to the studio vertically integrated oligopoly, one key aspect that defines the sector's culture is its high level of reliance on the 'individual' and the industry's own idiosyncratic 'network'. The role of talent (meaning specifically, individual writers, directors, producers, actors, production companies and entrepreneurs) and the means by which they interact has a direct impact on the independent film industry's architecture, creative opportunities within, and the shape of a new, emerging digital entertainment value chain model. As such, they can be seen as representing the 'human, intuition and experience based prescription', as opposed to the '*technical* value chain' (Hadida and Paris, 2013, italics added).

Digitization has eliminated some of the high sunk costs associated with film production, and distribution can be achieved through a new mix of old and new marketing techniques aided by the power of Internet search. However, leaping to the conclusion that disruption offers a panacea to the independent film-maker is too simplistic: are producers really less 'dependent' on public subsidy, finance/investment sources and distributors thanks to the falling production costs? Can they successfully bypass gatekeepers through multiple open-source routes to the market and their intended user base? The answers to these kinds of questions are more complex and nuanced than some academics have deduced to date (McPhillips and Merlo, 2008; Hilderbrand, 2010).

The impact of the current disruption and the issues it is raising about the creative economy is currently under discussion in both the scholarly literature and in media and creative industry practitioner circles. This chapter offers some insights into the changing dynamics taking place in the independent film sector, and forms part of a wider social and technological debate about the future of media and the creative economy.

THE SHAPE AND STRUCTURE OF THE INDEPENDENT FILM INDUSTRY AND ITS SIGNIFICANT CHARACTERISTICS

As a global research site, the film industry's shape, size and characteristics present a series of challenges for the researcher. The film market can be analysed from a horizontal perspective, which assists us in understanding global, multinational, and territory-by-territory strategies, and the respective values and potential competitive advantages offered by scale and reach. As such, the horizontal approach allows us a degree of 'macro' analysis, taking into account global trends, key territorial distinctions and, in the rare instance of an independent film that hits worldwide, an extraordinary penetration and super-returns resulting from *The King's Speech*-style universal exploitation. However, economic data points to the fact that the film industry is a failure-driven business, not a 'hit-driven' business, as practitioners tend casually to refer to it.

The film market can also be approached from a vertical perspective, which enables us to analyse specific film media characteristics and their relative values and roles within the film value and exploitation chain. Each film product is capable of being delivered and viewed a number of ways by the end user. Up until recently, and still predominant, is the sequentially-constructed 'window' exploitation chain shown in Table 1.1.

It is this chain, when analysed from vertical link-to-link, that helps us towards an understanding of how the revenue streams within the film business can be understood on a 'micro' basis. Film exploitation remains dependent on both the vertical and horizontal aspects. Up until recent times, it would be accurate to state that a film is nearly always released first in its domestic country of origin, and then subsequently exploited in additional territories. It was also accurate to state that a film is released first theatrically (if it succeeds in being booked in cinemas), and then through a sequence of 'windows', including DVD, pay TV and free TV.

Just as other associated media and information providers are losing control, the film industry's reliance on restricting user access, the creation of scarcity of access, and hence the control of pricing, is starting to collapse. There is a clear shift of power in the value chain. Changing technology and user demands are challenging the established 'windows' structure favoured by both the studios and all independent distribution incumbents.

Table 1.1   Historical window exploitation chain

Theatrical release →	DVD window →	Pay TV window →	Free TV window

Local audiences and communities are rising up, demanding culturally specific stories that explore their own communities (Tapscott and Williams, 2006).

Change has almost shot past much of the overall film industry: while studio incumbents struggle to turn their tankers around, the weaker independent players have also found themselves caught at the bottom of a V-shape: the current obsession with 3D – meaning higher ticket prices but also higher production costs; declining distribution advances (for example minimum guarantees that have historically been used to finance independent film production), a lack of bank appetite and lowering of expertise in lending and risk management, declining DVD revenues and free TV values, yet with no clear way to aggressively monetize emerging Video-On-Demand (VOD) and streaming. The studios are benefiting from new aggregators such as Amazon and Netflix, but independent companies lack the scale and volume to compete, at least to date.

The enduring strength of the independent sector's film value chain rests on its design and tacit understanding between players, which serves to combat uncertainty in the economic and risk management 'link' in the chain. Observers have argued that the value chain that connects the film producer/financier/seller/distributor exists in order to combat uncertainty: the film value chain model depends on conventions, where action is only rational between certain practitioners and is enabled through the use of evaluative frameworks that coordinate action and enable film-makers to operate under uncertainty. Such evaluative frameworks include budgets, financial plans, recoupment charts and sales estimates. Sales agents estimate the potential high and low prices that a film will sell for to a distributor in each territory around the world. These figures allow for coordinated action across segments of the value chain. Producers in turn depend on these estimates, combined with some pre-sales to test the commercial market appetite and pricing, alongside the 'reputation' and track record of the sales company attached. The sales company, or 'international distributor' has a historical and current understanding of what combination of prices it will attract in order to (a) service the production's ability to close its finance, and (b) contribute effectively to its own portfolio of product and ultimately capture value and profit for its own business operation (Biggart and Beamish, 2003; Franklin, 2012).

As the Internet starts to dominate both the support of theatrical film releases, but more importantly, all circulation and consumption options beyond the cinema, the context of existing evaluative frameworks can be questioned. Social media data for example is changing the relationship between upcoming product, appetite and performance. Terry Ilott, former director of the Cass Business School, City University London

Film Business Academy, has suggested that, given this level of disruption to traditional business-to-business middlemen and gatekeepers, the film industry will become less 'special' and more like other industries as larger parts of the value chain, freed from capacity and scarcity constraints and able to implement differential pricing based on a more direct relationship to the user, and thus enabled to take on so-called 'normal' commercial characteristics (Finney, 2010).

Convergence has placed the 'user' at the heart of any emerging business models, which are zeroing in on how well-informed consumers are using the functionality and content now available across the full range of devices, platforms and services that they own or receive. These new digital technologies have also concurrently shrunk and yet opened up key sections of the vertical chain model. Increasingly, films are distributed and circulated at different stages of the old value chain, and move on from there.

THE ESTABLISHED FILM VALUE CHAIN MODEL

The film value chain is a term that applies to all the various stages of creation, distribution and exploitation of product across the global film business. The primary products of the film industry are often described as a group or 'bundle' of rights. This group of related rights that constitutes a movie product can be broken down into three key parts: (1) the underlying rights; (2) newly created copyrights; and (3) exploitation rights. Before examining the broader implications of the film value chain, it is essential to ground the analysis in a legal and practical framework. The underlying rights to a film normally kick off in a pre-existing book, script (original or adapted), play or other source of material that has to be acquired, along with any underlying rights that are created or used within the film, including elements such as character, image, and music. These rights normally belong to third parties, and have to be legally acquired before they can be incorporated into a film.

Secondly, the right to utilize and exploit the work of writers, actors, directors and designers has to be acquired by legal contract. Writers, directors and creative artists normally are contracted through standard formatted contracts that are agreed across the industry.

Thirdly, it is often required that permissions must be sought and cleared from third parties – most notably when shooting on location. Service agreements have to be entered into for the use of studios, laboratories, visual effects houses, and so on. Once a film has completed production and post-production, an entirely new right is created: the film copyright. Other copyrighted elements may be included within the film, such as the soundtrack, costumes or characters. The film copyright and related copy-rights are then exploited by the licensing of various sales, distribution and merchandising rights to third parties active in film sales, distribution, exhibition, home entertainment, merchandising, prequels, sequels and other forms of ancillary exploitation.

This historical, entrenched structure has effectively withheld product from the market in a way that has suited the rights owner, licensor and creators, rather than the consumer/user. The copyright structure has also clashed with the 'open' Internet streaming of content via predominantly 'free' payment structures. Whilst subscription (Amazon, Netflix, iTunes) and ad-supported sites (YouTube, Facebook) are taking up the 'digital dime' slack, there is a fundamental mismatch between copyright structures and 'free' and 'open' information systems that has yet to be fully reconciled. The declining DVD revenues next to slow digital revenue growth are providing a challenge to film entrepreneurs keen to move away from a business model of 'uncertainty' to one that has a clear shot at sustainability.

The established structure and system for distributing independent films (see Table 1.2) is encountering a period of growing tension. There is rising pressure on the sales/territorial distributor relationship in the value chain, alongside escalating costs of marketing and distribution that have enabled the Hollywood studios to dominate theatrical distribution. Advances paid to acquire and distribute non-studio films have now dwindled to near extinction unless they are around the $10m plus budget level and have significant creative elements attached which need to confirm a combination of track record and a clearly intended market. Without pre-saleable elements such as stars, top directors or proven genre credentials (including the dominance of mainstream sequels, prequels, remakes, etc.), distributors have grown increasingly shy of paying advances to secure upcoming but yet-to-be-produced film product. The narrow, intensely competitive and studio-dominated theatrical window has also worked against the smaller, niche film that has traditionally struggled to find its audience in the first three weeks, let alone the first three days.

The long-existing approach of attempting to 'sell' films (which normally means 'licence') or minimum guarantees (i.e. advances against rights) in return for significant cash advances that in turn contribute towards repayment of the negative cost of the film or (in exceptional cases) take the film past break-even and into profit, is set for considerable change.

The growing importance of web streaming, supported for example by well-placed Google Ad Sense plugs, is in turn generating DVD sales but now, crucially, new streaming downloads. Messianic fervour often accompanies experiments that have worked: digital distribution 'is the difference between being able to pay the rent and not being able to pay the rent',

Table 1.2   The independent value chain model: from consumer to concept

FILM VALUE CHAIN MODEL (INDEPENDENT MODEL, BY ACTIVITY)

Element	Players	Support
Consumer	First time product is seen by end-user, and where true value can be assessed and realized. Time and money have been sunk at high level before this final contact with the consumer marketplace.	Media spend, press and publicity, social networking + traditional marketing tools
Exploitation	Exhibition/cinema release, DVD sales/rental, VHS, Sales/rental, pay-TV, Video on demand, Internet, Download, Free-TV, Syndication Library rights: ongoing exploitation opportunities for producer, financier; distributor's licence window. Remake, prequel, sequel rights + library sales.	Marketing by territory (distributor and separately by exhibitor)
Distributor	International sales agent; producer's rep; producer, Marketing and selling distribution rights and in return receiving commission.	Marketing By sales agent and international markets
Shoot/Post	Production company/Producer, Director, Cast, Crew, Studio Locations, Labs, Support services, Post Production, supervision, facilities. (Director, producer and financiers normally involved in final cut and sign-off of product.)	Marketing use of PR on shoot
Financing	Producer(s); Production company; package (including the script, director, cast, national and international pre-sales (if available), sales estimates, co-production, co-finance). Funds/partners, national subsidy finance, national broadcaster. Finance, equity, bank, gap finance, tax financing. Executive, Associate and Co-producers. Talent agent, talent manager, lawyers. Completion Bond. Insurance.	Lawyers, talent agents
Development	Concept, idea, underlying material producer (creative), Writer, development executive, script editor, development financier, agent, director (as developer with writer or as writer/director). Private equity rare at this stage.	Regional and national subsidy support and/or broadcaster support

explained film-maker Seth Caplan, whose *In Search of a Midnight Kiss* was heralded creatively, released theatrically by IFC in North America and won a Spirit Award. 'When it comes to indie films,' says Caplan, 'the drains are clogged. And what's been clogging them are these middlemen, these layers of sales agents and distributors, which soak up every cent on profitability. You just don't have that with digital' (Finney, 2010, p. 123). That sounds attractive, but the challenge of actually getting the film to its intended market without the aid of a globally focused international sales company and their network of distributors remains a significant challenge. Bucking the business-to-business stages of the existing value chain is neither simple nor straightforward.

THE PRESSURE AND SPEED OF CHANGE

The overall media environment, which includes film, television, music, games and user-generated content, is under considerable and increasing pressure, with many competitors for people's time, attention, money and loyalty. The production and distribution of audio-visual content in particular has been affected in the past decade by:

- technological change, including a considerable increase in bandwidth specifically within Western Europe and North America, but also many first and second world regions across the globe;
- audience fragmentation and migration;
- an increase in multi-tasking skills and multi-absorption of varying media simultaneously;
- a rise in social networking and associated user-generated content and collaboration;
- a rise in multi-channel, interactive broadcasting;
- an increase in populist, interactive programming involving the public as lead players and contestants;
- a change in payment/billing mechanisms;
- a rise in the public's ability to produce and distribute (often cost-free) their own creative endeavours, including music, words, photographs and video;
- an increase in file sharing and an associated increase in piracy;
- interchangeability between media, with decreasing and less clear boundaries between online networks, short films, recorded music, photos, etc.

The effect of the above changes has not in large part been driven by old style broadcasters and film-makers but by a range of new companies meeting consumer demands in ways the old systems did not (Finney, 2010). The supply-led to demand-led business trend is changing the exclusivity of existing suppliers and gatekeepers. And while broadcasters and film-makers have habitually referred to 'choice', what they usually mean is a choice of content. Films and programmes tend to be prototypical, one-offs that demonstrate little indication of future success. Hence the entertainment industries have downplayed retail management and failed to deliver customer service to a level that competitive *high street* brands have aimed to perfect. Control over distribution is now being forced to give way to retail branding and servicing power. Some have argued that 'share of mind' is the concept that captures the reality of the new market. . . replacing the conventional concepts of share of time and share of voice. The British Screen Advisory Council (BSAC) states that 'owners of mind have the power to decide what, when and how to pay attention to what is on offer. Producers and distributors have to maximise their share of mind, and monetise it' (Finney, 2010, p. 185). In conclusion, BSAC suggests that there is a new industry ecology emerging and that organizations in the market vary in terms of how successfully they are able to cope with the new conditions.

The new ecology consists of TV, film and video, the music industry, Internet Service Providers (ISPs like Orange, BT and Virgin), investors, computers, games and other sectors in puzzling and often volatile relationships. The new ecology is systemic in that it is not possible to isolate one niche from another. In order to make sense of what is happening, industry and regulators have to understand the new relationships, both of content and cash, between producers, distributors, users and re-users, as we have tried to do. There is a real danger that by focusing on preservation, it will be impossible to relish the new. Attack is often the best form of defence and always better than accepting failure.

All organizations have to work out how to establish a foothold in the new landscape. Revenues will be cannibalized as traditional business revenues begin to fail. 'We believe organisations that have a secure revenue base (e.g. the BBC) and newcomers that have no revenue base to cannibalise (e.g. Google) are the best placed' (Finney, 2010, p. 185).

DEVELOPING BUSINESS MODELS

Today's media incumbents are having considerable difficulty changing their own predispositions, assumptions and entrenched mindsets. Media companies creating, licensing and distributing Intellectual Property Rights (IPRs) have tended to rely on relatively complex business models, traditionally based on a mixture of advertising, subscription, licence fee (e.g.

Free TV), pay-per-view, sponsorship, sub-licensing and so on. None of these models necessarily placed the customer value proposition in poll position. And now the 'traditional' models are starting to either struggle, fail to adapt, acquire businesses they don't understand, or go bankrupt.

While there are key inherent dangers lurking in the bipolar positioning (where each side may well fail to see the future clearly), there are also positive areas of potential advancement. Specifically, barriers to entry for smaller and independent companies are lowering, and opportunities for creative talent to develop with fewer sunk-cost risks associated with physical production are promising. The arrival of a new, increasingly efficient market that is responding to the needs of new users provides for new commercial opportunities, which in turn also offer potential cross-media synergies for the entertainment industry, and lastly, but not least, the scope for interaction with other markets linked to core product, and able to be exploited and disseminated simultaneously across new platforms and accessed (and potentially paid for) by a myriad of user-friendly systems. Ultimately, the adoption of a more holistic approach towards IPR exploitation (in particular at the initial rights stage) and multi-platform promotion and circulation will be essential if the cost of new content is to be successfully amortized. Hardly new (the studios have been operating it for decades) is the much discussed '360 degree' model. In the 'future is now' multi-channel world, where the user has infinite choice, creative businesses need to compete not just against rival product, the maturing user-generated content and alternative entertainment providers, but with other non-media businesses competing for the user's 'share of mind' and marginal utility. This requires early consideration and assessment of all potential forms of exploitation, adoption and promotion of film in particular if the 'restructuring' value chain is to be mastered. How this fits with the kind of producer-entrepreneur who currently populates, for example, the UK independent film market, raises serious commercial questions.

'The 360-degree model only really makes sense if it is matched by a focus on brand, genre, talent and/or defined audience/community', explains Terry Ilott, former director of the Film Business Academy at Cass Business School. 'Drama does not lend itself to the 360-degree approach, yet it is what nearly all UK indie producers focus on. The 360-degree model also requires volume, which in turn means flexibility as to budgets, formats and platforms. Again, indie producers don't do volume.' Ilott goes on to underline recurring weaknesses in the producer value chain, as few production companies are appropriately resourced, few have business skills to match creative skills, and rarely is the independent film producer armed with equivalent knowledge and skill in television, games and new forms of content (Ilott, 2009).

Table 1.3   Integrated film value chain

Development	→	Financing	→	Production	→	Licensing-Distribution	→	Exploitation

Vertically integrated, multi-channel exploitation remains vital to the sustainability and commercial development of the independent film sector. New product has the potential to be positioned and accessed through a multiplicity of revenue channels. This strategy demands a certain level of knowledge of the market for each opportunity, but it is also possible to acquire this through a series of partnerships or joint ventures, something that is anathema to many SME-sized independent production-orientated outfits. By avoiding the integrated approach, such outfits are losing out from a direct relationship with their audience and the virtuous circle created as each strand of exploitation promotes and reinforces each other. True integration, however, is potentially more likely as the film value chain model starts to contract (see Table 1.3).

OPPORTUNITIES: THE NEW BATTLEGROUND

This author's work and this summarizing chapter explore key sections of the existing film value chain whilst noting where that chain is being restructured. It is clear that the early part of the chain will not face the same disruptive pressures that the later parts currently have to confront. Development and the production process remain constants, although formats and transmedia storytelling will start to have an impact on the selection process of material. Finance is definitely evolving and reacting to the uncertainty of digital revenue streams and the cannibalization of what used to be separate, controlled windows and profit pools, while distribution is facing a significant revolution.

The emerging film value chain (see Table 1.4) places the aggregator (e.g. Google, Amazon) at the centre of financing/distribution. We should watch out for consolidation and the emergence of 'super-independent' players that are linked to aggregators – who in turn control platforms and content

Table 1.4   The emerging film value chain

Producer	→	Aggregator	→	Consumer

Source: Finney (2010).

access – and are able to achieve scale and critical mass. These 'international distributors' will have the ability to release through third parties in appropriate theatrical territories, while concurrently exploiting their digitized libraries and new product on multiple digital outlets and platforms. In turn, the aggregators will have both a considerable impact and potential control over the industry's emerging structure.

However, it's not Google TV or Apple TV that are driving the filmed content business on new platforms. LoveFilm, the UK streaming service, was acquired by Amazon in 2011, while Netflix, the US-based subscriber movie service, has rolled out to numerous territories in 2011–12 and quickly overtook Apple's iTunes store as the largest VOD service by share (44 per cent of the market according to *The Guardian* newspaper, 11 June 2012). When the service moved into Canada in September 2010, it sprinted to a 20 per cent share of downstream Internet traffic during peak home Internet use during peak Internet hours across North America, compared to an 8 per cent share by Bit Torrent. Its launch in the UK in 2012 and anticipated global expansion will need to be matched by access to a compelling blend of new, high-end blockbusters, top TV programming and the cream of independent cinema if it is to service its subscribers and gain both loyalty and steeper membership rates to pay for that product.

The new information gatekeepers, including the 'open' face of Google and its acquired offspring YouTube and the 'closed' appliances of Apple (Wu, 2010), will play critical roles in determining how, which and if filmmakers and their consumers get access to what and, crucially, on what terms. The aggregator driven model is one that does not greatly encourage traditional film distributors. 'You're facing a situation where you make a film', explains Simon Franks, a successful entrepreneur and distributor, and chairman of Redbus.

> Let's say it does £5m at the UK box office, which is always the hurdle to profitability in most films, and there is still a prints and advertising loss at that level. But now you need to make all your prints and advertising back and pay for the film and the profit just from one source, which is the second and now only window. We don't know yet who that might be. I don't like the idea of that. I don't like the idea of having to rely on just one window and one entity in order to become profitable (Finney, 2010).

Since Franks made this analysis, it's important to note that the UK currently now has no less than four S-VOD (Subscription Video On Demand) operators now competing in the market: LoveFilm (acquired by Amazon in 2011); Netflix (launched in early 2012); Curzon-On-Demand (art house); and HMV-On-Demand, although the latter is struggling to build access to new product and has a limited library.

It is the potential tightening of the film value chain, whereby the producer is brought much closer to the consumer (and hence the revenue streams are being recouped) that is of significant interest. Niche audiences, once able to be tapped and marketed directly, have significant value if they can be reached less expensively. Communities offer the potential for fan bases and, on occasion, significant commercial core-audiences. As part of work published since the author's last book (Finney, 2010), it is instructive to see how Finney's own students are taking the argument forward.

Michael Franklin, a former Film Business Academy MSc student and now research fellow at St Andrews University, frames the new environment via the historical insecurity of the traditional film value chain:

> Recognising and interpreting new evaluative frameworks is becoming integral to managing uncertainty and reformulating the film value chain for the digital age. To put it simply, digital tools allow producers to react to consumer demand uncertainty in two ways. Firstly, by engaging with the potential audience earlier and to a greater degree; through interactive media and extended content producers create greater demand and thus increase revenues. Secondly, in order to claim a larger share of revenues, filmmakers pro-actively pursue disintermediation by circumventing some segment(s) of the traditional film value chain via the Internet. The success of this second strategy often relies on the success of the first. The removal of the traditional sales agent, distributor or exhibitor, who traditionally funds and executes all marketing activities, means that their marketing role and resources must be replaced (Franklin, 2012).

The above argument will depend on independent film producers striving to achieve a 'hybrid' model – one that Franklin notes and this author has been using as a model when training and teaching at an MBA level and to professional trade associations. By 'hybrid' I mean that producers and entrepreneurs in the film space need to understand and master traditional and current tools for selling and marketing their films, but concurrently start designing and working on digital and social media aspects that are growing increasingly critical to finding and winning an audience. They may also need to consider traditional 'cornerstone' finance next to new pools of finance from crowd-sourcing and crowd-funding for example. What is less clear, however, is how typical loan finance (senior and junior debt for example) will read the unsteady and unproven revenue streams as the window system collapses. The market seems to imply that alternative financiers will replace the entertainment banking structures and take higher risk in return for higher pricing, as indicated by the changing Film London Production Finance Market's (PFM) financier profile over the past five years (the author is the project manager of the PFM).

Whether the fall-out from disruption offers investors and entrepreneurs enough upside and opportunity in the film sector is open to debate. Alongside the potential 'opening' of the market, with the distributor's role potentially being taken over by either side – by the consumer-aware producer and the digitally-programmed exhibitor – it is reasonable to surmise that new kinds of investors may become interested in investing directly in film and content. These new opportunities are not limited to financiers and equity investment. The potential upside may well be of interest to large retail brands, for example, looking for new sponsorship and marketing opportunities. In turn, the challenge for the producer is to find an alignment of interest with either investment and/or aggregators, and to maximize the new, digitally flexible exhibition circuit to showcase their product prior to distribution via the Internet and new forms of portable delivery, such as the iPad and smartphone.

New devices that play movies when and where the user wants are exploding, including computers, laptops, net books, iPads, hand-held DVD players, smartphones, games consoles, cable set-top boxes and of course the re-tooled television set that is now capable of playing 3D images, and soon to be consumed without the ubiquitous glasses. It can be argued that providers of technology both in terms of 'playability' but also, crucially, 'connectability' could potentially become involved in generating and delivering content, hence becoming involved much earlier in the value chain, though evidence will need to be carefully tracked and calibrated.

Ultimately, Internet marketing and its growth in sophistication and specific demographic reach and targeting will encourage end-users such as cinema owners and chains, pay-TV operators and even video/streamed game operators to enter the production market themselves. Global aggregators, such as Google and Apple, may also decide to prime the pump. A world where these players decide to buy shares in companies that commission development and feature films which in turn help drive their respective platforms will cut out third party distribution completely. Such a move in strategy by players operating with global scale and reach would signal a very different, restructured film value chain.

NOTE

1. By 'independent' the author refers to all film product made outside the Hollywood development and production system. Certain independent films, however, enter the studio distribution system but are still deemed 'independent'.

REFERENCES

Biggart, N. and Beamish, T. (2003). 'The Economic Sociology of Conventions: Habit, Custom, Practice, and Routine in Market Order'. *Annual Review of Sociology* 29: 443–64.

Bloore, P. (2009). *Re-defining the Independent Film Value Chain*. London: UK Film Council. Available at: http://www.ukfilmcouncil.org.uk/12384.

Cave, R. (2000). *Creative Industries*. Cambridge: Harvard Business Press.

Finney, A. (2010). *The International Film Business – A Market Guide Beyond Hollywood*. Abingdon/New York: Routledge.

Franklin, M. (2012). 'Internet-enabled Dissemination: Managing Uncertainty in the Film Value Chain', in Iordanova, D. and Cunningham, S. (eds), *Digital Disruption – Cinema Moves On-Line*. St Andrews: Dina Iordanova.

Hadida, A. and Paris, T. (2013). 'Managerial Cognition and the Value Chain in the Digital Music Industry'. *Technological Forecasting and Social Change* (in press).

Hilderbrand, L. (2010). 'The Art of Distribution: Video On Demand'. *Film Quarterly* 64(2).

Ilott, T. (2009). '50 Theses On Film'. Unpublished paper.

McPhillips, S. and Merlo, O. (2008). 'Media Convergence and the Evolving Media Business Model: An Overview and Strategic Opportunities'. *The Marketing Review* 8(3): 237–53.

Rayport, J.F. and Sviokla, J.J. (1996). 'Exploiting the Virtual Value Chain'. *The McKinsey Quarterly* 1.

Tapscott, D. and Williams, A.D. (2006). *Economics: How Mass Collaboration Changes Everything*. London: Atlantic.

Wu, T. (2010). *The Master Switch: The Rise and Fall of Information Empires*. New York: Vintage.

2. Business innovation in the film industry value chain: a New Zealand case study

Natàlia Ferrer-Roca

INTRODUCTION

There is no question that new technologies are transforming conventional market boundaries and business models and, at the same time, are changing the value chain relations of established industry structures. National film industries are being particularly affected by these changes, partly due to the rapid transformation of production and distribution technologies, which influence almost all parts of this chain. This chapter illustrates how the film business is undergoing a process of disruption and transformation due to, on the one hand, the technology of the Internet and a change in existing social forces driven by social media and, on the other hand, the decreasing costs of information and communication. Drawing on a case study from New Zealand (*How to Meet Girls from a Distance*), the chapter demonstrates how new business opportunities can arise when technologies are used in an entrepreneurial and innovative way, in the process demonstrating the capacity to reduce entry barriers for new film-makers into the New Zealand film industry and market. This is exemplified by a new approach to content creation which is showing the ability to overcome some of the limitations of the traditional film business model by innovating in different parts of its value chain. This chapter aims to link Schumpeter's arguments about entrepreneurs and new technologies to a communication and media studies framework and to offer a point of liaison with business scholars of the academic study of innovation through disruptive media and platforms.

APPROACH

In many respects it is clear that new business models have already overtaken well-established structures of the twentieth century, but the question is how such significant changes will evolve in the future. In such uncertain times, case studies provide a useful tool through which to demonstrate what may or may not work in future business environments. Harvard Business School Professor, Clayton Christensen, is well known within the business academic community for promulgating the theory of disruption (1997; 2003). His book *The Innovator's Dilemma* (1997) explains 'how, under certain circumstances, the mechanism of profit-maximizing resource allocation causes well-run companies to get killed', while *The Innovator's Solution* (2003) offers 'a set of theories that can guide managers who need to grow new business with predictable success – to become the disruptors rather than the disruptees – and ultimately kill the well-run, established competitors' (Christensen, 2003, pp. 17–18). A key focus in Christensen's research is profit-maximization and strategies for creating and sustaining successful business growth. This focus has its strengths, such as predicting the shape of market competition and how to challenge incumbent competitors. Although this is a natural priority from a business perspective, my approach as a media studies scholar is slightly different.

This chapter adopts Joseph Schumpeter's (1883–1950) view of innovation and entrepreneurship as key drivers of markets,[1] but challenges the idea that technology is the key driver of business innovation – also known as technological determinism.[2] For Christensen (2013), 'a disruptive technology or disruptive innovation is an innovation that helps create a new market and value network, and eventually goes on to disrupt an existing market and value network.' Apart from using a somewhat tautological definition, it seems as if 'technology' and 'innovation' are in this context synonyms. Nevertheless, Christensen (2013) goes on to clarify that 'although the term *disruptive technology* is widely used, *disruptive innovation* seems a more appropriate term in many contexts since few technologies are intrinsically disruptive; rather, it is the business model that the technology enables that creates the disruptive impact'. Indeed, this implicitly seems to agree with Schumpeter's idea of entrepreneurship as a key driver of markets, because entrepreneurs are the agents that enable new business models.

According to Schumpeter, it is important to distinguish between invention – 'the discovery of new technical knowledge and its practical application to industry', and innovation – 'the introduction of new technical methods, products, sources of supply, and forms of industrial organization' (Schumpeter, 2000, p. 51). The entrepreneur is seen as a mediator, the liaison between the initial invention and the final innovation or, in other words, as 'the personification of innovation' (Hagedoorn, 1996, p. 889), who needs to have the ability 'to combine already existing resources in creative ways' to become 'the source of all economic change' (Schumpeter,

2000, p. 51). Put differently, the entrepreneur provides the social linkage that allows the innovation to be implemented. As Hagedoorn explained (1996, p. 890), the Schumpeterian entrepreneur is not 'necessarily a strictly rational economically maximizing subject', but rather is 'both a rationally and irrationally motivated economic agent who seems to be never satisfied by results based on existing innovations but who keeps searching for new opportunities' (see also Elster, 1983; Santarelli and Pesciarelli, 1990).

Invention then is necessary to create new technologies, but it is innovation that is the key to creating new business models, which will not succeed without some form of entrepreneurship.[3] At some stage a company or a group of people might be able to use a new technology, but the disruptive innovation in a market will not occur until the right entrepreneur challenges the conventional business environment and thus implements a new business model, appropriate to and feasible within a particular environment. These new business models may grow to represent a certain proportion of the market, but they may fail 'to completely overtake the traditional way of competing' (Markides, 2006, p. 21). Put differently, a new business model may develop by complementing – but not replacing – already well-established business models, as the case study in this chapter suggests. Moreover, an innovation that might create a particular disruption must always be viable within a particular institutional context,[4] including its regulations and policy framework, or as Schumpeter put it (1949, p. 71), 'every social environment has its own ways of filling the entrepreneurial function'. The case study presented in this chapter is specific to New Zealand and has been viable within this particular social, historical and institutional environment.

METHODOLOGY

Drawing on findings derived from a combination of scholarly books and articles, policy analysis, archival research and interviews, this chapter takes an institutional and political economy perspective to illustrate how innovative business ideas are complementing conventional business models. Using a case study as part of my research strategy has proved particularly useful for its 'emphasis on understanding processes alongside their [. . .] contexts' (Hartley, 2004, p. 324). Together with the institutional and political economy perspectives central to my work, the use of a specific case study offers the tools necessary to understand the institutional agents, their pressures and priorities. The case study presented here was selected for its novelty and originality within the New Zealand socio-political and economic context. Descriptive data used in the case study was collected from the website www.makemymovie.co.nz, in addition to online interviews with Ant Timpson (2012) and New Zealand On Air personnel.

THE NEW ZEALAND FILM INDUSTRY CONTEXT

New Zealand has to face significant challenges to overcome the various constraints for its film-makers. It has a relatively young and small film industry, a small national population with limited economies of scale. Although English speaking, New Zealand is also geographically isolated from its most significant overseas markets. The case study looked at in this chapter, *How to Meet Girls from a Distance*, was funded and supported by the New Zealand Film Commission (NZFC). Established in 1978 as a publicly financed agency, the purpose of the NZFC is to 'encourage, participate and assist in the making, promotion, distribution and exhibition of films' made in New Zealand by New Zealanders (NZFC, 1978). The NZFC provides financial assistance only to films with 'a significant New Zealand content', but not to New Zealand 'national cinema', a term that is deliberately not used in official policy, due to its ambiguity. As Higson (1989, p.36) affirms, 'there is not a single universally accepted discourse of national cinema'. Therefore, more accurate might be the term 'New Zealand-domiciled' or 'locally-produced', coined by Dunleavy and Joyce (2011, p.20) who argue that 'Both of these terms. . . describe productions whose conception, narratives, financing, development, and completion are centred upon New Zealand culture, creative personnel and institutions'. Using this alternative rather than the contested term 'national cinema' allows a clear differentiation between foreign-funded screen productions occurring in New Zealand, such as *The Hobbit*, and locally produced feature films like *Boy* whose public funding requires them to pursue New Zealand-specific cultural objectives. The case study corresponds with the New Zealand-domiciled feature film definition.

New Zealand's film industry can be considered relatively youthful if compared to those of other countries. In fact, before the 1970s, the New Zealand government had little interest in the promotion of films, even if film-making had occurred in New Zealand since the early twentieth century (Ministry of Education, 1997). It was in 1971 that the Film Industry Working Party recommended government support of film focusing on a social rationale, instead of economic gains. They argued that 'motion pictures are the most potent communications force for social development and change', and that a film industry would help to 'ensure that New Zealanders are not subjected to a constant diet of programmes from other cultures' (Waller, 1996, pp. 245–6). This could be interpreted as a soft defence against American or British cultural imperialism. In 1972, the Reid Report[5] was published, which provided an analysis of the current state of the film production industry in New Zealand, initiating a debate about whether or not a local film commission was really necessary (NZOS, 2012). Five years later, in 1977, film-makers signed a petition to parliament supporting the introduction of a film commission and, at the end of the same year, the National Party-led government introduced legislation to establish such a body (Shelton, 2005, p. 11).

The NZFC has been the primary public funder for films in New Zealand. In the 35 years since its inception, it has funded more than 300 feature films and certified 60 co-productions.[6] Considering the current economic climate, it aims to invest in at least four feature films per year, in addition to offering opportunities for talent development, administering grants for big budget feature films, and managing New Zealand film certification and co-productions (NZFC, n.d.a). The NZFC budget varies every year. In financial year 2012/2013, 28 per cent of the budget came from the NZ government, 68 per cent from the New Zealand Lottery Grants Board, and the remaining 4 per cent from returns on film investments and interest (NZFC, n.d.a). NZFC's seven-member board – members being appointed by the Minister for Culture and Heritage (MCH) – is a statutory body providing governance and policy direction, and is responsible for making final funding decisions after considering staff recommendations. The Commission's current challenge is to sustain the growth of the New Zealand film industry in a country that is characterized 'not only by its limited population size but also by its geographical distance from the large markets which continue to dominate international feature film production' (Dunleavy and Joyce, 2011, p. 259).

BUSINESS CHALLENGES OF NEW ZEALAND-DOMICILED FEATURE FILMS

New Zealand is a comparatively small English-language cinema market, sustained by a population of only 4.4 million (Statistics New Zealand, 2012). Although this limits the economy of scale domestically, the main export advantage of being an English-language cinema is the 'relatively uncomplicated linguistic access' to other English-speaking markets (Babington, 2007, p. 9), such as the UK, Canada, Australia, Ireland or the USA, which allows film productions to have a significant 'advantage in the international marketplace' (O'Regan, 1996, p. 83). Nevertheless, New Zealand's characteristic English accent – or Kiwi accent – might not be easily understood by other English-speaking countries, which was confirmed at the American release of NZ-domiciled feature film *Boy*, during which writer-director-actor Taika Waititi received mixed feedback from the audience when they were asked whether they found it difficult to understand the Kiwi accent (Lichman, 2012). In this regard, while New Zealand might benefit from English-language markets, its accent – not to mention productions made in the indigenous Māori language – might still pose commercial barriers.

Just as locally produced New Zealand feature films can be distributed to other English-speaking countries relatively easily, New Zealand's film market also provides easy access for English-language films from abroad. Due to free trade agreements,[7] there is no barrier to importing foreign English-language audio-visual products into New Zealand (apart from the classification system[8]). Furthermore, New Zealand's writers and producers also face the issue regarding whether New Zealand films should cater predominantly to a domestic audience, or whether films should target an international audience in order to cover expenses.[9] It is almost impossible for locally produced feature films to cover their initial production costs by relying on New Zealand's domestic market alone,[10] which makes buying foreign productions more economically viable and attractive (Harvey and Tongue, 2006, p. 227).

While countries in the European Union and Canada overcame the issue of economies of scale by introducing a local content quota in both the broadcasting and cinema sector, New Zealand failed to include such a clause to protect its culture in the General Agreement on Trade in Services (GATS), with the consequence that local content quota for feature films are now legally impossible (Kelsey, 2003, p. 7). Moreover, while Canada and the European Commission included 'an Annex that would exempt cultural services from the most-favoured nation (MFN) obligation to treat services suppliers from all foreign countries equally', New Zealand followed the example of the USA and opposed these proposals (Kelsey, 2003, p. 5). Even if New Zealand's government were to impose a local content quota, it would not only 'breach the market access and national treatment provision of the GATS', but also the Closer Economic Relations (CER) Agreement with Australia (Kelsey, 2003, pp. 7–8). The larger cinema chains and private broadcasting companies would also be likely to oppose such policies.

New Zealand films compete, on the one hand, with high-budget Hollywood productions and, on the other hand, with foreign art-house feature films, most of which have higher budgets than most New Zealand productions. Most New Zealand-domiciled films have serious difficulties due to a lack of funding, which diminishes New Zealand's competitive position in the international sphere to 'a very small-budget player in a higher-budget market' (Babington, 2007, pp. 11–12). This also affects their capability to sustain and deploy talent when making a film in New Zealand, which is even more challenging since foreign-financed feature film projects pay crew members much higher rates than most New Zealand productions could ever afford, creating expectations impossible to meet for local producers and budgets (Shelton, 2005, p. 53).

Moreover, New Zealand's film industry has to manage the advantages and challenges of the additional opportunities offered by New Zealand's hosting of major foreign-funded productions (Babington, 2007, p. 10). Due to economic growth agendas, attracting international large cinema productions has become a priority for many governments,[11] as the Global Guide to Soft Money suggests (Screen International, 2011). Foreign-financed productions, such as 'runaway-Hollywood' feature films, are considered not only to generate domestic investment and employment, but also to stimulate the domestic film industry, strengthening its infrastructure and assisting the host country's tourism industry (Barrett, 2011). Nevertheless, hosting international productions may also have unpredictable side-effects for the local film industry, such as changes/clarifications[12] of the employment law in order to retain foreign film productions, as has happened in New Zealand with *The Hobbit* (see Conor, 2011; McAndrew and Risak, 2012).

Internationally, New Zealand-domiciled feature films have to find their way into an overseas media market where trade channels are dominated by media conglomerates primarily domiciled in the USA (Hoskins et al., 1997).[13] Those Hollywood majors are able to defend their internationally dominant position partly because of the control they exert over distribution (Wasko, 2003) or, in other words, because they are vertically integrated, controlling almost all parts of the film value chain: from conception/development and production to international distribution. Each of them possesses a global distribution network to make sure that its products are made available to final consumers (Hoskins et al., 1997). They choose the theatres in which the film will be exhibited, as well as the release date, basing their decision on previous high-demand periods, such as Easter or Christmas (De Vany, 2004). Many New Zealand-domiciled feature films depend on overseas distribution deals for international release, the majority of which are made in festival circuits (Babington, 2007; see also Shelton, 2005). Success in one of the world's top film festivals, such as Cannes, Toronto, Sundance, Berlin or Venice, can lead to wider theatrical distribution. This situation affects all production companies in the world without distribution capability (Hoskins et al., 1997).

While the political economy of New Zealand's film industry shares some characteristics with other countries, such as Ireland, which also has a small-sized English-language cinema market with limited economic resources and a small domestic market, it also shows some distinctive trends, such as international recognition through its hosting of major foreign-funded productions. Zanker and Lealand (2009, p. 156) regard New Zealand as 'open to the world but also struggling to find its place in a globalized world of corporate economics and mass-distributed media'. The current challenges for New Zealand are to provide adequate institutional mechanisms, policy and economic resources – such as updating the 1978 NZFC Act and re-focusing its objectives – to maintain New Zealand-domiciled films and, at the same time, come up with new ways to encourage foreign-funded film projects to come to New Zealand. The following case study shows how a small country with few resources can create innovative business ideas to overcome some of these limitations.

OVERCOMING CHALLENGES: *HOW TO MEET GIRLS FROM A DISTANCE* (2012) AS A CASE STUDY

The New Zealand-domiciled feature film *How to Meet Girls from a Distance* was the first of its kind produced thanks to the *Make My Movie* (MMM)[14] scheme, 'an innovative multi-platform project that utilizes graphic design, social networking, a web series, and the public to decide which idea should receive NZ$100 000[15] to be used to create a low budget feature film' (MMM, 2011a). The project was initiated by Ant Timpson,[16] a well-known Kiwi producer, creator of the country's 48 Hours Short Film Competition and programmer at the New Zealand International Film Festival (NZIFF), together with Hugh Sundae, the Entertainment Editor of *The New Zealand Herald*, New Zealand's main newspaper. Both of them functioned as entrepreneurial agents in terms of the innovation, having first come up with the idea of *Make My Movie* in 2011, put the application including budget together and then approached the NZFC and New Zealand On Air (NZoA) for financing, which both bodies provided. Although NZoA is a public broadcast funding agency, it often provides a limited amount of 'top-up' funding to support the production of feature films that fit its 'cultural identity' remit, accepting that these have an 'after-life' on New Zealand broadcast television (Dunleavy and Joyce, 2011, pp. 144 and 257). So in this case, the primary funder was the NZFC with 'top-up' finance from NZoA.

MMM's main innovation is shifting the film value chain by allowing the audience to be a significant partner in the film-making process – from its inception right through to its release – while simultaneously building up the audience for theatrical release and using the national newspaper as means of promotion. Any New Zealand resident can enter MMM by uploading a movie idea containing a title, a logline,[17] a poster and a synopsis. These ideas are then shared via social media networks, such as Facebook and Twitter, to gauge the general public interest. The MMM team then whittles down around 760 entries to 12,[18] using data from social networks and industry advisors, including one from the NZFC and from NZoA respectively. Considering that the NZFC is on average only able to fund four feature films per year, 760 entries indicate that a considerable number of prospective producers in New Zealand are willing to make a low-budget movie.

The top 12 finalists are presented on *New Zealand Herald*'s newspaper website, subjected to comments and feedback from the public, then further reduced to the top two by a panel of five (of which public feedback represents one vote). The winning team receives NZ$100 000 to complete a feature film. In the inaugural 2012 competition the winner was the romantic comedy *How to Meet Girls from a Distance*. The finished feature film – which was written, filmed and edited in only six months – had its world premiere at the 2012 New Zealand International Film Festival, was also selected for the 3rd Beijing International Film Festival, and featured as part of Melbourne Film Festival's Breakthrough Screenings. It was picked up by Madman Entertainment, one of Australia's leading distributors of independent films,[19] which released it in New Zealand cinemas in November 2012 and made it available on DVD in March 2013. Following such success, the NZFC has announced its support for a further competition in 2013/2014 (NZFC, 2013, p.7).

REDUCING UNCERTAINTY BY ENGAGING WITH AUDIENCES

During the entire project, from the official launch of MMM to the final editing of the selected film, short videos – also called web series or webisodes – were uploaded on the official *Make My Movie* website. The first webisode showed how the project was born in an informal way, while the second video interviewed well-established directors and producers giving their (positive) opinion about the MMM project. This was useful for engaging with both future audiences and aspiring film-makers, as well as to gain legitimacy from industry experts and credibility through the involvement of public funding agencies. Other web series produced for the project showed how the MMM team went to the largest genre film festival in the US, the Fantastic Fest in Austin, to give some examples of how great movies can be made with little money and end up in international festivals.

Another showed how the MMM panel of experts deliberated which of the 760 entries would make it into the final top 12. Afterwards, the posters of the 12 finalists were shown to industry professionals, mainly exhibitors and marketing experts, who commented on their marketability and general appeal. Another webisode showed the panel of experts[20] debating how to reduce the 12 finalists down to the top two, which were announced at the end of the same web series. Once the feature film idea was selected, the web series continued to be published online and on the newspaper website, informing the audience about the entire process of film-making, including interviews with the producers, writers, the main actor, the director and some of the main crew members.

This non-stop flow of information created several market-oriented filters. On the one hand, asking exhibitors and marketing professionals to comment on the posters' marketability and general appeal was clearly a market-oriented filter for decision-making. It helped decision-makers not only to 'greenlight' ideas to allocate funding for production, but also to justify their funding decisions in a tight fiscal climate where public funding is under increased pressure to deliver measurable outcomes. This simultaneously minimized both commercial as well as political risk. Another way to minimize risk was by identifying the most popular film idea and also by enhancing creativity by inviting a wider range of proposals. On the other hand, all online and offline communication tools and marketing strategies, such as offering an inside perspective through the web series, a lively interaction through social media, such as Facebook and Twitter, and using the national newspaper as a broadcaster (whose step-by-step coverage of the film aimed to bring it to the reach of a broader 'offline' audience), created market-oriented filters by building an audience through the entire film-making process. Building up audiences and directly engaging with them even prior to production meant that audience appeal limited production viability, although there was the danger that audience feedback might not be representative of the general public. Nevertheless it can be argued that, by creating a fan-based audience before going into production, film business is less risky for all – funders, marketers and distributors.

ENTREPRENEURSHIP AND COMMUNICATION

New technologies have allowed a considerable increase in audio-visual content availability, both in terms of production and distribution, resulting in ever more online platforms competing for audience attention. As Ant Timpson (2011, 1:36–1:41min) clearly stated in MMM's web series 2: 'He can make a film, you can make a film, I can make a film, finding an audience for that film – that is the hard part'. Rather than producing, the real challenge thus seems to be to convince people to watch the film and pay for it. In other words, distribution and marketing are the main problem, especially for 'indie' and low-budget films.

Lack of vertical integration being a main cause for this market barrier, the entrepreneurs Ant Timpson and Hugh Sundae created the MMM project not only by persuading public funders that their business idea was feasible and possibly successful in a particular context, but also by creating communication channels for social and institutional interaction, necessary to implement such a project. There is no doubt that 'the entrepreneur brings in his personality' (Schumpeter, 2003, p. 101), but it does much more than that. Apart from bringing up new ideas, seeing a new market possibility and being the linkage that allows the innovation to be implemented, an entrepreneur also creates new social codes and meanings and channels of interaction that enable market actors to reshape market activity and thus create new revenue streams. In this case, the entrepreneurs created a new path for institutional communication – between NZFC and NZoA – and social interaction – with audiences. Implicitly, there is also a persuasive element here, because the entrepreneur has to be successful in persuading institutional decision-makers in order to change the scope of what is considered legitimate action in a certain context. Put differently, the entrepreneur does not only recognize new business models and their market potential, but also creates communication channels and mediation processes for social and institutional interaction, which are necessary to successfully implement a new business idea. This process may or may not include a new technology, but the entrepreneur needs to see how to deploy a technology in a creative way in order to create a new business model. Or, as Schumpeter (2000, p. 51) put it, the entrepreneur needs to have the ability 'to combine already existing resources in creative ways' to become 'the source of all economic change'.

DIFFERENCES AND SIMILARITIES WITH CROWD-FUNDING AND CROWD-SOURCING

Other chapters in this volume focus on crowd-funding and crowd-sourcing initiatives, such as Luka in Chapter 9 and Roth and Kimani in Chapter 10 respectively. The case study presented in this chapter shares more similarities with crowd-sourcing projects and less with crowd-funding initiatives. On the one hand, crowd-funding is 'a collective effort by consumers who network and pool their money together, usually via the Internet, in order to invest in and support efforts initiated by other people or organizations'

(Ordanini et al., 2011, p. 443). However, the production of *How to Meet Girls from a Distance* was financed institutionally via public money by the NZFC and NZoA. Audiences did not need to pool their money together in order to see the production made and released, and thus behave in an entrepreneurial way. Both cases nevertheless involved their active participation through social networks. Crowd-sourcing, on the other hand, is 'the act of a company or institution taking a function once performed by employees and outsourcing it to an undefined (and generally large) network of people in the form of an open call' (Howe, 2006a). While the employees/in-house concept does not apply in the MMM project because all film-makers are contractors, some of the advantages of crowd-sourcing are very similar. The MMM project also gained 'access to a very large community of potential workers who [had] a diverse range of skills and expertise and who [were] willing and able to complete activities within a short time-frame and often at a much reduced cost' (Howe, 2006b quoted in Whitla, 2009, p. 16). Indeed, the film-makers that made *How to Meet Girls from a Distance* had only six months to write, film and edit the movie and did all that with a very small budget.

DISCUSSION AND CONCLUSIONS

The case study illustrates how digital technologies are reducing the entry barriers into the New Zealand film market: young and mostly non-professional film-makers have been able to make a low-budget film, access public funding, and reach new audiences by reducing communication costs as well as securing international distribution. This is especially important in the context of New Zealand, in view of the general shortage of funding for feature film production, the limited economies of scale arising from a small domestic market, and the dependency of New Zealand films on overseas distribution deals for international release. More broadly, this case study shows how new ways of using the Internet and social media can offer opportunities not only for promoting and marketing feature films (and doing so right from the beginning of the film-making process), but also for creating an accessible and highly effective point of entry to the film industry for aspiring new film-makers. Apart from making revenue available prior to development and production, generating an online audience in advance of the completion of production can minimize the considered risks for funders, marketers and distributors. This case study also reveals that the traditional value chain sequence of feature films – entailing the processes of conception and development, production, distribution, exhibition and consumption – need not necessarily remain strictly

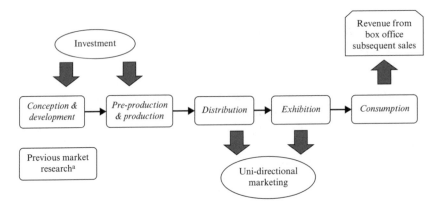

Note: a.   Big Hollywood corporations conduct market research before a feature film is eventually produced or released (Wasko, 2003; Miller et al., 2005), which undoubtedly creates a flow of information from the audience to the producers/distributors. While this is also a risk-reduction strategy, it is nevertheless a completely different kind of communication flow compared to the one presented in value chain B.

Figure 2.1   Film value chain A

linear, in view of the additional opportunities of an Internet era. With the low-budget 'indie'-styled film being an indicative example, the Internet is facilitating a departure from the traditionally linear chain of production, to create innovative ways of developing, producing, financing and marketing a feature film.

Although one must be cautious of over-generalizing, the film value chain A (Figure 2.1) shows how conventional film business models (notably the 'Hollywood model' and most independent films prior to the mainstream take-up of new media) have traditionally used uni-directional marketing strategies at the distribution and exhibition stages of the film value chain. The communication channels are uni-directional because information is produced by distribution and marketing experts, and sent to – and consumed by – audiences. Moreover, from the point of view of a funder/investor, monetary streams are mainly used 'up-front' for conception and development (processes which include acquiring rights, preparing synopses and budgets, acquiring finance, and writing successive screenplay drafts), and pre-production and production (processes including the preparation of final budgets and shooting schedules, hiring crew, actors and equipment needed, and the shooting of a film), whereas revenue streams are generated at the end of the value chain, being derived mainly from box office and subsequent sales.

In the case of the *Make My Movie* project (film value chain B, see

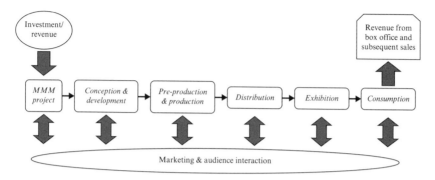

Figure 2.2   Film value chain B

Figure 2.2), however, marketing played a much more important role from the beginning of the feature film-making process, its influence continuing right through to the film's release. In order to minimize both commercial and institutional risks, this process departed from a uni-directional approach to embrace multi-directional ways of marketing and interacting with audiences (Figure 2.2). The communication channels are multi-directional because information is produced by both distribution and marketing experts, as well as by consumers and audiences. There already exists some marketing and audience interaction prior to the funding decision, so conception is tested before funding. Furthermore, from the point of view of a funder/investor, monetary streams are generated 'up-front' to enable project implementation. Some revenue streams may also emanate from the box office, but this post-release source is able to play a secondary role, because contrary to the conventional film business model that is demonstrated here as film value chain A (Figure 2.1), the primary public funder is not expecting to recoup their initial investment.

In this case, both entrepreneurial agents – Ant Timpson and Hugh Sundae – not only created new communication channels for institutional interaction with their public funders, but also used new media to create new communication channels through which to directly access potential audiences. These two entrepreneurs also persuaded both funders that their business idea had market potential and would possibly be successful in certain kinds of audience contexts. In this case study, then, the new business idea did not involve a new technology since the Internet and social media were both well established before the MMM initiative. Rather, both entrepreneurs combined already existing resources (these including the potentials of New Zealand's public funders to provide financial support for screen production) with the newer potentials of the Internet and social media to reach a range of potential audiences. They did this in such a creative way that it enabled them to successfully test and implement a new business idea. Simultaneously, this approach was able to reduce commercial and political risk for all parties involved – the creators, funders, marketers and distributors.

As Christensen (2013) put it, 'it is the business model that the technology enables that creates the disruptive impact', and not the technology per se. In this case study, however, we cannot talk about a complete 'disruptive impact' to the traditional business model, but rather, it would be more accurate to say that a new business model can complement, though not replace, conventional businesses, nevertheless triggering an adjustment to the value chain that, before the Internet, few could have anticipated. The case study also demonstrates how the entrepreneur can function to link the innovation with a new business model and, simultaneously, as the creator of communication channels between agents and actors located in quite different parts of the traditional value chain. For good reasons, New Zealand's screen production funding agencies, NZFC and NZoA, operate most strongly in the areas of conception/development and the facilitation of production, whereas audiences (even if these are important when considering what kinds of New Zealand productions should receive public finance) become more important at the consumption end of the film value chain. Both Timpson and Sundae acted as the main performers in this particular instance, in that they were able to persuade different social and institutional actors to work together so as to create a new business model.

As previously mentioned, the MMM project shares some features from both crowd-funding and crowd-sourcing initiatives. The case study presented in this chapter is nevertheless limited in that it is specific to the institutional arrangements for the film sector in New Zealand, which might not apply to other national film markets. New Zealand might yet well serve as a useful example for other small countries which need to develop alternative feature film business models. Some ideas, such as marketing and interacting with audiences during the whole film-making process, might be replicable in other countries of proximate population size. In the end, the main limitation of this business idea is funding availability, and more research is needed to establish whether or not this model would also be successful in other social, political and economic contexts. The case presented here is, however, indicative of the ways in which new business models and strategies within some parts of the film value chain may be able to change and what they might look like in the near future.

ACKNOWLEDGEMENTS

Special thanks go to Dr Peter Thompson and Dr Trisha Dunleavy for their valuable, extensive, critical and constructive comments. The usual disclaimer applies.

NOTES

1. Balabkins (2003) suggests that Schumpeter got the idea of the innovating entrepreneur from Albert Schäffle's work (1831–1903).
2. The term 'technological determinism' was coined by the American sociologist and political economist Thorstein Veblen (1857–1929).
3. For a further analysis of Schumpeter's notion of entrepreneurship see Ebner (2003).
4. Veblen also makes strong arguments for looking at the institutional context as a shaper of social-economic agency.
5. John Reid was commissioned by the Queen Elizabeth II Arts Council to write this report. His biography is available on New Zealand On Screen, http://www.nzonscreen.com/person/john-reid/biography.
6. Sixty co-productions as follows: 24 with Canada, 19 with the UK, 11 with Australia, 5 with France, 5 with Germany and 1 with Singapore. New Zealand also maintains co-production agreements with South Korea, Spain, Italy, Ireland, China and India (NZFC, 2012).
7. GATS (General Agreement on Trade in Services) and CER (Closer Economic Relations Agreement with Australia).
8. 'Under the Films, Videos, and Publications Classification Act 1993, films which receive an unrestricted rating (G, PG, or M) in Australia are automatically cross-rated to receive the same rating in New Zealand. [. . .] Therefore the majority of unrestricted films do not come to the Classification Office' and can therefore be automatically distributed in New Zealand (Office of Film and Literature Classification, 2012).
9. Arguably the best strategy for New Zealand so far has been to make out significant 'overseas audiences without diminishing local interests' (Babington, 2007, p. 266).
10. Recent NZFC calculations show that from 1993 until 2012 New Zealand films only took 2.5 per cent of the overall New Zealand box office (NZFC, n.d.b).
11. The countries covered in this report are the UK, Ireland, France, Germany, Austria, Italy, Spain, Malta, Belgium, Luxembourg, Iceland, Hungary, the Czech Republic, South Africa, Australia, New Zealand, the US, Mexico and Canada.
12. The New Zealand Government claims that the employment law was only *clarified*, whereas the Unions and Actors Equity assert that the employment law was *changed* to reduce workers' rights.
13. According to Hoskins et al. (1997, pp. 37–50), a large domestic market with a common language, high per capita income, and the vertically integrated nature of the major studios explain US dominance over international media trade.
14. More information is available at http://www.makemymovie.co.nz.
15. Equivalent to US$78 890, £52 210 or 59 780 euros (2 August, 2013).
16. To find out more about Ant Timpson see: http://www.timpsonfilms.com/default,22,bio.sm.
17. A logline is a brief summary of a feature film, often providing both 'a synopsis of the program's plot, and an emotional "hook" to stimulate interest' (MMM, 2011b).
18. Data from the MMM 2012 round.
19. Interestingly, the cinematic release of the first MMM winner is still dependent on a

foreign – Australian – distribution company, a situation caused by a lack of vertical integration of New Zealand's feature film value chain.

20. The MMM panel of experts consisted of Ant Timpson (the MMM creator and executive producer), Jonathan Dowling (Co-producer of winning movie), Rachel Gardner (Producer), Andrew Miller (Event Cinemas), Lisa Chatfield (NZFC) and Glenn Usmar (NZoA). The meeting was held in an informal setting, exemplifying the low-budget characteristic of the project.

REFERENCES

Babington, B. (2007). *A History of the New Zealand Fiction Feature Film.* Manchester, UK: Manchester University Press.

Balabkins, N.W. (2003). Adaptation Without Attribution? The Genesis of Schumpeter's Innovator. In J. Backhaus (ed.), *Joseph Alois Schumpeter, Entrepreneusrhip, Style and Vision* (pp. 203–20). Boston, Dordrecht, London: Kluwer Academic Publishers.

Barrett, J. (2011). Conflict in "Middle-earth": Employment Law, Globalisation and Independent Film Workers. *Web Journal of Current Legal issues*, 1. Retrieved from: http://webjcli.ncl.ac.uk/2011/issue1/barrett1.html.

Christensen, C.M. (1997). *The Innovator's Dilemma: When New Technologies Cause Great Firms to Fail.* Boston, Massachusetts: Harvard Business School Press.

Christensen, C.M. (2003). *The Innovator's Solution: Creating and Sustaining Successful Growth.* Boston, Massachusetts: Harvard Business School Press.

Christensen, C.M. (2013). Disruptive Innovation. In M. Soegaard and R.F. Dam (eds), *The Encyclopedia of Human–Computer Interaction* (2nd edn). Aarhus, Denmark: The Interaction Design Foundation. Retrieved from: http://www.interaction-design.org/encyclopedia/disruptive_innovation.html.

Conor, B. (2011). Problems in "Wellywood": Rethinking the Politics of Transnational Cultural Labor. *Flow TV*, 13(7). Retrieved from: http://flowtv.org/2011/01/problems-in-wellywood/.

De Vany, A. (2004). *Hollywood Economics. How Extreme Uncertainty Shapes the Film Industry.* London, UK: Routledge.

Dunleavy, T. and Joyce, H. (2011). *New Zealand Film & Television; Institution, Industry and Cultural Change.* Bristol, UK: Intellect.

Ebner, A. (2003). The Institutional Analysis of Entrepreneurship: Historist Aspects of Schumpeter's Development Theory. In J. Backhaus (ed.), *Joseph Alois Schumpeter: Entrepreneurship, Style and Vision* (pp. 117–39). Dordrecht, the Netherlands: Kluwer Academic Publishers.

Elster, J. (1983). *Explaining Technical Change.* Cambridge: Cambridge University Press.

Hagedoorn, J. (1996). Innovation and Entrepreneurship: Schumpeter Revisited. *Industrial and Corporate Change*, 5(3), 883–96.

Hartley, J. (2004). Case Study Research. In C. Cassell and G. Symon (eds), *Essential Guide to Qualitative Methods in Organizational Research* (pp. 323–33). London, UK: Sage Publications Ltd.

Harvey, S. and Tongue, C. (2006). Trading, Cultural Commodities or Promoting Cultural Diversity? UNESCO's New Convention. In S. Harvey (ed.), *Trading*

Culture: Global Traffic and Local Cultures in Film and Television (pp. 221–30). Eastleigh, UK: John Libbey Publishing.

Higson, A. (1989). The Concept of National Cinema. *Screen*, 20(4), 36–46.

Hoskins, C., McFadyen, S. and Finn, A. (1997). *Global Television and Film. An Introduction to the Economics of the Business*. Oxford, UK: Oxford University Press.

Howe, J. (2006a). Crowdsourcing: A Definition. *Wired Blog Network: Crowdsourcing*. Retrieved 17 May, 2013, from: http://crowdsourcing.typepad.com/cs/2006/06/crowdsourcing_a.html.

Howe, J. (2006b). The Rise of Crowdsourcing. *Wired*. Retrieved 17 May, 2013, from: http://www.wired.com/wired/archive/14.06/crowds.html

Kelsey, J. (2003). Lessons from New Zealand: The Saga of the GATS and Local Content Quotas. Paper presented at the Conference on Cultural Diversity, Paris, 2–4 February.

Lichman, J. (2012). Taika Waititi Talks About Making The Smash Hit New Zealand Film 'Boy' & His Plans To Reunite With Jemaine Clement. 2 February. Retrieved 24 January, 2013, from: http://blogs.indiewire.com/theplaylist/taika-waititi-talks-about-making-the-smash-hit-new-zealand-film-boy-his-plans-to-re unite-with-jemaine-clement.

Markides, C. (2006). Disruptive Innovation: In Need of Better Theory. *The Journal of Product Innovation Management*, 23, 19–25.

McAndrew, I. and Risak, M. (2012). Shakedown in the Shaky Isles: Union Bashing in New Zealand. *Labor Studies Journal*, 37(1), 56–80.

Miller, T., Govil, N., McMurria, J., Maxwell, R. and Wang, T. (2005). *Global Hollywood 2*. London, UK: BFI Publishing.

Ministry of Education. (1997). *Tracking Time. 100 Years of Film in Aotearoa New Zealand*. New Zealand: Learning Media/New Zealand Film Archive.

MMM. (2011a). MMM About. Retrieved 22 April, 2013, from: http://www.make mymovie.co.nz/about/.

MMM. (2011b). MMM FAQ. Retrieved 13 December, 2012, from: http://www.makemymovie.co.nz/faq/.

NZFC. (n.d.a). *NZFC Key Facts*. Retrieved from: http://www.nzfilm.co.nz/about-us/key-facts.

NZFC. (n.d.b). *New Zealand Feature Films Share of New Zealand Box Office*. Retrieved from: http://www.nzfilm.co.nz/sites/nzfc/files/NZ%20Feature%20 Films%20Share%20of%20NZ%20Box%20Office.pdf.

NZFC. (1978). *New Zealand Film Commission Act 1978*. Retrieved from: http://www.legislation.govt.nz/act/public/1978/0061/latest/DLM23018 html?search=ts_act_ New+Zealand+Film+Commission+Act+(1978)_resel.

NZFC. (2012). *NZ Official Co-productions Summary May 2012*. New Zealand: NZFC.

NZFC. (2013). *NZFC Statement of Intent 2013–2016*. Retrieved from: http://www.nzfilm.co.nz/sites/nzfc/files/NZFC%20Statement%20of%20Intent%202013% 20-%202016_0.pdf.

NZOS. (2012). John Reid Biography, New Zealand On Screen. Retrieved 27 January, 2012, from: http://www.nzonscreen.com/person/john-reid/biography.

O'Regan, T. (1996). *Australian National Cinema*. London, UK: Routledge.

Office of Film and Literature Classification. (2012). What does M mean? *Office of Film and Literature Classification*. Retrieved 30 April, 2013, from: http://www.censorship.govt.nz/news/news-what-does-M-mean.html.

Ordanini, A., Miceli, L., Pizzetti, M. and Parasuraman, A. (2011). Crowd-funding: Transforming Customers into Investors through Innovative Service Platforms. *Journal of Service Management*, 22(4), 443–70.

Santarelli, E. and Pesciarelli, E. (1990). The Emergence of a Vision: The Development of Schumpeter's Theory of Entrepreneurship. *History of Political Economy*, 22, 677–96.

Schumpeter, J. (1949). *Economic Theory and Entrepreneurial History – Change and the Entrepreneur, Postulates and Pasterns for Entrepreneurship History.* Cambridge, MA: Harvard University Press.

Schumpeter, J. (2000). Entrepreneurship as Innovation. In R. Swedberg (ed.), *Entrepreneurship – A Social Science View* (pp. 51–7). Oxford, UK: Oxford University Press.

Schumpeter, J. (2003). The Theory of Economic Development. In J. Backhaus (ed.), *Joseph Alois Schumpeter, Entrepreneurship Style and Vision* (pp. 61–116). Boston/Dordrecht/London: Kluwer Academic Publishers.

Screen International. (2011). *Screen International's Global Guide to Soft Money 2011.* Retrieved from: http://softmoney.screendaily.com/.

Shelton, L. (2005). *The Selling of New Zealand Movies.* Wellington, New Zealand: Awa Press.

Statistics New Zealand. (2012). Estimated Resident Population of New Zealand, Statistics New Zealand, Tatauranga Aotearoa. Retrieved 6 March, 2012, from: http://www.stats.govt.nz/tools_and_services/tools/population_clock.aspx.

Timpson, A. (2011). *Make My Movie Webisode 2: The Next Chapter.* New Zealand. Retrieved from: http://www.makemymovie.co.nz/webisodes/.

Timpson, A. (2012). Interview with Ant Timpson. Medium: Skype. 20 December.

Waller, G.A. (1996). The New Zealand Film Commission: Promoting an Industry, Forging a National Identity. *Historical Journal of Film, Radio and Television*, 16(2), 243–62.

Wasko, J. (2003). *How Hollywood Works.* London, UK: Sage Publications Ltd.

Whitla, P. (2009). Crowdsourcing and its Application in Marketing Activities. *Contemporary Management Research*, 5(1), 15–28.

Zanker, R. and Lealand, G. (2009). New Zealand as Middle Earth: Local and Global Popular Communication in a Small Nation. In T. Miller (ed.), *The Contemporary Hollywood Reader* (pp. 155–61). Abingdon, UK: Routledge.

3. A case study of business model innovation and transformation in China's film industry

Tuen-Yu Lau and Axel Kwok

INTRODUCTION

China's population of 1.35 billion people has always been attracted to all kinds of businesses, and the film industry in China is no exception (National Bureau of Statistics of China, 2013). While the film industry in some parts of the world is declining, the Chinese film industry is currently experiencing a period of rapid growth. China's State Administration of Radio, Film and TV (SARFT) statistics from 2011 showed that a total of 791 films were produced during the year, and box office revenues amounted to approximately RMB 13 billion (USD 2 billion), representing a year-on-year increase of 29 percent. About 803 new cinemas with 3030 new screens were built in 2011, which resulted in a 43 percent growth of the number of screens, and reaching a total of 9286 screens in the country (Li, 2012). This growth continued the following year, and SARFT 2012 statistics reported that a total of 893 films were produced, and box office revenues totaled approximately RMB 17 billion (about USD 2.7 billion), representing an increase of 30 percent from the previous year. About 3832 new screens were built in 2012, reaching a total of 13 118 screens, which is a 41 percent growth (Li, 2013).

This growth started when China entered the World Trade Organization (WTO) in 2001, which initiated the reformation of the film industry in 2002. Today, China is the world's second largest film market, with the third largest number of film productions. During the past ten years, the Chinese film industry has not only grown, it has also experienced technological change that has transformed and increased the number of content delivery formats. Two of the most significant aspects of this transformation are manifested by the development of Internet access in China and the rapid growth of the mobile telephony and data communication. The China Internet Network Information Center's (CNNIC) 2013 report showed that about 40 percent of the Chinese population uses the internet, with the country's online population reaching 591 million by the end of June 2013, and mobile phones (464 million users) have overtaken desktop computers as the primary channel for Internet access (CNNIC, 2013). These developments enable entirely new routines and methods for film production, distribution and consumption, which will be discussed in this chapter. First the chapter will present the major components of the regulatory transformation of China's film industry. The chapter will then turn the focus to market conditions and the development of digital technologies followed by an analysis of traditional and online film distribution and particularly how Chinese censorship of these channels shapes the production of film in China. The chapter continues by analyzing two film productions, one from 2002 and another from 2011, which illustrates how the Internet and particularly social media have transformed the industry during this decade.

REGULATING THE CHINESE FILM INDUSTRY

The market environment in China has changed fundamentally since 11 November 2001, when the Minister of Foreign Trade and Economic Cooperation of China signed the WTO Accession Protocol in Doha (Tan and Geng, 2001). China's film industry was expecting to face a serious challenge from its Hollywood peers and hence a market-orientation reformation of the film industry officially began. From 1990s onwards, China's reformation path started by learning from successful overseas peers' operational experience, which was then applied to its domestic situations. The reformation of China's film industry and its future development became a significant item on the Chinese government's agenda.

The General Office of the Central Committee of the Communist Party of China, the highest authorities, and the State Council, the chief administrative authority, are involved in forming the policy for China's film industry. The State Council's executive branch, the State Administration of Radio, Film and Television (SARFT), with a main task being the administration and supervision of state-owned enterprises engaged in the television, radio and film industries, promulgated a series of reformation rules and regulations in 2000 and 2001.

The first reformation (Opinions on further reform of the film industry, SARFT No. 2000–320) enabled the film industry to establish film production companies and to invite external shareholders. It also proposed the establishment of cinema theater chains that enabled efficient film distribution, and it revised the regulations that governed the import of foreign films (SARFT, 2000). This regulation, issued in 2000, set the scene for future reformations of the film industry and made it possible for additional reforms to be implemented.

Following this major regulatory change, two additional changes were implemented in 2001 that intended to increase the internal efficiency of the broadcasting and film industries and to strengthen the industry's market orientation (General Office of the CPC Central Committee, 2001; SARFT, 2001a).

The regulatory changes continued with a focus on film distribution and particularly cinema theaters (Implementation details of film distribution and exhibition (cinemas) reform, SARFT No.2001–1591). This regulation enabled the rapid establishment of cinema theater chains. In regions with feasible conditions, two or more cinema chains were established. The regulation also encouraged major cinema chains to extend their operations across multiple provinces. The regulation kept the existing China Film Group as the original distribution company for imported films but at the same time, it also established another distribution company (consisting of various shareholders) to import films, thus initiating competition, by integrating planned and market-oriented film distribution mechanisms (SARFT, 2001b).

These regulations provided general direction for all regulatory reformations of the Chinese film industry that were to follow. The objective of the regulatory changes was to help establish China's film industry as a strong competitor to foreign films and to improve the marketing channels so that the film industry was working more effectively in a market-oriented economy.

After ten years of reform and the formation of industry groups of the Chinese film industry, the 2010 box office revenue exceeded RMB 10 billion, about USD 1.59 billion (SARFT, 2010). In 2010, one significant policy directive specifically for the film industry was released (The General Office of the State Council guidance on promoting the prosperity and development of the film industry, State Council No. 2010–9). This policy formally established the film industry as a national strategic industry, which means that the film industry gained significant national support with added resources for its development (General Office of the State Council, 2010).

CENSORSHIP OF CHINESE FILM PRODUCTION, DELIVERY AND CONSUMPTION

The market-related regulations of the Chinese film industry may have changed as presented in the previous section, but the censorship of

Chinese film production and distribution remains largely unchanged. This section will briefly explain how Chinese film censorship works, both related to traditional and online film distribution.

The Censoring of Offline and Online Film Production and Distribution

All films produced in China must go through a process of review before the content is approved. In China, all films have to go through a SARFT censor board to determine whether they can be shown in cinemas publicly. The SARFT Film Review Board consists of 36 members, who are film censors. Not all board members are SARFT officials, but they are from various professional organizations in order to facilitate diversified review of the films that are under consideration. The board includes members from the Department of Education, the Supreme People's Procuratorate (which is the highest agency at the national level responsible for both prosecution and investigation in the People's Republic of China), National Union's Education and Propaganda Department, the Supreme People's Procuratorate press office, and academic scholars from the Communication University of China, Beijing Film Academy, and China Art Research Institute and film directors (Baidu, 2013a).

The State Council issued the 'Movie Administration Regulations' on 25 December, 2001, consisting of 11 regulations to set the standards for films to meet specific requirements under SARFT's internal policies (State Council, 2001). Only one of these 11 regulations is focused on technical standards, such as color, sound, and video technology issues, and the remaining ten regulations are focused on content and ideology. These regulations are intended to ensure that the content does not leak state secrets; endanger national security; harm national honor and interests; incite ethnic hatred; undermine national unity; propagate obscenity, gambling, or violence; or instigate crimes, subordination, superstition and cult (State Council, 2001).

Those films that pass the examination will receive the 'Film Examination Decision Letter' and the 'Film Public Screening Permit', which are to be shown at the opening of the film. Productions that fail to pass the review may re-submit the film for a second review within 30 days after having re-edited as instructed by the board's decision (cf. Cain, 2011).

Censorship of Online Film Distribution

Because of the rapid growth of the Internet and new media in China, films are not only shown in cinemas. Film content delivery today has switched from one-way, single-channel communication to interactive, multiple and integrated media. Internet and online streaming of audio-visual content has become popular in China because of the high penetration of internet broadband connections. However, the Internet has been controlled and censored in China since the first day the technology was available in the country. In recent years, many regulations have been enacted and implemented, covering film content and its dissemination via the Internet (National People's Congress, 2000; Net.china.com.cn, 2013). A 2012 study published by the 'OpenNet Initiative', co-founded by Harvard Law School, Cambridge University and the University of Toronto, concluded that China has the world's most advanced Internet filtering system which also includes the filtering of audio-visual content (OpenNet, 2012). The system blocks or deletes any online content that violates certain regulations such as those presented above. As a consequence, film-makers have resorted to self-censorship to make sure that their productions are not removed from online distribution by the authorities.

CHANGING MARKET CONDITIONS

In addition to the new policies, the market conditions in China's film industry have also undergone major changes. As presented in the introduction of this chapter, the Chinese film industry produced 893 films during 2012 and total box office revenues reached RMB 17.1 billion (Li, 2013). Domestic films were able to generate RMB 8.27 billion in box office revenues, about 48 percent of the total revenues. These numbers should be compared to the total box office revenues in 2002, which were no more than RMB 920 million (USD 146 million). In other words, compared to ten years ago, 2012 total box office revenues increased 18.5 times, with an average annual growth rate of almost 34 percent.

Chinese film production has been resilient to the competition from foreign film, but some of this growth is nevertheless generated by foreign film import. On 18 February 2012, China and the United States resolved the WTO film issues by reaching a memorandum of understanding (MOU) that was an extension of the 2001 WTO agreement. This MOU required China to further lower the barriers of entry for US film-makers (The White House, Office of the Vice President, 2012). As a result of this agreement, the Chinese government has agreed to import 14 foreign films in addition to the original agreement of 20 films per year based on a revenue-sharing model. The agreement further specified that these additional 14 films had to be 3D or IMAX productions and that the box office revenue-sharing ratio should be increased from 13 percent to 25 percent. This 12 percent increase would facilitate American film companies to gain an additional USD 20–40 million in revenue from the Chinese market (Yi, 2012). The imported films have certainly increased competition, but it also shows that domestically made Chinese films were ready to face competition from Hollywood and other outside sources.

DIGITAL TECHNOLOGIES

Ever since Zhang Shuxin founded the first Internet service provider – Infohighway – in 1995, people in China have been heavy Internet users (Baidu, 2013a). In the past three years, the access to the Internet has moved from the wired desktops to mobile Internet connected devices such as iPads, iPhones and other smartphones (Jia and Zhang, 2012). At the same time, 3G networks have been developed, which increased the capability of mobile devices. In order to contextualize the two cases that will be presented later in this chapter, it is important to understand how digital technologies have influenced innovation and reformation of China's film industry.

According to the China Internet Network Information Center (CNNIC) report released in July 2013, the total number of Internet users in China reached 591 million by the end of June 2013, which means that China is the country with the highest number of Internet users in the world. We have already reported in this chapter that the mobile phone has replaced the desktop computer to become the most common Internet access tool, with 464 million mobile phone users.

As in most advanced mobile telephony markets in the world, mobile applications (e.g., QQ, WeChat, Weibo, which are all Chinese social media services) are becoming increasingly popular and widely used in China (Yang, 2012). Figure 3.1 shows how these mobile devices were used in China to access audio-visual and other content. It shows that close to 70 percent of the usage was used to access music, video and films.

The regulatory and technological transformations discussed above have significantly changed consumer behavior in China. The Internet has enabled the use of new social media tools, and allowed consumers to become active participants in information creation, gathering and exchange. Tang (2013) states that this transformation 'has changed the Chinese people's lack of a public exchange to a community-based way of life'. The two cases presented below will show the effect of how this new consumer behavior using new media tools transformed the marketing and promotion of films in China.

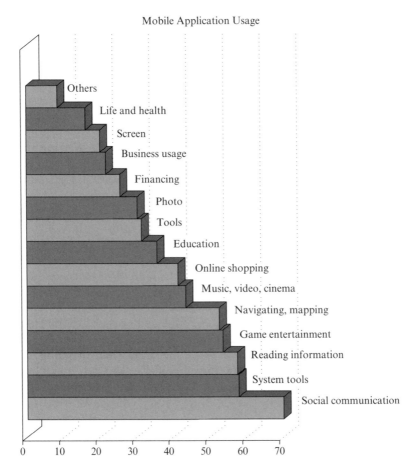

Mobile Application Usage

Others
Life and health
Screen
Business usage
Financing
Photo
Tools
Education
Online shopping
Music, video, cinema
Navigating, mapping
Game entertainment
Reading information
System tools
Social communication

0   10   20   30   40   50   60   70

Source: Yang (2012, p. 299).

Figure 3.1   Mobile application usage in China

MARKETING STRATEGIES BEFORE AND AFTER THE INDUSTRY TRANSFORMATION

With these changing regulatory and social communication patterns as a backdrop, we will examine two successful films produced in China in 2002 and 2011. These two films are selected as case studies because they were highly successful in box office revenues generation. One of the films (*Hero*) was produced in the very early days of the transformation of the film industry in China, and the other film was produced about a decade later when the new Chinese film industry was established as the world's number two. The analysis will use the two films to illustrate what has been argued throughout the chapter, namely how regulatory and technological change during the past decade has transformed the way films are produced and distributed in China.

Case 1: *Hero*, 2002

Hero is a story that takes place in ancient China during the Warring States Period, and is focused on the life of the swordsman 'Nameless' who came to the Qin state to assassinate the emperor. After several assassination attempts, no visitors were allowed to be close to the emperor within 100 steps. Nameless claimed that he had killed three assassins and offered his stories to the emperor one after another in order to be allowed to get closer and closer to the emperor. However, when Nameless was close enough to make his assassination, the emperor convinced Nameless that the state would become chaotic again if he would die. Finally, Nameless did abandon his assassination plans due to his respect for the emperor's reasoning. He earned the emperor's respect and received a hero's funeral. The emperor ended the Warring States Period and became Qin Shi Huang (Wikipedia, 2002; Cinema.com, 2013).

The USD 30 million production was directed by Zhang Yimou, a successful director who also was the director of the 2008 Olympic Games opening show in Beijing. The cast included stars from Mainland China and Hong Kong, including Jet Li, Tony Leung, Maggie Cheung, Chen Daoming, Donnie Yen and Zhang Ziyi. The film was able to generate RMB 250 million (USD 40 million) in box office revenues in China and USD 177 million worldwide. *Hero* was nominated and received a number of accolades and awards all over the world. For instance, it was nominated for the Best Foreign Language Film Oscar at the 2003 Academy Awards and Zhang Yimou won the Alfred Bauer Award at the Berlin International Film Festival in 2003 for his work. The National Society of Film Critics awarded Zhang Yimou the Best Director award and The New York Film Critics Circle recognized cinematographer Christopher Doyle with its award for Best Cinematography. *Hero* received seven Hong Kong Film Awards in 2003, including Best Cinematography, Best Art Direction, Best Visual Effects and Best Sound. The movie was also nominated for seven other awards, including Best Picture, Best Screenplay, Best Actress, Best Song and Best Director.

Hero was produced during the time when China was pushing for a market-oriented and market-led environment. *Hero* used a comprehensive integrated marketing approach constituted by a number of components that was both innovative and pioneering in the Chinese marketplace at the time. First, it had a RMB 10 million (USD 1.58 million) marketing campaign budget, which included television commercials in national TV networks (CCTV1, CCTV3, CCTV8), and provincial TV networks (Beijing TV, Guangdong TV, Shanghai TV, etc.). It was the first time that film promotion publicized widely on such a large scale. Other advertising outlets included various media, such as websites, billboards and subway light boxes. Second, it used large-scale public relations activities, included spending RMB 11 million (USD 1.75 million) for Beijing's Great Hall premiere. The Great Hall had traditionally been used exclusively for party leaders to meet and have official parties. Third, it was the first film project in China that created ancillary content products, including books, Internet games, 'the-making-of' documentaries, concerts, theme song albums and so on. These products generated revenues of RMB 17.8 million (USD 2.83 million), including revenues from domestic audio and DVD copyrights. The licensing revenues generated by *Hero* were 44 times bigger than what was the norm for similar films before it. Fourth, because of the success of the film's huge promotion and publicity campaign, *Hero* itself also became a well-known brand, and other commercial products made several promotional collaborations with the *Hero* production. They included Lenovo, which made three products, mobile phones, computers and digital cameras; as well as China Mobile, MMS, Beijing Netcom; and the Great Wall brand of red wine. The film also teamed up with international brands such as Procter & Gamble, Unilever, Citroën, Hyundai and Toyota. These Chinese and international companies created these co-branded products simultaneously with the film.

Conclusively, before the rise of new media in China, *Hero* managed to make a strong marketing impact, thanks mainly to a large promotional budget and the overwhelming publicity with full and effective use of actors and directors. Its branding synergy effectively integrated the film's content with various platforms, which penetrated the consumers' life with various value-added products (Huang, 2003).

Case 2: *Love is Not Blind,* **2011**

Love is Not Blind is a story about Huang Xiaoxian, a single young woman who had a bad break-up following her seven-year romantic relationship. Her work colleague, Wang Xiaojian, supported her during this difficult period and eventually they began a new relationship together (Wikipedia, 2013; Elley, 2012). The RMB 9 million (USD 1.4 million) production was directed by Teng Huatao and the cast included Wen Zhang, Bai Baihe and

Zhang Jiayi. The film was not internationally distributed but generated RMB 350 million (USD 56 million) domestically.

In 2011 when *Love is not Blind* was produced, social media started to play an important and widespread role in China. Unlike *Hero, Love is Not Blind* was not a big budget production and the film's production team did not spend large amounts of money producing promotional material in the same way as for *Hero*. Rather, the social media became a primary tool in the publicity and promotion of *Love is not Blind*. The way the film uses new content distribution channels, including social media tools, illustrates how these new tools have made a revolutionary breakthrough in China's film industry.

Love is not Blind used social media and interactive communication to reach out with its themes focusing on 'nostalgia, romance and emotions'. They used websites such as Weibo and Renren.net as the main dissemination outlets and tried to appeal to college students born between 1985 and 1990, as well as to white-collar workers. *Love is not Blind* was produced in the year called 'The Century of Unattached Singles' in China. The break-up story of the film fitted perfectly with this theme and the film quickly developed into a very successful Internet meme.

The production team created a number of videos, called 'Break-up Stories', along with the film's trailers that were posted on online video and social networking sites. Weibo was also used to strengthen the film's romantic theme and to collect fans' reactions and comments immediately to interact with them in order to expand the film's content coverage.

Furthermore, at the early stage of the promotion and publicity of *Love is not Blind*, a mobile application, 'Cheap Cat Version I', was pre-sold on China's largest online retailer, Taobao, website. It had accumulated 56 823 downloads and showed nearly 1.5 million search results. Mobile applications started to become an important promotional and sales channel for films in China, exceeding the reach of similar techniques used in Hollywood films (Chen, 2011).

Love is not Blind has also demonstrated a different way to create promotional content. Using Weibo in its promotional campaigns, the film used three types of Weibo formats: official Weibo, public Weibo and actors Weibo, to gain exposure to different audience segments. That means a combination of players was used to generate attention and content. They also used various types of Weibo applications, for example online voting and activities to establish an interactive communication base on which to post text, pictures, music, video and other forms of transmission, making breaking-up love stories and any words related to the film omnipresent on Weibo (Weibo.com, 2013).

Another innovative idea was to set up a 'Break-up Museum' website, which played publicity materials at the movie, and collected break-up love stories, healing songs, and moods after break-up on Weibo. It has made the 'Break-up Museum' an interaction center for people who have suffered an unpleasant break-up (Sina.com, 2013).

In addition, the film crew went to seven major box office markets in three months to produce 14 'break-up love stories' videos. It recruited volunteers to participate in the video through the largest website, Sina.com, and its advertising clients' own websites. So, the publicity and video-making were conducted concurrently, making it an instant interactive process. Some Internet users made their own 'break-up love stories' videos to post online, adding to the importance of user-generated content to promote the film (Sina.com, 2013).

The examples presented above show that promotional content does not need to be produced by the film companies. The key success of *Love is not Blind* was due to effective user-generated content distributed via social media. The successful creation of user-generated content distributed via social media made consumers participate interactively and resonate with the movie, and thus paved the way for the film's great success.

CONCLUSIONS

We have used two films, *Hero* (2002) and *Love is not Blind* (2011), as two examples to show a change in the business models in China's film industry. Based on our focus of content creation, content delivery and content consumption, we can see that the emergence of user-generated content and consumer-generated media, which were based on an emergence of new content distribution channels, have made a revolutionary breakthrough in the distribution and marketing processes of films in China.

These two case studies show that innovation of business models in China is driven by the development of new media. Though there were policy changes in terms of the film industry in China, the original creation of film content is still highly censored and content delivery channels are monitored by the government. But film content is no longer a product that users simply buy and consume. Instead, new media users use the content and stories interactively. These factors, when combined, contribute to an innovation and reformation of China's film industry.

REFERENCES

Baidu (2013a). Internet in China. http://baike.baidu.com/view/38177.htm.
Baidu (2013b). SARFT censor board. http://baike.baidu.com/view/10018083.htm.

Cain, Robert (2011). 'How to be Censored in China: A Brief Filmmaking Guide'. 30 November. http://www.indiewire.com/article/how-to-be-censored-in-china-a-brief-filmmaking-guide.

Chen, Liming (2011). 'Box office of "Love is not blind" over RMB 300 million mobile applications of innovative marketing concepts'. 29 November. http://dh.yesky.com/7/30936507.shtml.

Cinema.com (2013). Hero (2002) Synopsis. http://cinema.com/film/7975/hero/synopsis.phtml.

CNNIC (2013). The China Internet Network Information Center (CNNIC) report 2013. http://www.cnnic.cn/hlwfzyj/hlwxzbg/hlwtjbg/201307/P020130717505343100851.pdf.

Elley, Derek (2012). 'Charming, unpretentious rom-com boosted by subtle chemistry between its leads. Asian events.' http://www.filmbiz.asia/reviews/love-is-not-blind.

General Office of the CPC Central Committee (2001). Several opinions on further reform of news publishing, TV broadcasting and film industry. The General Office of the CPC Central Committee No. 2001–17. http://hk.lexiscn.com/law/law-chinese-1-70020.html and http://www.lawyee.org/Act/Act_Display.asp?ChannelID=1010100&RID=203540.

General Office of the State Council (2010). General Office of the State Council guidance on promoting the prosperity and development of the film industry guidance. State Council No. 2010–9. http://www.gov.cn/zwgk/2010–01/25/content_1518665.htm.

Huang, Jiangwei (2003). 'Analysis of the Successful Marketing of "Hero"'. 7 January. http://www.emkt.com.cn/article/91/9199.html.

Jia, Jinxi and Zhang Yi (2012). 'Mobile and Electronic Media, Annual report on development of new media'. Beijing: Social Sciences Academic Press, pp. 280–83.

Li, Ting Jun (2013). SARFT Annual Press Conference 2013. *China Film Daily*. 14 January. http://www.dmcc.gov.cn/publish/main/175/2013/201301141774537702165813/20130114174537702165813_.html.

Li, Xiaodao (2012). '2011 National box office revenues reached an all-time high of 13.1 billion, and 20 Chinese-made films exceeded revenues of RMB 1 billion'. 9 January. http://news.mtime.com/2012/01/09/1479569.html.

National Bureau of Statistics of China (2013). Statistical Communiqué of the People's Republic of China on the 2012 National Economic and Social Development. Beijing, National Bureau of Statistics of China, 22 February. http://www.stats.gov.cn/english/ pressrelease/t20130222_402874590.htm.

National People's Congress (2000). National People's Congress decision on safeguarding Internet security, 28 December. http://big5.xinhuanet.com/gate/big5/news.xinhuanet.com/it/2006-04/30/content_4495376.htm.

Net.china.com.cn (2013). 'Internet Message Services Management Methods'. http://net.china.com.cn/zcfg/txt/2005–06/02/content_206761.htm.

OpenNet (2012). 'China country profile. OpenNet Initiative', 19 March 2014. https://opennet.net/research/profiles/china.

SARFT (2000). Several opinions on further reform of the film industry. SARFT No. 2000–320. http://www.gov.cn/gongbao/content/2001/content_60781.htm.

SARFT (2001a). Principles of further formation of the Film Groups. SARFT No. 2001–126. http://www.sarft.gov.cn/catalog.do?catalogId=20070831154622180039&pageIndex=15.

SARFT (2001b). The implementation details of film distribution and theater reformation. SARFT No.2001–1591. http://www.sarft.gov.cn/.

SARFT (2010). The 2010 Radio Film and Television Industry Development Overview, Radio, Film and Television Development Research Centre, SARFT. http://www.sarftrc.cn/templates/T_content/index.aspx?nodeid=95&page=Cont entPage&contentid=518.

Sina.com (2013). '33 days of activities of sad love failures'. http://video.sina.com. cn/z/wdyslbwg/.

State Council (2001). PRC State Council document No. 342. 25 December. 20 March 2014. http://www.sarft.gov.cn/articles/2007/02/16/20070913144431120333.html.

State Council (2005). PRC State Council document No. 342. 21 August. http:// www.sarft.gov.cn/articles/2007/02/16/20070913144431120333.html.

Tan, Wei Ping and Geng Zhen Jin (2001). Minister of Foreign Trade and Economic Cooperation of China Shi Guang Sheng: Enter World Trade Organizations document will be announced next month. 19 November. People.com.cn quoted *Beijing Youth Daily*. http://www.people.com.cn/BIG5/jinji/31/179/20011119/608046. html.

Tang, Hao (2013). 'From top social structure design to low level design'. *South Reviews Magazine*. 26 February. http://www.nfcmag.com/article/3907.html.

Weibo.com (2013). Weibo Search result of 'Love is not Blind'. 8 July. http://s. weibo.com/weibo/%25E5%25A4%25B1%25E6%2581%258B33%25E5%25A4% 25A9&Refer=index.

White House, The, Office of the Vice President (2012). United States Achieves Breakthrough on Movies in Dispute with China. February. http://www.ustr.gov/ about-us/press-office/press-releases/2012/february/united-states-achieves-break through-movies-disput.

Wikipedia (2002). 'Hero' (2002 film). http://en.wikipedia.org/wiki/Hero_%282002_ film%29.

Wikipedia (2013). 'Love is not Blind'. http://en.wikipedia.org/wiki/Love_Is_Not_ Blind.

Yang, Binyan (2012). 'Report on Mobile Application Software used in China'. In Annual Report on Development of New Media, Beijing: Social Sciences Academic Press, pp. 297–311.

Yi, Dong Fang (2012). 'China and the United States resolve WTO movies agreement with a Memorandum of Understanding'. *Beijing Times*. 19 February. http://media.people.com.cn/GB/17152162.html.

4. The power of Japanese film production consortia: the evolution of inter-firm alliance networks and the revival of the Japanese film industry

Naoki Wakabayashi, Jin-Ichiro Yamada and Masaru Yamashita

INTRODUCTION

Japanese films are increasing in popularity, not only at the Cannes Film Festival but also in the Japanese market. At the Japanese box office, Japanese films have regained over half their market share since 2006, overtaking Hollywood movies, which made up the major share of films from 1975 to 2005. Several major factors account for the current success of the Japanese film business (Tanaka, 2010; Yamashita and Yamada, 2010). First, major Japanese TV stations wanted to cut costs and to buy inexpensive Japanese films rather than expensive Hollywood productions. Second, the growth of cinema complexes provides many more screens and increasing opportunities for Japanese film-makers in their home market. Third, many cultural critics suggest Japan's younger generation shows a greater interest in domestic culture than the previous generation. Finally, one of the main factors for the resurgence of the Japanese film market is the new business approach that is practiced within Japanese film production today. Japanese film production has shifted from being organized as independent film studios to joint ventures that involve both media and non-media companies. This new structure enables films from these joint ventures to generate greater revenues than was possible in the era when film studios held a monopoly in the Japanese market. These film-making joint ventures are referred to as 'Film Production Consortia' (FPC) or, in Japanese, *'Eiga Seisaku Iinkai'*. A typical FPC is a temporary organizational body for a joint venture project, led by a major TV broadcasting company, and consisting not only of film business companies, but also other media companies and non-media sponsor companies in manufacturing and service industries. FPCs are now the dominant organizational form for Japanese film production and they currently provide the majority of the most popular movies in the Japanese market. FPCs are effective inter-firm alliances that can pool resources (financial as well as non-financial) from member companies; share business risks; coordinate internal deals that involve the use of content across different media; enable merchandising and sponsorship opportunities; and practice cross-media promotion of the film that is produced. FPCs are quite new to the Japanese film industry and to our knowledge FPCs have not been seen in the global film industry either, especially not in Hollywood, where major TV broadcasting companies have tended not to take many initiatives to organize joint inter-firm film-making projects for box office films.

FPCs open the formerly closed world of the Japanese film business to outside companies working in non-film-related industries and provide new and creative opportunities for commercial film production. An FPC forms an inter-firm strategic alliance for film production, including a short-term arrangement with a dynamic network that connects an array of companies across diverse industries. Many FPCs are organized in a particular manner in order to attract a given category of potential new enterprises operating outside the film business. As FPCs can mobilize and combine financial and non-financial resources for film production through their network of companies, they could be construed as a network resource or 'social capital' in the Japanese film industry.

For the production of large commercial films, FPCs have gradually become the standard alliance strategy in the Japanese film business. This chapter examines three aspects of this strategy. First, their unique features and main advantages for Japanese film production will be presented. Next, the historical development of these inter-firm alliances is explored, looking specifically at their contributions to the upturn and revival of Japanese film-making in Japan. Lastly, as an FPC is largely an inter-firm project team consisting of corporate producers from a number of member companies, the role of the producer in Japanese film production consortia will be discussed.

ADVANTAGES OF FILM PRODUCTION CONSORTIA

Unique Features

FPCs are the most rapidly increasing form of alliance amongst current firms in the Japanese film industry, providing Japanese film-makers

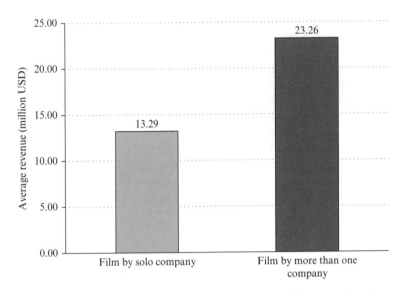

Note: This comparison is calculated by the authors, using the data from 300 films (the annual top 30 commercial films from 2000 to 2009 as ranked by the industry statistics compiled by the Motion Picture Producers Association of Japan: http://www.eiren.org/ toukei/data.html). 1 USD = 97.64 JPY.

Figure 4.1   Comparison of average revenue in the 2000s

numerous advantages in film production. After a long downturn in the big Japanese studios, FPCs allowed the creation of a new system of commercial film production, invigorating the Japanese film industry by increasing the production and sales of Japanese commercial films. In the 2000s, the average revenues of films made by such alliances were nearly twice as high as those produced by one film studio or a solo company (Figure 4.1). Moreover, in Japan, beyond the film business, this style of inter-firm alliance is now widely applied to the content production in other genres, including TV programs, animation, video games and online motion pictures. Therefore, it is relevant to address this academically not only in a Japanese context, but also in a context of global media business transformation.

An FPC is defined as a temporary, inter-firm project organization employed for film production joint ventures. Companies across different industries jointly organize in order to collectively plan, provide financial and non-financial resources, share profits and own intellectual property from the project. FPCs exist in various corporate forms, including voluntary partnerships, anonymous associations, limited liability partner-

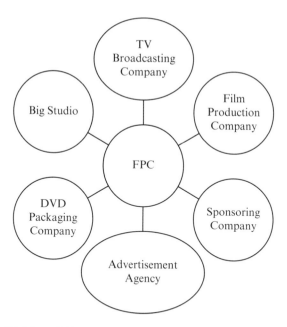

Source: Modified from *Nikkei Entertainment* (2009, September, p. 103).

Figure 4.2   Typical set-up of a film production consortium

ships or limited partnerships for investment among member companies (Kishikawa, 2010, p. 160). They are typically led by a major TV broadcasting company and consist of a publisher, a big film studio, a film production company, a video or DVD packaging company, an advertising house, and sometimes a video games company. One or two (non-media) sponsor companies are often also part of the FPC to promote their products or services, mainly via the advertisement company in the FPC consortium (Figure 4.2).

Looking inside, the FPC is typically organized as a temporary project team composed of corporate producers from member companies. In FPCs, activities and roles in the value chain are mainly structured as follows: original novels or comic books are provided by a publisher; film-making by a production company; film distribution by a film company; and broadcasting by major TV stations. Furthermore, an advertisement agency mediates promotional requests between non-media and media companies involved in sponsorships. In some Hollywood blockbuster films, film studios and sponsor companies collaborate for advertisement; however, initiatives by major TV stations to produce large numbers of commercial films are not globally seen except in the Japanese film industries.

A good example of an FPC is the production of the popular comic-based live action film, *Death Note* (2006). One of the major Japanese TV stations, Nippon Television Network Corporation (NTV), led the consortium and provided promotion and distribution via its nationwide TV network. The other member companies in the FPC included: Shueisha, a publishing company which provided original comics and new guidebooks; Shochiku and Warner Brothers, both film studios, which were responsible for distributing the film worldwide and in Japan; Horipuro, a large talent agency, which allocated available actors; and Konami Entertainment, a video games company, which led the video game production.

Collective Advantages

FPCs consist of companies not only in the film industry, but also in media industries (e.g. TV broadcasting, publishing, advertising, video packaging and video game designing); manufacturing industries; and non-media service industries. TV broadcasting companies often initiate FPCs, but as these are not long-term or regular partnerships, they differ from so-called *keiretsu* relationships, which are fixed, limited and continuous linkages between a major core company and regular subcontractors or retail agents, as typically seen in the Japanese automotive, electronics and manufacturing industries. Although potential partner companies for FPC alliances are relatively limited within traditional media industries and sponsoring non-media industries, the partner companies can be combined in numerous different ways. According to Japanese regulations only a single company from a particular industry can participate in an FPC. For example, the major TV broadcasting company previously mentioned (NTV) participated in several film projects during a certain year, but it collaborated with a different set of partners from project to project.

Currently, many commercial films in Japan are produced via FPCs since they are considered to offer four distinct advantages in the film production business in terms of finance, risk-sharing, intellectual property rights and new promotional opportunities. First, while the production costs of an average Hollywood movie vary from 50 to 100 million USD per film, in comparison, popular Japanese commercial films cost only 3 to 5 million USD per film. Within an FPC, a film-making project is able to cover these costs with contributions from a range of companies from different industries as presented above (Tohmatsu & Co., 2003, ch. 3). The FPC allows joint investments in film productions to be made, and have been able to avert the economic slump that faced big Japanese studios and film companies during the 1970s, which led to a severe shortage of production money and the production of only one or two films per year. FPC member companies may also contribute to a film project with non-financial resources, for example providing new technology, support for ticket sales and celebrity endorsements and offering other promotional activities. A film project may also enjoy earnings from merchandized characters and publicity goods (including toys, stationery and other related items) and commission fees from collaborating with the promotional activities of sponsoring companies. FPCs facilitate the collaboration between film production companies and sponsoring companies related to so-called 'product placement' and 'branded entertainment' projects (Albarran, 2001, p. 124). These projects involve product and services companies in the script development which means that the product and services companies get joint ownership of the intellectual property that is generated during the projects.

Second, joint investment and film production allows FPCs to share the business risks associated with the high uncertainty in financial performance typically found in the film business (Yamashita and Yamada, 2010, p. 88). From the 1960s to the 1980s, Japanese film studios independently financed the majority of commercial films but faced financial losses if their films were unsuccessful.

Third, as FPC member companies jointly own the intellectual property rights of a film they can freely use scenes and snapshots for their own media or business. In media studies, these deals are a very unique phenomenon and are termed 'multi-use of content' in different media and business contexts (Tanaka, 2010, pp. 161–7). Furthermore, FPCs allow these member companies to diversify and share revenues from TV licensing, DVD sales, character goods, advertisement and promotion fees, in addition to box office sales from movie theaters.

Fourth, FPCs are able to practice nationwide, short-term cross media promotions to attract audiences, as not only mass media companies (such as TV stations, publishers and radio stations) but also non-media companies (such as toy manufacturers, nationwide franchised convenience stores, mobile phone companies and Internet service providers) are also FPC members. As Steinberg (2012) shows, in the case of animation films, a toy manufacturer often takes exclusive distribution rights for character toys and uses aggressive cross-media promotion through several types of mass media. Sponsoring, non-media companies provide additional promotional opportunities such as storefronts, mobile phone advertising and online websites. For example, nationwide chains of convenience stores show film previews on LCD screens installed in their stores for several weeks as well as engaging in intensive sales campaigns involving original character goods at media events. These promotions may attract customers to movie theaters and lead to increased sales at box offices.

Finally, the majority of companies that formed FPCs found new business opportunities within the current era of digital technology innovation and the industrial transformation of media industries, creating new alliances between traditional visual media industries and new information industries. The wide application of digital technologies leads to a rapid restructuring and transformation of the visual media industries. Aris and Bughin (2012, pp. 26–33) stress that an important aspect of this transformation is that traditional platform service providers such as TV broadcasting and satellite TV services branch out into new media channels and integrate their current platform businesses with online TV services and digitally distributing films. Since FPCs are in a position to arrange multi-use deals using new, integrated services, scenes and film snapshots are distributed in both old as well as new, emerging media formats (such as Internet websites and digital mobile phones).

FPCs as Social Capital for Japanese Film Production

FPCs provide an 'organizational architecture' of linked internal and external elements that the organization creates and uses to achieve its goals (Buchanan and Huczynski, 2010, p. 519). As Cattani et al. (2008) argue, linkages for instance between film production and their distribution companies (such as big studios, major TV stations and CATV operators) are essential relationships. Based on an analysis of historical changes to distribution relationships between film production and distribution companies in Hollywood, Cattani et al. (2008) argue that many production companies which lost support of distribution companies eventually declined. The FPCs differ considerably from this traditional stable structure as they have a very short lifecycle and are established and dismantled over a short period of time. Distribution companies thereby do not hold on to their production partners for long periods of time but change their partner production companies every time a new FPC alliance is formed.

FPCs shape the unique social capital of film production as they connect and reconnect companies from different industries and allow access to different and greater resources, information and opportunities than film studios alone could access in their traditional networks. Interpersonal and inter-firm networks that provide valuable managerial resources that enable organizations to reach their goals are referred to as 'organizational social capital' (Tsai and Goshal, 1998). Since FPCs started to emerge, various combinations of companies from different industries have appeared, which has allowed the development of a more open and fluent film business ecosystem. This has also led to the evolution of interpersonal networks between corporate producers in those industries. Inter-firm networks formed via FPCs grew in number during the 2000s and an analysis of the

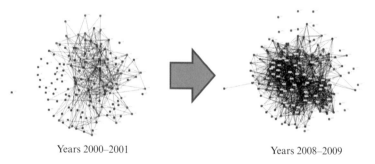

Years 2000–2001   Years 2008–2009

Note: Calculated using Netdraw.

Figure 4.3   *Evolution in film production consortium networks among organizations*

138 companies that jointly produced the annual top 30 box office sales films during the 2000s shows that the number of inter-firm ties has grown significantly between an early period (2000 to 2001) and a later period (2008 to 2009) (Figure 4.3). The comparison between these periods shows an increase in inter-firm ties from 694 to 2362, respectively, with an average number of partner companies increasing from 4.42 to 15.04.[1] By the end of the 2000s, FPCs had become widely institutionalized in the Japanese film business and the first step when shooting a successful film was the formation and management of an FPC. An FPC network is often also a breeding ground for new combinations of alliances in the film business. In these networks the intangible assets, such as knowledge, value, trust and custom support, shape the new FPCs that are allowed to develop. Thus, they provide a unique social capital for Japanese film production that allows for inter-firm alliance across industries, and that significantly widens the film business community by including media, manufacturing and new service companies in Japanese film production.

THE DEVELOPMENT OF FPCs IN THE JAPANESE FILM INDUSTRY

Decline and Revival of the Japanese Film Industry

The emergence of FPCs was in response to a long-term economic slump for the big Japanese studios, which made modernization of the Japanese film industry a necessity. Figure 4.4 shows the decline of the domestic market share of Japanese films during five decades. Since the 1960s, the

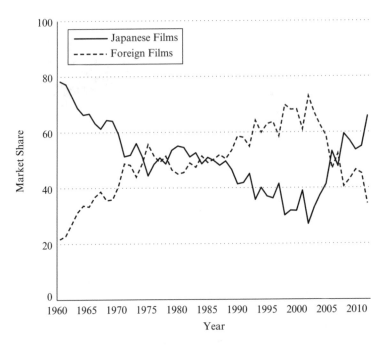

Source: Industrial statistics provided by the Motion Picture Producers Association of Japan, from http://www.eiren.org/toukei/data.html.

Figure 4.4   Revival of the market share of Japanese films

market share of Japanese films in Japan decreased from around 80 percent to less than 40 percent, whilst over the same period the market share of Hollywood films increased.[2] Major Japanese film studios, Toho, Shochiku and Toei, relied on their nationwide networks of theaters for their long-term survival during this downturn. They concentrated their resources on maintaining and strengthening the film distribution networks, and downsized and outsourced their in-house film production to independent production companies (Okada, 1991).

As a result of this outsourcing, a number of film creators working for the major studios were made redundant and transferred to small production firms or were given independent status. Film creators working in small firms and those with independent status were unable to market their own products unless they were distributed through the national theater networks operated by major film studio companies. Among domestic (Japanese) movies, 90 percent of the market share was still held by these 'big box' studio firms (Murakami and Ogawa, 1999). Therefore, these film creators had no option other than to be dependent on the 'big box' studio operators who dominated the copyrights of major films as well as the nationwide film distribution networks. This imposed hardship, both financially and motivationally, on most of the film creators running either independently or in small companies. They made dozens of 'economically viable movies' in subcontracting deals with major film studios, solely for their survival rather than focusing on their artistic desires and abilities.

However, these Japanese movies that were produced during the 1970s failed to attract audiences, and during the 1980s Japanese studios increasingly allocated their financial resources to importing Hollywood films rather than to creating domestic productions. Japanese studios purchased the distribution rights to Hollywood films and distributed them to their own cinema chains (Okada, 1991), which contributed to the growing market share of Hollywood productions in the Japanese film market.

The Japanese film industry has witnessed a series of structural changes since the 1990s, one being the emergence of 'cinema complexes' run by foreign affiliated companies. Major Hollywood studios also expanded independently to distributing their films directly in the Japanese market. These firms rapidly increased their market share, at the expense of Japanese theater owners. This led to a decline of the major local studios' market presence. At the same time, a group of new, large-scale media firms (publishers, TV stations, and advertising agencies) entered into the film production sector and further diminished the overall influence of major local studios over the clusters of independent film creators. The domination of the film production sector thus transferred from the traditional film studios to these media companies, in particular, major TV stations, which capitalized on their expertise and their access to vast resources available for promotional activities of the films they supported (Yamashita and Yamada, 2010). This shift in market dominance was the beginning of the Film Production Consortium (FPC) in Japan.

Changing Marketing Practices

The Japanese TV broadcasting companies considered the pre-FPC promotion plans put forth by the big Japanese studios old fashioned and ineffective. Thus, using their promotion expertise they provided more effective media channels to boost the advertising's effectiveness. In this regard, the TV broadcasting companies retained a bigger say among the FPC members. Initially however, when broadcasting companies began collaborating with film studios, they passively provided their own media channels for the studios' out-of-date promotion plans. Later, the TV broadcasting companies believed the promotional plans to be problematical. This was linked to the fall in the studios' presence in the Japanese film industry. Ultimately the TV broadcasters planned their own promotions. For instance, when the Japanese film *Shall we Dance?* was released in 1996, NTV, a major Japanese TV broadcasting company and an FPC member for the film, arbitrarily made a TV program designed to promote and televise the movie. The director and the producer, however, complained, since the TV program content differed markedly from their original movie concept. Despite this, the movie reaped considerable revenues, partly because of the TV program's influence on the audience.[3]

The start of participation of major advertising agencies in FPCs during the 2000s completed the ideal model of a consortium. Before then, the Japanese advertising agencies had usually coordinated animation projects between the production companies, sponsors (especially toymakers) and the publishers that held the original rights to the 'manga'. Such agencies are employed to coordinate the companies from various industries and to develop a trusting working relationship. Needless to say, they also have expertise in coordinating effective promotion plans applicable to various media. It was sensible for major advertising agencies to join an array of FPCs. This allowed FPCs to connect consortium member companies in order to undertake large-scale promotion campaigns of their films.

For example, the Japanese film *Socrates in Love*, released in 2004, is a typical film created via an FPC.[4] Shogakukan, one of Japan's major publishers in 2001, published the original novel. Although initially the film rights were not in demand, Haruna, the corporate producer at Hakuhodo, a major Japanese advertising agency, decided that the novel would make an attractive film and arranged to obtain the film rights from Shogakukan. Shimatani, the executive producer of Toho, a major Japanese film studio, asked if he had any new and interesting proposals for new films and Haruna proposed *Socrates in Love*. The executive producer considered this proposal, and then invited Haruna to commence the project. Haruna invited not the professional film producers, but instead a TV producer, Hamana, based at Tokyo Broadcasting System Television (TBS), a major Japanese TV broadcasting company, to join the FPC. Hamana participated in the consortium because he thought TBS would automatically obtain the rights to broadcast the film as well as to broadcast a TV drama version of *Socrates in Love*. Shogakukan, the publisher of the original novel, also decided to join to act as an agent for the novel's author and to ensure that the original author's vision endured. TBS employed their own media channels and promoted *Socrates in Love* both as a film and as a TV drama. The FPC also allowed the publisher to publish a script of the film, aggressively promoting it in every bookstore, which proved to be a great promotional arena at that time. Hakuhodo, an advertising agency firm, coordinated all the consortium members' promotional activities. Eventually *Socrates in Love* gained revenues of 85 million USD at box offices in Japan. It was the biggest box office hit in 2004 in Japan.

It is important to recognize that the majority of films made by FPCs are aimed at the Japanese market and hence are not exported overseas. The goal for an FPC project is success in the Japanese market rather than in the global market. Most FPC member companies tend to focus on and operate within the domestic market and are consequently unwilling to make and promote films targeting foreign markets. As a result, most Japanese productions that are represented at international film festivals are independent projects rather than FPC projects.

THE ROLE OF THE PRODUCER IN A FILM PRODUCTION CONSORTIUM

The revival of the film industry was brought about by film producers who shaped FPC into an alternative to the distributor/studio-driven subcontracting system in Japan. In terms of managing creative FPC projects, the producers succeeded in the integration of commerce and art, improving the artistic recognition and audience appeal of Japanese films.

The role of the producer in film projects has received a lot of scholarly attention. For instance, studies have explored the relationship between the director and the producer and how they connect the creative and the business side, respectively, in their cooperation with each other (Faulkner and Anderson, 1987; Baker and Faulkner, 1991; Yamashita and Yamada, 2010). Faulkner and Anderson used quantitative analysis to identify instances of cooperation and role allocation between the director and producer. The research identified the strongest and the weakest director–producer relationships and showed that high-achievers in both professions choose to work together most frequently. Producer–director combinations are temporary working relationships but their interaction process is crucial to the overall project's success. It is clear that in this apparently fluid mix there are stable patterns from each professional's contribution (Jones, 1996; DeFillippi and Arthur, 1998).

The media sector's production process is composed of various inter-firm relationships (Lampel and Shamsie, 2003). It is vital for artists, creative professionals and stakeholders in these industries to know how to utilize their individual resources and also how to manage the collaboration across sectors and functions, while they at the same time are able to hold on to their own identities and ideals. Research conducted at the micro-level has indicated the challenges associated with contractual, temporal project-based network organizations (Antcliff et al., 2008; Manning, 2005; Windeler and Sydow, 2001). What has not been highlighted sufficiently by these scholars is that dynamic career-long collaborations can also appear between professionals in firms that bring complementary skills, logic and networks into the film projects. Although FPCs may appear to be temporary organizations, they are actually involved in a considerably long-term systematic relationship linked to a project's accomplishments and within which both key and temporary staff gather and then scatter (DeFillippi and Arthur, 1998; Jones, 2002). The success or failure of long-term creative content production is not only determined by producers' ability to collaborate with other professionals representing different firms' interests and rights, but also their ability to support the advancement of the other partners' careers.

Aspiring producers usually start their careers with odd jobs at small production companies or part-time jobs at filming sites. A young producer at a production company has to develop their experience as a producer and at the same time to build a network of creators that they can collaborate with, but production companies usually have a range of ongoing projects and thus producers have plenty of opportunity to work with many different creators. It is common practice in the Japanese FPC system to promote internal staff to producer roles rather than giving the role to external candidates. As a consequence, there are very limited career opportunities for independent producers who want to gain access to the FPC system. An alternative to the gradual career development as a producer at a smaller production company is to get employed by a major production company involved in the production of multiple films. However, since it is difficult to enter a major production company as a producer without a track record it is more likely that the aspiring producer will start out in the accounting or sales department of the major production company and then slowly work his/her way into producer roles.

This background may be useful in an FPC system where the producer role is very much to be responsible for increasing the likelihood of film profitability by ensuring access to the film theaters associated with the big film studios and maximizing the PR activities of the TV broadcasting companies.

The producer has to be able to manage the tension between art and commerce that is inherent in most commercial media projects, but perhaps even more so in an FPC. For example, as a typical film only appears in theaters for a short period of time, usually a month or so, it is difficult to generate substantial PR and marketing activities during this short period. However, by producing and broadcasting a TV drama version of the film, TV stations are able to increase the advertisement and PR income substantially. As a consequence of this separation of the TV version and the theater version of the film, it is possible to consider the theater version as an art form rather than as an advertising commodity. However, the separation also generates internal tensions between commerce and art, which the producer has to be able to manage. In order to manage these tensions the producer assembles a team with multiple functions and types of expertise that is able to understand and communicate and negotiate with representatives from different FPC member companies. These negotiations may be very complex as FPCs involve collaboration between multiple stakeholders in various markets and industries. The creative content may originate from the film-making process, but based on this content it is possible to identify several opportunities that can be commercially exploited without violating core artistic values. In this sense, the work of corporate producers is a type of cross-media marketing role aimed to engage with all FPC stakeholders.

CONCLUSIONS

This chapter has presented how the FPC system has proven to be a very effective film production alliance in Japan and how it has invigorated the Japanese film industry. FPCs deliver films as new services and promotional avenues for sponsoring companies in other media and non-media industries that potentially attract audiences for not only large but also small- or medium-sized films. FPCs may also invite investment for films from outside the film business. The FPC system has now extended beyond the film industry in Japan and is now spread widely to other industries producing TV programs, video games, animation programs and so on.

FPCs and the FPC producer balance art and commerce or film-making and the multi-use demands from sponsoring FPC member companies. Member companies use FPCs as social capital, or as a networking resource for creating films as media events for their businesses. In FPCs, member companies act not only as financial actors in setting up a joint venture, but also as joint creators of media events, connecting their ideas, resources and opportunities via corporate producers.

NOTES

1. This was calculated by the authors using data from the industrial statistics compiled by the Motion Picture Producers Association of Japan. A total of 138 companies jointly produced the top 30 commercial films during 2000–2001 and 2008–2009. Analysis of the network expansion from the earlier period to the later period was determined using UCINET and NETDRAW.

2. Based on industrial statistics from the Motion Picture Producers Association of Japan.
3. The description of this case is based on our original interview with Mr Masui, the producer of the film *Shall we Dance?* on 10 August, 1998.
4. Details of this case are based on our original interview with Mr Haruna on 24 July, 2008 and Mr Hamana on 30 September, 2008. The Japanese title of this film is *Sekai no Chushin de Ai wo Sakebu.*

REFERENCES

Albarran, A.B. (2001) *Media Economics: Understanding Markets, Industries and Economics.* Ames, IA: Iowa State Press.
Antcliff, V., Saundry, R. and Stuart, M. (2008) 'Networks and social capital in the UK television industry: The weakness of weak ties', *Human Relations*, 60 (2), 371–93.
Aris, A. and Bughin, J. (2012) *Managing Media Companies: Harnessing Creative Value*, 2nd edn, Chichester, UK: Wiley.
Baker, W.E. and Faulkner, R.R. (1991) 'Role as resource in the Hollywood film industry', *American Journal of Sociology*, 97, 279–309.
Buchanan, D.A. and Huczynski, A.A. (2010) *Organizational Behavior*, 7th edn, Harlow, UK: Pearson Education.
Cattani, G., Ferriani, S., Negro, G. and Perretti, F. (2008) 'The structure of consensus: Network ties, legitimation, and exit rates of U.S. feature film producer organizations', *Administrative Science Quarterly*, 53, 145–82.
DeFillippi, R.J. and Arthur, M.B. (1998) 'Paradox in project-based enterprise: The case of film making', *California Management Review*, 40, 125–39.
Faulkner, R.R. and Anderson, A.B. (1987) 'Short-term projects and emergent careers: Evidence from Hollywood', *American Journal of Sociology*, 92, 879–909.
Jones, C. (1996) 'Careers in project networks: The case of the film industry', in M.B. Arthur and D.M. Rousseau (eds), *The Boundaryless Career: A New Employment Principle for a New Organizational Era*. New York: Oxford University Press, pp. 58–75.
Jones, C. (2002) 'Co-evolution of entrepreneurial careers, institutional rules and competitive dynamics in American films, 1895–1920', *Organization Studies*, 22 (6), 911–44.
Kishikawa, Z. (2010) *Content Business Tokuron* [Content Business], Tokyo: Gakubunsha.
Lampel, J. and Shamsie, J. (2003) 'Capabilities in motion: New organizational forms and the reshaping of the Hollywood movie industry,' *Journal of Management Studies*, 40 (8), 2189–210.
Manning, S. (2005) 'Managing project networks as dynamic organizational forms: Learning from the TV movie industry', *International Journal of Project Management*, 23, 410–14.
Murakami, Y. and Ogawa, T. (1999) *Nihon Eiga Sangyo Saizensen* [Japan Movie Now], Tokyo: Kadokawa Shoten.
Okada, Y. (1991) *Eiga Sozo no Bizinesu*, [Movie, the Creative Business], Tokyo: Chikuma Shobo.
Steinberg, M. (2012) *Anime's Media Mix: Franchising Toys and Characters in Japan*. Minneapolis: University of Minnesota Press.

Tanaka, E. (2010) '*Media mix no sangyo kozo*' [Industrial structure of media mix], in H. Deguchi et al. (eds), *Content Sangyo Ron* [Content Industry], Tokyo: Tokyo University Press, pp. 159–86.

Tohmatsu and Co. (eds) (2003) *Kontentsu Bizinesu Manezimento* [Content business management], Tokyo: Nikkei Shinbunsha.

Tsai, W. and Ghoshal, S. (1998) 'Social capital and value creation: The role of inter-firm networks', *Academy of Management Journal*, 41, 464–76.

Windeler, A. and Sydow, J. (2001) 'Project networks and changing industry practices: Collaborative content-production in the German television industry', *Organization Studies*, 22 (6), 1035–61.

Yamashita, M. and Yamada, J. (2010) *Producer no Career Rentai* [A sense of solidarity that guides careers of producers: Strategic collaborative organization of creative individuals in the Japanese film industry], Tokyo: Hakuto Shobo.

5. European audio-visual production companies adapting to strategic challenges

M. Bjørn von Rimscha, Patrik Wikström and Lucia Naldi

1. INTRODUCTION

These are turbulent times for audio-visual production companies. Radical changes, both inside and outside the organizations, reach across national markets and different genres. For instance, production methods are changing; the demand from audiences and advertisers is changing; power relations between the actors involved in the value chain are changing; and increasing concentration makes the market even more competitive for small independent players. From a perspective of the structure–conduct–performance paradigm (Ramstad, 1997) it is reasonable to expect that these changes on a structural level of the industry will cause the production companies to adapt their strategic behaviour.

The current challenges for media companies are a combination of rising complexity and uncertainty in the market (Picard, 2004). The increasing complexity can for instance be observed in the growing number of market segments and in the continuing trend towards cross-media strategies where media companies operate in multiple markets and on multiple platforms. The market uncertainty is reflected in the increasing market volatility, which requires media managers to be more innovative and to accept greater risk exposure. The problem for media companies is in the contradictory nature of an adequate reaction to increasing complexity on the one hand and rising uncertainty on the other. Complex markets require organizations to keep tight control over strategy and production while market uncertainties require organizations to be agile and flexible. Interestingly, the industry on an aggregate level responds relatively slowly to the changing business environment conditions. One way to explain this behaviour is by pointing to a fundamental set of deficiencies that impede many media companies' strategic response, namely that 'media managers' knowledge of strategy and strategy processes are limited and most media firms do not have strategy units or organized business intelligence activities' (Picard, 2004, p. 2).

This observation is even more true for small production businesses or self-employed producers. The disadvantage of being small is amplified by a strategic orientation where creativity is regarded as equally important as profit maximization (von Rimscha and Siegert, 2011). The production companies' room for strategic manoeuvring is also relatively constricted due to high dependence on broadcaster clients (Lantzsch, 2008, pp. 95–100) and the close ties in partner networks created by repeated collaborations (Manning and Sydow, 2007). Considering that production companies currently operate in such difficult conditions, it is reasonable to assume that there is a strong incentive to use the ongoing environmental transformation to break loose from the existing constraints, to gain a better position in the value network, and to start building market power. In this chapter we present a study of European audio-visual production company behaviour. The questions addressed concern how these companies adapt to industrial change and how they assess two strategic options suggested by theory.

The chapter is structured as follows: first we describe the major changes in the industry in terms of technology, economy and regulation (section 2). We then discuss two possible extensions to the business model of audio-visual production companies, namely advertiser funding programming (AFP) and online self-distribution (section 3). We present the findings from a survey of how 154 production companies in eight European countries (section 4) assess and implement the aforementioned business model extensions (section 5). The chapter closes with a discussion of the findings (section 6).

2. STRUCTURAL CHANGES IN THE EUROPEAN AUDIO-VISUAL INDUSTRY

The structural changes in the European audio-visual industry concern the three areas: technology, economy and regulation. These areas are presented in the sections below.

2.1 Technological Changes

Digitization (Negroponte, 1995) affects production and workflow in all media industries, including the audio-visual industry sectors, as new techniques for content presentation, storage and distribution emerge (see the

special issue of *Popular Communication* on 'Digitizing audio-visual production' edited by Gripsrud, 2010). Digital production is faster and tends
to be cheaper than analogue production. In addition, media users expect
to be able to access content via a range of media platforms and devices.
In short: production companies gain new opportunities in terms of the
product range and simultaneously the audience gains new usage opportunities. The development of mobile multimedia devices and the proliferation of fixed and mobile broadband Internet drive this development.
Consequently, production companies no longer have broadcasters as their
only possible distribution partners. Digitization enables the emergence of
new distributors and even allows production companies to manage the
distribution of their content themselves.

2.2   Economic Changes

As early as 1993, Tunstall took note of a development towards a 'publisher television' where broadcasters retreat from production activities
and instead focus on packaging programmes commissioned or bought
by independent production companies. Since Tunstall observed this
trend on the British market, the model has been adopted across Europe
by both commercial and public service broadcasters, creating an industry based on so-called 'networked production' (Altmeppen et al., 2007;
Fuller-Love, 2009; Manning, 2005). The relation between broadcasters and independent production companies differs between countries
depending on the market's maturity and the aggregated market power
of the independent production sector. For instance, in the UK total buy-
out contracts, where all rights to the production are transferred to the
broadcaster, have become a rather rare exception, while such contracts
still prevail in Germany. From the production companies' perspective,
this development has both pros and cons. On the one hand the end of
the total buy-out means more freedom and the possibility to build and
exploit a library of proprietary programme rights. On the other hand it
means less security and the need to collect funds from a multitude of
sources by marketing content rights (Schaal, 2010). Production companies can recoup the cost of a series pilot only if the series is actually
picked up. But if they develop a successful programme they can generate
additional revenues by selling it to distributors in different media or different regions. In other words, a considerable share of the development
risk has been transferred from the broadcasters to the production companies (von Rimscha, 2008).
   In addition to these changes, there are other almost equally fundamental
developments taking place in the advertising market. New technologies

and devices such as DVRs make it possible for the audience to avoid the television commercials and lower the attractiveness of the traditional thirty-second spot (Mandese, 2004). While new advertising formats integrated in the programme are getting increasingly important (Russell and Belch, 2005) it is unclear which party is to implement the integration (e.g. product placement vs. split screen advertising) and who is to receive the revenues from these advertising formats – the broadcaster or the production company (Newell et al., 2006).

2.3 Regulatory Changes

Changes in the regulatory framework impact on how production companies are allowed to act. Traditionally, media regulation focuses on industry structures rather than content and usually it is the distribution that is regulated rather than the production. With the convergence of traditional media and the Internet, regulatory boundaries become blurred, creating a tendency towards a more relaxed regulatory policy. European harmonization of regulation has in fact led to less regulation in general as national regulation regimes converge to the lowest common denominator. A relaxed advertising regulation as implemented in the EU's Audio-Visual Media Services Directive (AVMSD 2010/13/EU) blurs the separation of advertising and editorial content by allowing product placements under certain conditions. This also challenges the traditional separation of the roles of production companies as content suppliers, and broadcasters as advertising platform. If an advertising message is an integral component of the programme, it is relevant to question why the message should be inserted only at the level of programme packaging and distribution and not already during the actual production.

The current regulation of the production processes is often benefiting rather than restricting the actions of independent producers. Several countries have quotas requiring broadcasters to commission a certain percentage of their programmes to independent domestic production companies (Doyle and Paterson, 2008; Fernández-Quijada, 2011). Further, there is no specific concentration regulation for production companies as is common for broadcasters in many countries and cross-media ownership rules usually do not apply to the establishment or the acquisition of production companies by broadcasters. Thus, the level of concentration in the audio-visual production industry has been rising in recent years and the lax regulation regime could eventually lead to a few strong independent production corporations or to a reintegration of production resources into the distributors (Baya, 2008, p. 45; Fernández Quijada, 2008; Pätzold and Röper, 2008).

3.   PRODUCTION COMPANIES' STRATEGIC RESPONSE

As mentioned above, production companies face several difficult challenges caused by changes in the industry. It is however not clear how production companies perceive these industry dynamics – if they experience a pressure to innovate, and if they have the capabilities required to be innovative. A limited number of studies have looked into these questions. Chaston (2008) concludes that the innovativeness of small creative firms in the UK by and large is limited to the creative content and that they are not prepared to cope with industry change and cannot be considered entrepreneurial. Rott and Zabel (2009) suggest different business model revisions for production companies in the German market. In their study, they interviewed industry representatives to assess the attractiveness of the suggested revisions and concluded that broadcasters are willing to engage in online streaming but remain sceptical about production company engagement in distribution. The broadcasters rather suggest production companies ought to focus on finding new customers via emerging online distribution channels. Przybylski (2010) describes how the relationship between production companies and broadcasters may evolve from a partnership to direct competition. Based on her interviews with production companies, Przybylski concludes that they prefer to concentrate on their traditional production activities and have limited interest in self-distributing their content. However, she does observe some willingness to open up to advertising and corporate communication as new revenue generators.

These few explorative studies are pessimistic about the likelihood that production companies will engage in business innovations. However, there are at least two possible business model extensions that stand out. These will be discussed below and empirically examined. As illustrated in Figure 5.1, the two strategic options involve: (a) extension into advertiser funding as a replacement for declining broadcaster funding; and (b) extension into distribution by starting an in-house online distribution business.

3.1   Extension into Advertiser Funding

As discussed previously, broadcasters' risk aversion increases along with their reluctance to fully fund the productions. The shrinking revenues from broadcasters need to be replaced by new revenues. One option is to turn to advertising as a new source of revenue. Advertising is already the primary funding mechanism for television production, especially in markets such as Germany where pay TV penetration is low. However, advertisers finance

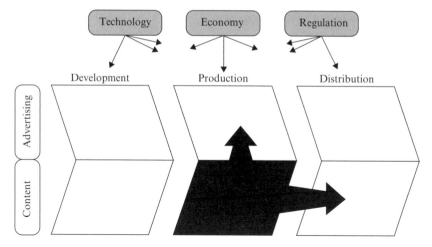

Figure 5.1   Possible business model extensions for production companies

the productions indirectly by buying advertising slots on broadcast schedules. This means most of the advertising revenue remains with the broadcaster who commissions the production companies. At the same time advertisers show a growing disaffection with the traditional spot advertising and are seeking a closer integration with the content. These problems could be addressed if advertisers fund the production directly rather than indirectly via broadcasters.

There are different ways the commercial message can be integrated into the production, from a simple props placement, via a scripted placement where the brand is an integrated part of the narrative, onto branded entertainment programming where the brand replaces the screenplay as the starting point for the production (Hudson and Hudson, 2006; Lehu, 2007).

Several problems emerge with this strategy, however. First, neither advertisers nor producers are used to collaborating with each other. Advertisers are used to telling advertising production companies exactly what they want and buying advertising space in bulk. Producers on the other hand are used to a high degree of creative freedom and have no experience in selling their product to customers other than the broadcasters. Further, broadcasters still act as gatekeeper to the viewers. In an asymmetric market with many production companies and relatively few broadcasters, the broadcasters hold on to powerful positions that they are eager to defend. They do not gently hand over the advertising business to production companies but use all the clout they possess in order to keep the status quo.

3.2   Extension into Distribution

While television usage is stagnant or – for younger audiences – declining, video consumption via the Internet is on the rise. For production companies it offers an opportunity to bypass the broadcasters and to get a direct connection to the audience.

Again several problems emerge with this strategy. Production companies are not used to dealing with the consumer. They do not control well-known and trusted brands like the broadcasters. If they have programmes that constitute their own brands they still rely on broadcasters to build these programme brands. Often they do not even own the rights to distribute their productions online, because they have sold them to the broadcaster in a total buy-out contract. Even if production companies do own the rights, most of them face the problem of not having the critical mass of video content. Small production companies do not have a big enough portfolio to attract consumers that are used to the vast choice of video portals such as *YouTube* or *vimeo*.

4.   METHOD

4.1   Research Design

We combined qualitative and quantitative methods, that is, expert interviews and a survey. First, expert interviews were conducted with representatives from production companies and other industry actors. These interviews were used to facilitate the theory-driven design of the survey questionnaire.

4.2   Sample

We selected eight European countries that represent the variance in the industry. The country sample differs in terms of their market size, concentration level, broadband penetration, and regulatory tradition but the sample also represents the popular distinction of media systems proposed by Hallin and Mancini (2004). It comprises Croatia, Germany, Ireland, Norway, Spain, Sweden, Switzerland and the United Kingdom. Spain and Croatia represent the 'Mediterranean or Polarized Pluralist Model', Germany, Norway, Sweden and Switzerland represent the 'Northern European or Democratic Corporatist Model', and finally the UK and Ireland represent the 'North Atlantic Liberal Model'. The latter two countries and especially the UK are often regarded as more production company-friendly and their regulatory framework in term of rights retained by the production companies serves as an ideal for industry associations in the other countries.

The companies were identified using the national industry associations' membership databases. We addressed the general management or the person concerned with the company's strategic development. The study was supported by the industry associations, which sent out recommendation letters to the respondents in order to increase the turnout. While the invitations to the survey were in the local languages, the actual questionnaire was the same for all participants and completely in English. Of a total of 1383 production companies contacted we received 154 completed questionnaires, a response rate of 11.1 per cent.

4.3 Measures

Industry dynamism was measured as an index based on a set of six questions (Miller and Friesen, 1982). For each question, the respondents were asked to rate which one of two statements they believed was the most accurate description of their industry.

We use the term *AFP* to refer to all elements of advertiser funding within the programme. Thus we choose to neglect the fact that any programme on a free-to-air commercial channel is advertiser funded. We distinguish between two levels of advertiser involvement: 'product placement' and 'branded entertainment'. 'Product placement' means that products or services are only included after the script is written and 'branded entertainment' means the brand is the starting point of the production and the storyline is scripted around the brand.[1] Due to the lack of established measures on the other aspects covered in the survey we created all other measures ourselves. These measures are defined when first mentioned in the results section below.

5. RESULTS

This section presents the results from the study structured into three areas. First, the respondents' perception of the dynamism in the TV production industry; second, their understanding of how the industry and their own organization will be affected by these dynamics; and last, how they respond to these changes.

Table 5.1   Index of perceived industry dynamism

1 Country	2 n	3 Mean	4 SD
United Kingdom	16	3.48	0.85
Ireland	25	3.34	0.87
Spain	22	3.37	0.53
Norway	6	3.22	0.40
Sweden	15	3.11	0.67
Switzerland	18	3.09	0.65
Germany	35	3.03	0.58
Croatia	17	2.65	0.91
Total	154	3.16	0.73

Note: Cronbach's α of the index = 0.80.

5.1   The Production Companies' Perception of the External Dynamism

The European TV production companies that participated in the study perceive their industry as only moderately dynamic (3.16 on a scale from 1 to 5). The companies only marked one (technology) of the six items that constitute the Miller and Friesen (1982) dynamism index, as clearly above the scale centre (3.56). The other items in the index – competition, consumer behaviour, regulatory framework, product maturity rate, and marketing – were all considered to be less dynamic.

We were able to find some significant differences (F = 2.44, p < 0.05, η^2 = 0.11) between the countries in the sample.

Production companies in the UK and in Ireland (adhering to the North Atlantic liberal media model) perceive the industry as more dynamic than in the other countries (Table 5.1). When scrutinizing the answers to the specific items in the index, production companies report a higher frequency of changes in marketing activities, a more rapid product maturity rate, less predictable competition, and more rapid technology development. This could be a consequence of the relatively early deregulation of these media markets and accordingly the early establishment of a functioning market for independent TV production that followed.

We also asked whether production companies perceived that production costs (Table 5.2) were rising or shrinking; if the complexity of the production workflows were increasing or decreasing; if the broadcasters' expectations of the productions' technical quality were increasing or decreasing; and if the regulations in general were becoming tighter or weaker. Again the responses were relatively close to the scale centre. The greatest deviation from the scale centre concerned technology and production costs. The

Table 5.2   Perceived change in production costs

Country	n	Δ cost	SD
Spain	22	3.77	1.72
Sweden	15	3.60	1.55
Switzerland	18	3.39	1.42
Norway	6	3.17	1.48
Germany	35	3.03	1.71
Croatia	17	2.76	1.56
Ireland	25	2.40	0.87
United Kingdom	16	2.37	1.31
Mean	154	3.01	1.53

Note: Scale from '1: cheaper production' to '7: more expensive production'.

production companies perceived that technological development in general was able to reduce these costs (3.04 on a scale from 1 to 7).

Also here we could identify some differences across countries ($F = 2.42$, $p < 0.05$, $\eta^2 = .10$). Production companies in the UK and Ireland expect greater cost savings through technological change while those in Sweden and Spain identify only limited potential for savings. We also noted that production companies in the Nordic countries perceive a pressure from the broadcasters to deliver content with higher technical quality while production companies in Britain and Ireland do not perceive such a pressure at all.

We also asked the respondents specifically how they perceived the development within the two areas that are at the core of this study, namely AFP and online distribution.

The production companies indicated that AFP, at least for the time being, is not as important as other available funding sources; however, its importance is considered to be on the rise. In 2007 the share of productions containing any element of AFP on average was at 9.2 per cent (SD 21.3) of all productions. This figure increased to 11.9 per cent (SD 23.8) in 2009 and it was expected to further increase to 15.7 per cent (SD 25.2) for 2011. The share of production companies making use of advertiser funding for at least one production rises from 35.8 per cent (2007) to 42.8 per cent (2009) and 59.1 per cent (2011). Thus, a growing share of the production companies use advertiser funding in their productions, but the funding mechanism still is limited to a relatively small part of the companies' total production portfolio. While advertiser funding is less common in Germany and Ireland than in other countries, no differences between the countries were statistically significant.

In regard to distribution, the production companies see no growth potential in traditional channels over the next three years. On a scale from −3 (strong decrease) to +3 (strong growth), production companies expect stagnation in TV (−0.06, SD = 1.34) and a small decline in cinema distribution (−0.31, SD = 1.06). Growth is expected to come from mobile (1.41, SD = 1.06) and – even more so – online distribution (1.78, SD = 1.23). While production companies agree in their assessment of cinema, online and mobile distribution, their expectations about the development of TV as a distribution channel differ significantly across countries (F = 3.66, p < 0.01, η^2 = 0.18). While production companies in Germany (−0.63, SD = 1.03) and Switzerland (−0.67, SD = 0.91) expect a shrinking TV market, production companies in southern European countries (e.g. Spain, 0.50 (SD = 1.37) and Croatia, 0.65 (SD = 1.80)) still perceive some growth potential.

5.2   How the Growth of AFP and Online Distribution will Impact the Industry

5.2.1   AFP

To examine how the power relationships within the industry might be affected by new funding schemes, we asked which party (production company, broadcaster or advertiser) initiates the development of a new production and which party green-lights the production. We asked how these roles change in productions with three different funding models: 'traditional' without advertising elements inside the programme (no AFP); product placement; and branded entertainment; see Table 5.3.

In productions without advertiser funding, production companies perceive themselves as initiators (76.6 per cent). Broadcasters initiate (20.2 per cent) of productions and all other actors are negligible. This changes for productions with product placements: here the share of the production

Table 5.3   Changing roles due to new funding schemes

	Initiation			Green-light		
	No AFP	Product placement	Branded entertainment	No AFP	Product placement	Branded entertainment
	n=94	n=84	n=79	n=94	n=84	n=76
Production company	76.6%	63.1%	48.0%	43.6%	40.5%	26.3%
Broadcaster	20.2%	14.3%	6.7%	52.1%	40.5%	35.5%
Advertiser	3.2%	22.6%	45.3%	4.3%	19.0%	38.2%

companies drops to 63.1 per cent and that of the broadcaster to 14.3 per cent while the advertiser category (including advertising agency and media agency) together account for 22.6 per cent of the productions initiated. The role of the latter is even more pronounced with branded entertainment productions where these actors initiate 45.3 per cent of the productions. Production companies seem to have an active role in seeking advertiser funding since they claim to be the initiating actor even for 48.0 per cent of the branded entertainment productions. If we use the green-light decision rather than the initiative as a measure, a similar picture emerges. The commissioning broadcaster gives the green-light for 52.1 per cent of the productions without advertiser funding. Obviously not all shows are fully funded by the broadcaster since 43.6 per cent get their green-light from the production company. For productions with product placement, advertisers and their agencies do have some influence (19.0 per cent) of the green-light decision. However, this influence is more pronounced for branded entertainment productions as advertisers and their agencies decide on the green-light more often (38.2 per cent) than the production company (26.3 per cent) and are even more influential than the broadcasters (35.5 per cent).

Some differences between the countries included in the study emerge but due to the small number of participants none of them is statistically significant. More important and significant (F = 6.80 −8.72, p < 0.01, η^2 = 0.08 −.10) differences emerge between how AFP is used in different genres. First of all, non-fiction productions are more likely to contain some kind of advertiser funding than fiction productions and documentaries. For production companies focusing on non-fiction, the share of productions containing some advertiser funding increased from 20.16 per cent in 2007 to an expected 30.35 per cent in 2011. For fiction productions this figure increased from 4.91 per cent to 12.64 per cent and for documentaries from 7.81 per cent to 10.04 per cent. Furthermore, advertisers and their agencies play a more important role in initiating and green-lighting non-fiction productions. There are at least two ways to explain these findings: either non-fiction formats are perceived as more attractive by advertisers or non-fiction production companies are more prepared to open their development to advertisers.

The study showed that the introduction of advertiser funding is not perceived as a way to achieve more freedom from the broadcasters. Actually, production companies are even less involved in the initiation and the green-light of advertiser-funded productions than in production using other funding mechanisms. Thus we can observe a power shift from the broadcaster to the advertiser. When advertisers replace broadcasters as financiers, they also take over their decision-making authority. Production companies remain in a dependent relationship, only the master is changing.

*Table 5.4   Distribution of advertising revenues between the production
company and the broadcaster*

Country	n	mean	SD
United Kingdom	8	5.88	1.36
Norway	6	5.33	2.16
Switzerland	9	5.22	2.11
Sweden	13	4.62	1.94
Spain	21	4.38	1.53
Germany	16	4.19	1.60
Croatia	12	3.58	1.51
Ireland	10	2.50	1.65
Total	95*	4.35	1.87

Notes:
Scale from '1: all revenues remain with the broadcaster' to '7: all revenues remain with the
production company'.
* Only companies with first-hand experience of advertiser funding were asked this question,
thus the reduced sample size.

Even when only considering the financial terms, advertiser funding is not
clearly beneficial for production companies: broadcasters are often able to
retain a significant share of the advertising revenues generated in the production stage. Most likely their prevailing market power allows them to get
compensated for revenues lost in the diminishing appeal of the traditional
30-second advertising spot. On a seven-point scale (with 1 being broadcaster only and 7 production company only) the respondents on average
indicate that production companies are at least able to keep more of the
AFP revenues than the broadcasters (4.35). The study shows that there are
significant differences between the sampled countries ($F = 3.65$, $p < 0.01$,
$\eta^2 = 0.23$) as illustrated by Table 5.4.

In Ireland and Croatia the broadcaster receives a bigger share of the
advertiser funding than the production company, while British, Norwegian
and Swiss production companies manage to keep the bulk of the advertiser
revenues for themselves.

5.2.2   Online distribution

Production companies expect the online market will be somewhat more
competitive than traditional distribution (0.5, $SD = 1.16$ on a scale
from -2 to 2, where -2 equals lower competition and 2 indicates fiercer
competition). The differences between countries are significant only at the
10 per cent level. While British and Croatian production companies perceive the same level of competition online and in traditional distribution

channels, their counterparts in Germany (0.57), Switzerland (0.72), Spain (0.77) and Ireland (0.80) expect a higher level of competition in the online market. However, these responses must be regarded as speculations, since only 28 per cent of the production companies have first-hand experience of online distribution.

The production companies also expect to have a less powerful position in the online space compared to the traditional market. While they expect to become slightly more relevant (0.28, SD = 1.16) themselves, they believe new actors such as telecommunication operators (0.92, SD = 0.86) and Internet platforms (1.30, SD = 0.83) such as Google and Apple will gain even more relevance. Relevance also translates into revenues: when asked to rank the involved actors according to their revenue shares in an online entertainment market, production companies rank themselves only in fifth position after Internet platforms, telecommunication operators, broadcasters/publishers and advertisers. Only users/viewers who create user-generated content are expected to gain less. All in all, production companies expect the Internet to have the same effect on audio-visual production as has been experienced by the music and the newspaper industries. This bleak outlook is widely shared across countries and genres. Only Spanish production companies are more optimistic, ranking themselves third after Internet platforms and telecommunication operators. Swedish production companies expect broadcasters/publishers to be able to secure the biggest revenue share. It is possible that our respondents have different business models in mind for online distribution when they respond to this question. While Spanish production companies seem to envision a model where they deal directly with the distributors and Swedish production companies expect the broadcasters to control the market in an online pay TV scenario, production companies in the other countries consider themselves as the start of the value chain, focusing exclusively on the actual production.

One reason for these differences might be the amount of online rights a production company is able to retain. Spanish production companies retain significantly more online rights than production companies in other countries (Table 5.5). One interpretation of these results is that production companies consider online rights to be of minor importance, since they on average retain less online rights than broadcast rights.

5.3 How TV Production Companies Respond to the Change

In looking at how production companies respond to change we focus on two areas: first, whether and how the production companies have revised their business models; and second, whether and how they believe they need new competences to cope with the changes in business conditions.

Table 5.5   Share of (online) rights retained by the production company

5 Country	n	6 Rights retained		Online rights retained		Δ online rights
		mean	SD	mean	SD	
Switzerland	18	5.22	1.96	5.39	1.88	0.17
Norway	6	4.50	2.26	2.33	1.75	−2.17
United Kingdom	16	4.06	1.98	3.81	1.72	−0.25
Spain	22	3.95	1.73	4.32	1.99	0.37
Germany	35	3.63	1.91	3.03	2.15	−0.60
Sweden	15	3.60	1.92	3.13	1.85	−0.47
Ireland	25	3.44	1.78	3.68	2.48	0.24
Croatia	17	3.41	2.12	3.18	2.19	−0.23
Total	159	3.88	1.95	3.68	2.18	−0.20

Note: Scale from '1: no (online) rights at all retained' to '7: all (online) rights retained'.

5.3.1   Business models

We asked the production companies what parts of their business model they have revised during the last three years (Table 5.6). The results largely follow the production companies' perception of the general dynamism of their industry, as reported above, but we were unable to find any significant differences between the countries. Table 5.6 also shows that there are no major differences between how much the different business model areas have been changed. The minor differences that can be observed concern the two financial areas (cost structure, revenue streams) that have been slightly more revised than the average and the area which production companies define as the 'key activities' in their business model which has been revised to a lesser extent than the average for all the business model areas.

Production companies expect that their product will have to be adjusted for online distribution. For instance, budgets will have to shrink – especially for non-fiction programmes – and individual episodes will have to be shortened. This expectation should be combined with the earlier observation that production companies have negative expectations of what online distribution will mean to their business. Conclusively they expect that they will be forced to adapt their product to cater to the online market, which they are unfamiliar with and which does not offer them any big additional rewards. Production companies also consider their present business model with its distinct bundle of resources and competences incompatible with the needs of an in-house online distribution (2.49 SD = 1.35 on a scale from 1: not at all compatible, to 5: very compatible.). The production com-

Table 5.6   Business model revisions during last three years

	7 mean	8 SD
Cost structure	3.23	1.01
Revenue streams	3.06	0.95
Partner network	2.96	1.11
Channels	2.89	1.12
Market/customer segments	2.86	1.04
Value proposition	2.84	1.07
Customer relationship	2.75	0.99
Key resources	2.73	1.07
Key activities	2.47	1.06

Note: Scale: from '1: not changed at all' to '5: changed completely'.

panies were consequently not very enthusiastic about a forward integration of their businesses into an online distribution business (2.92, SD = 1.23), measured on a scale from 1: not at all important, to 5: very important.

5.3.2   New competences needed?

A total of 88.3 per cent of the production companies believe they need new skills in their organization in order to cope with the new business conditions. Approximately one-fifth of the respondents believe their training programmes need to be revised, and that a closer cooperation with advertising agencies should be established (Table 5.7). Two-fifths of the respondents perceive a need to build a marketing division for the production company and 76 per cent expect that in order to respond to the growth in AFP and online distribution, each employee needs to develop their own competencies, become more versatile, and be able to cope with a range of different areas of the business. One way to interpret this response is that a professionalization and functional differentiation within the companies is dismissed in favour of the stereotype of the ingenious all-rounder. Here it is important to recognize that many companies in our study are small in size, and lack strict functional division of roles and responsibilities.

There are no significant differences between countries in this question except for the item related to the necessity of a marketing division. As Table 5.8 indicates, production companies in the UK and in Ireland do not perceive the need to set up a marketing division as strongly as production companies in other European countries do. However, it is possible that production companies in Britain and Ireland already have implemented a marketing division and thus no longer perceive its creation as a pressing need.

Table 5.7   Areas where production companies perceive a need for enhancing their capabilities and skills

9 Area	Agreement
No changes necessary	11.7%
Training programmes have to be adjusted	19.5%
Stronger cooperation with advertising agencies needs to be built	20.8%
A marketing division is required	42.2%
Each person needs new skills	76.0%

Table 5.8   The necessity of a marketing division

10 Country	11 Necessity
Croatia	64.7%
Germany	60.0%
Spain	45.5%
Sweden	40.0%
Switzerland	38.9%
Norway	33.3%
United Kingdom	25.0%
Ireland	16.0%
Mean	42.2%

We also asked a specific question about the need to build new skills and capabilities to cope with AFP. More than a quarter (26.4 per cent) of the respondents believe their companies do not need new competences. In Germany (34.3 per cent), Ireland (36.0 per cent) and Switzerland (44.4 per cent) more than a third of the respondents subscribe to this opinion. However, this does not necessarily mean that production companies in these markets have these capabilities in place. Respondents may be particularly sceptical about AFP and have no intention of engaging in that kind of business. Among those who believe new competences have to be acquired, a majority (58.2 per cent) prefers to hire staff to have them in-house rather than buying them on the market via an outsourcing agency (42.8 per cent). This can be understood as an indicator that these production companies perceive AFP competences as part of their core competences since they prefer to keep them in-house rather than outsourcing them to an external agency. There are only two exceptions to this rule, namely Germany and Norway, where a majority of production companies (65.2 per cent and 80 per cent respectively) would rather buy the new competences on the market.

6. DISCUSSION

This chapter reports from one of the first empirical studies of how European independent production companies in the audio-visual industry perceive and cope with the ongoing transformation of their industry.

In the first part of the study we explored how production companies perceive the dynamism in their industry and concluded that they generally perceive it to be only moderately dynamic. This is interesting given that production companies expect important changes in the two areas in focus in this study: online distribution and AFP.

Next, the study examined how at the time of the survey the production companies perceive themselves to be affected by the growing use of ADF and how they expect to be affected by it in the future. The study showed that when advertisers replace broadcasters as financiers, they also take over their decision-making authority and the production companies remain as the dependent party in the relationship. Production companies actually have less ability to influence initiation and green-lighting decisions in advertiser-funded productions compared to traditional productions commissioned by a broadcaster. In addition, AFP does not mean that production companies are able to retain a greater share of the advertising revenues since broadcasters – based on their strong gatekeeper position – are able to capture a significant share of the AFP revenues and thereby to compensate for the shrinking revenues from sales of traditional thirty-second spots.

The study further showed that the production companies' outlook on the opportunities created by online distribution is almost as bleak as their expectations on advertiser-funded programming. The production companies expect the online market will be more competitive than the traditional distribution markets. They also expect new players, such as Google and Apple, will enter and dominate the market and hamper the production companies' ability to disintermediate traditional middlemen and connect directly with the audience.

In conclusion, production companies consider the two business model extensions proposed by this study to be threats rather than opportunities.

In its third part, the study turned to the question of how the production companies have responded, or how they intend to respond, to the developments in the two areas of AFP and online distribution. The study examined which business model areas the production companies would revise in order to cope with the new conditions, and if the production companies expected they needed new competencies in their organizations in order to realize this transformation of their businesses.

Production companies expect to revise their cost structures and revenue streams to a greater extent than the business model areas they refer to as their key activities. It may be assumed that key activities are related to the actual production of audio-visual programming, and while they believe this part of their operations will be least affected by the development of the industry, they foresee considerable changes to the productions in order to adapt them to the requirements created by new distribution channels, such as online and mobile. These changes will not be made with any great enthusiasm since the production companies dread the growing influence of the new distribution channels, which they expect to be even more competitive and difficult than their traditional markets.

Production companies further perceive that their current competencies are poorly adapted to the emerging audio-visual industry and that they need new skills in order to cope with the new business conditions. While some production companies had clear ideas of what those skills might be, the most common answer was that each person in the organization needed to expand their skill set in general.

All in all, the study paints a picture of a European audio-visual industry that expects a period of radical transformation. The production companies in this survey doubt that they are prepared to face this transformation, which they expect to have radical and primarily negative consequences for their businesses. The study gives empirical support to the findings presented by previous exploratory studies presented earlier in this chapter. These studies concluded that the production companies' innovative capabilities are focused on creating new content and that their entrepreneurial orientation is very limited. While those priorities might be desirable from a cultural perspective, this puts the industry in a very dangerous situation in times of change. Those production companies who are unable to adapt to the new business conditions run a considerable risk of being acquired by competitors or put out of business.

Although there are some differences between countries and genres covered by the study, the similarities between genres and countries are more striking than the differences. The European audio-visual industry seems to be increasingly coherent where the differences between countries primarily are caused by the varying maturity of the markets rather than by fundamental structural distinctions. It is likely that the homogenization of the European audio-visual industry will increase even further as regulatory differences between countries are reduced and the industry consolidation continues. Such a consolidation process may either be a passive process where small production companies struggle to survive and are forced to sell out or merge, or an active strategy driven by bigger production companies aiming to build market clout and to deal on a par with broadcasters and advertisers. While there are cross-ownership rules and strict concentration control in most broadcasting markets, the production market is less regulated, suggesting that this type of concentration will not be restricted by governments.

6.1 Limitations

There are obviously a number of limitations of this study. One weakness is the relatively low response rate. However, an inspection of the participant list suggests that the most important production companies in the respective countries have participated in the survey. The countries are not equally represented since the share of companies that are organized in the industry association and the scope of the associations differ substantially. This bias in the sample might lead to an underestimation of the importance of advertising revenue and online distribution, since companies planning to expand in these areas may not feel represented by traditional associations and do not join.

We did not experience any problems of a social desirability bias related to the separation of advertising and editorial programming. In the interviews conducted prior to the survey, industry representatives did not voice any concerns about editorial independence. Advertiser funding is considered legal, perfectly acceptable and unproblematic in an entertainment context. A bias in the survey results is more likely to result from strategies of self-portrayal by the production companies. They often boast about their creative expertise (cf. von Rimscha and Siegert, 2011) and might be tempted to overstate their capabilities in this area. A comprehensive survey that included all stakeholders in the value network might be able to balance the actors' internal and external perspectives and control for potential distortions caused by flawed self-representations.

NOTE

1. The literature on advertiser funded programming is full of colourful but not selective and not mutually inclusive terms to describe different variations of advertiser inclusion (see for example Galician, 2004). Some authors regard branded entertainment as another variety of product placement (Hudson and Hudson, 2006); however, we believe our distinction is reasonable since different business processes are implied when you start with the story or the brand.

REFERENCES

Altmeppen, K-D., Lantzsch, K. and Will, A. (2007). Flowing networks in the entertainment business: Organizing international TV format trade. *The International Journal on Media Management*, 9(3), 94–104.

Baya, A. (2008). The UK market for independent production: Toward a local Hollywood? *International Journal of Communications Law & Policy*, (12), 39–52.

Chaston, I. (2008). Small creative industry firms: A development dilemma? *Management Decision*, 46(6), 819–31.

Doyle, G. and Paterson, R. (2008). Public policy and independent television production in the UK. *Journal of Media Business Studies*, 5(3), 17–33.

Fernández Quijada, D. (2008). Independent television production in Catalonia in a changing market. *Quaderns del CAC*, (30), 91–101.

Fernández-Quijada, D. (2011). Quoting television: A cross-national analysis of regulatory intervention in the independent television production industry in the UK and Spain. *International Journal of Cultural Policy*, 1–20.

Fuller-Love, N. (2009). Formal and informal networks in small businesses in the media industry. *International Entrepreneurship and Management Journal*, 5(3), 271–284.

Galician, M-L. (2004). *Handbook of product placement in the mass media: New strategies in marketing theory, practice, trends and ethics.* Binghamton, NY: Best Business Books.

Gripsrud, J. (2010). Understanding the digitization of production. *Popular Communication*, 8(1), 1–3.

Hallin, D.C. and Mancini, P. (2004). *Comparing media systems: Three models of media and politics. Communication, society and politics.* Cambridge: Cambridge University Press.

Hudson, S. and Hudson, D. (2006). Branded entertainment: A new advertising technique or product placement in disguise? *Journal of Marketing Management*, 22(5/6), 489–504.

Lantzsch, K. (2008). *Der internationale Fernsehformathandel: Akteure, Strategien, Strukturen, Organisationsformen. The Business of Entertainment.* Wiesbaden: VS Verlag.

Lehu, J-M. (2007). *Branded entertainment: Product placement & brand strategy in the entertainment business.* London: Kogan Page.

Mandese, J. (2004). See spot run – or not. DVRs impact ad viewing, but is it time to panic? *Broadcasting & Cable*, 134(48), 22.

Manning, S. (2005). Managing project networks as dynamic organizational forms: Learning from the TV movie industry. *International Journal of Project Management*, 23(5), 410–14.

Manning, S. and Sydow, J. (2007). Transforming creative potential in project networks: How TV movies are produced under network-based control. *Critical Sociology*, 33(1–2), 19–42.

Miller, D. and Friesen, P.H. (1982). Innovation in conservative and entrepreneurial firms: Two models of strategic momentum. *Strategic Management Journal*, 3(1), 1–25.

Negroponte, N. (1995). *Being digital.* New York: Hodder and Stoughton.

Newell, J., Salmon, C.T. and Chang, S. (2006). The hidden history of product placement. *Journal of Broadcasting & Electronic Media*, 50(4), 575–94.

Pätzold, U. and Röper, H. (2008). Fernsehproduktionsmarkt Deutschland 2005 und 2006. *Media Perspektiven*, (3), 125–37.

Picard, R.G. (ed.) (2004). *JIBS Research report Series. Strategic responses to media market changes.* Jönköping: Jönköping International Business School.

Przybylski, P. (2010). *Heute Partner – Morgen Konkurrenten?: Strategien, Konzepte und Interaktionen von Fernsehunternehmen auf dem neuen Bewegtbild-Markt. The Business of Entertainment*. Wiesbaden: VS Verlag.

Ramstad, G.O. (1997). A model for structural analysis of the media market. *Journal of Media Economics*, 10(3), 45–50.

Rott, A. and Zabel, C. (2009). Marktentwicklung als strategische Option für TV-Produktionsunternehmen: Perspektiven, Probleme und empirische Evidenz. In J. Krone (ed.), *Fernsehen im Wandel. Mobile TV & IPTV in Deutschland und Österreich* (pp. 93–106). Baden-Baden: Nomos.

Russell, C.A. and Belch, M. (2005). A managerial investigation into the product placement industry. *Journal of Advertising Research*, 45(1), 73–92.

Schaal, U. (2010). *Das strategische Management von Contentrechten*. Wiesbaden: VS Verlag.

Tunstall, J. (1993). *Television producers. Communications and society*. London: Routledge.

von Rimscha, M.B. (2008). Risikomanagement in der Produktion und Entwicklung audiovisueller fiktionaler Unterhaltung. In G. Siegert and M.B. von Rimscha (eds), *Zur Ökonomie der Unterhaltungsproduktion* (pp. 178–203). Cologne: Halem Verlag.

von Rimscha, M.B. and Siegert, G. (2011). Orientations of entertainment media workers. *Media, Culture & Society*, 33(7), 1009–26.

6. When disruption is driven by established firms: the case of French multiplex theatres

Pierre Roy

INTRODUCTION

This chapter deals with a concept – disruptive strategy – that lies in a new stream of research in strategic management. The emergence of a new type of environment over the last twenty years has had a major impact on how firms compete with each other and how market dynamics are operating. Thus, some researchers have highlighted the fact that firms are more and more aggressive on their markets and tend to take more risks in order to build and/or defend a competitive advantage. In this context, a disruptive strategy can be defined as 'the capacity to reconceive the existing industry model in ways that create new value for customers, wrong-foot competitors, and produce new wealth for all stakeholders' (Hamel, 1998, p. 8).

In recent years, many industries have experienced such a fundamental change in their competitive rules of the game. Good examples include the airline transportation industry (Ryanair), the newspaper industry (Metro) or the computer industry (Dell). Cultural industries are no exception if we consider the transformations of the book-selling business (Amazon.com), music (iTunes), photography (smartphones) or video games (Nintendo Wii). These companies have completely changed the rules of the game in their respective industries by introducing new key success factors and new customer behaviours. Most of the time, technology-based disruptions are the causes of these business (r)evolutions. But non-technology-based sources can also have a major impact on the way a product or service is conceived or sold to customers.

In the existing literature, this new technique is discussed in terms of industry conditions that facilitate the introduction of a disruption, key success factors and consequences for firms' performances (Schlegelmilch et al., 2003; Kim and Mauborgne, 2005; Markides, 2008). These authors agree on the fact that exploration of new empirical fields is essential if theoretical knowledge of this phenomenon is to be expanded. For example, a dominant perspective is adopted by the literature about the profile of the disrupter. Most of the time, it is challengers or new entrants who introduce the disruption (Markides, 1997). I believe that more research should be focused on the role played by established firms. Therefore, this chapter intends to shed light on the following research questions: what are the conditions, drivers and consequences of a disruption when established companies introduce it?

In order to explore this perspective, I selected the film industry as an interesting empirical field. Over the last twenty years, many evolutions have fundamentally altered the way films are produced, distributed or broadcast to audiences. Recent evolutions reveal the emergence both of new technologies and newcomers in the film industry. These include, for example, digital cinema, movie downloading via the Internet, 3D cinema, and new media for film watching (smartphones and tablets). These evolutions are currently changing the way the film industry operates but I decided to study a previous evolution of the market, namely the transformation of movie theatres into multiplexes in France over the last twenty years. Mostly driven by established companies, this sector renewal has completely altered the rules of the game in the French film industry. Firms' strategies and competitive dynamics but also customer behaviours and professional practices have been impacted. Therefore, this case study offers a great opportunity to bring some answers to my research question. The chapter discusses results associated with the selected case study (section 3) after a review of the theoretical literature (section 1) and some details about the research methodology (section 2).

1.   THEORETICAL BACKGROUND

This research is directly rooted in a new stream of research in strategic management which intends to study the way firms are able to substitute new rules of the game in a given industry in order to reach a high level of performance. This refers to the concept of disruptive strategy and its synonyms that can be found in the literature such as 'strategic innovation' (Markides, 2008), 'disruptive technology' (Christensen, 2000) or the well-known 'blue ocean strategy' (Kim and Mauborgne, 2005). According to these authors, managers are nowadays facing a new challenge due to a high level of competition (D'Aveni, 1994): they must be able to disrupt the competitive status quo in order to outcompete other companies and create new value for all stakeholders.

A New Strategic Thinking

The emergence of a new type of environment over the last twenty years had a major impact on firms' competitive behaviour. New external parameters are the result of different evolutions such as market deregulation, global competition and the fact that supply is exceeding demand in most industries (Prahalad and Hamel, 1994). A high level of turbulence and the specific role of innovation became the key characteristics of a new competitive landscape (McCann and Selsky, 1984). Firms have to be more flexible and creative in an increasingly challenging context.

In terms of research topics, the evolution of both the environment and firms' behaviour led academics to develop new strategic approaches able to deal with the dynamic and multidimensional nature of modern competition. The aim is to go beyond the limits of mainstream strategic literature (that is, models mainly inspired by industrial organization economics), especially the view of strategy as a defensive process. Indeed, classical strategic views are focused on building and protecting a competitive advantage by creating barriers to entry and limiting the degree of competition within the industry. Porter's early models illustrate this dominant vision of strategy which becomes quite obsolete when firms are facing a high velocity environment and when protections against potential competitors become no longer sustainable.

Since the early 1990s, firms' strategies have become more and more proactive. Thus, researchers have investigated themes such as firms' competitive interactions (Smith et al., 1992), the impact of aggressiveness on performance (Ferrier, 2001) or the use of disruption as a way to make competition irrelevant (D'Aveni, 1994; Markides, 1997; Hamel, 1998). These proactive views of strategy are mainly inspired by two major publications, namely D'Aveni's *Hypercompetition* (1994) and Hamel and Prahalad's *Competing for the Future* (1994). These authors developed a similar thesis that maintains that the source of competitive advantage no longer lies in firms' ability to protect an economic rent on the market but rather in their ability to disrupt the competitive status quo in order to take control of the source of turbulence. According to them, in the twenty-first century, the competitive advantage is hardly sustainable over a long period of time and firms should rather struggle for a collection of short-term advantages (D'Aveni, 1994). In this context, the literature increasingly suggests that market leaders should adopt the same behaviour as challengers in order to maintain their advantage. The use of surprise and disruptive strategies may be a powerful way to reinforce a market position for established firms (D'Aveni, 1994; Nault and Van Den Bosch, 1996).

In this new type of environment, technological innovations obviously represent a major source of change (Bettis and Hitt, 1995). But actually, every type of innovation may be useful whether it is managerial, organizational or in marketing. This idea that innovation is playing a major part in the competitive process is not new if I consider the work of Austrian economists such as Schumpeter. Indeed, Schumpeter maintained that innovation is the essential source of competition between firms and the only source of major performance improvement. Throughout the process of creative destruction, firms are competing for the next source of major industry change that will disrupt the routine and design a new industry model. The literature on disruptive strategy is directly rooted in this entrepreneurial and dynamic perspective. Competition between firms is based on their ability to change the rules of the game in their industry. To achieve this challenge, firms have to be creative in order to innovate in terms of technology, but also in terms of business model and/or management techniques.

The strategic literature offers many definitions of 'disruptive strategy' and even many similar concepts such as 'disruption', 'strategic innovation', 'value innovation' and so on. Hamel (1998, p. 8) defined this type of strategy as 'the capacity to reconceive the existing industry model in ways that create new value for customers, wrong-foot competitors, and produce new wealth for all stakeholders'. Many examples are used in the literature to illustrate this phenomenon such as Amazon.com in the book-selling industry, Dell in the computer industry, Ikea in the home furniture industry, and Ryanair in the airline industry. These examples show that the core of the disruption is not always rooted in the product or service itself but also in the way a firm is organized to create value. Thus, I believe that a powerful disruptive strategy is frequently a combination of different types of innovation (technological, managerial, organizational or in marketing).

The increasing body of literature on disruptive strategy suggests that no industry is protected and that most established firms are threatened by the fact that a newcomer can disrupt the rules of the game at any moment (D'Aveni, 1994). This fact led a few authors to stress the importance of established firms being prepared for these strategic surprises and even to introduce the disruption themselves within their own industry (D'Aveni, 1994; Nault and Van Den Bosch, 1996). The next section discusses the specific challenges for established companies.

The Case of Established Firms

Introducing a disruption

The strategic literature suggests that there are two main factors that can enable an established company to change the rules of the game in its industry (Schlegelmilch et al., 2003). First, the company's top-management team must be unsatisfied with the competitive status quo. This feeling may for example be related to the fact that the firm's performance is threatened by the maturity or decline of the industry. In such a context, high entry barriers, a dominant business model and well-known key success factors often characterize the competitive game. Thus, improving the level of performance generally implies a complete change in thinking in the industry. Introducing a disruption may appear as a solution for newcomers as well as established firms to regenerate the industry. Bringing a new value proposition to customers can be a powerful way to increase the industry's demand and create new growth perspectives. For established firms, this technique is highly strategic in so far as they usually are the main victims of an industry crisis given the volume of assets engaged in the activity. I also believe that the feeling of dissatisfaction leading to a disruption can be related to the fact that an established firm is intending to improve its relative position within an oligopoly. Indeed, the will to win in terms of relative market power may be a motivation to change the rules of the game in order to destabilize the other market leader(s). A challenger within an oligopoly may use disruption in order to create new opportunities and to take control of newly created rules (D'Aveni, 1994; Hamel, 1998; Ferrier, 2001).

The second element to consider regarding the introduction of a disruption is the capacity of the established firm to implement such a strategic renewal. The literature evokes different organizational and cultural elements that facilitate the process. These elements are quite similar to those developed in the innovation literature. Indeed, authors stress the importance of entrepreneurship, adopting a questioning attitude, creativity, cross-functional dialogue and integrating capabilities from external partners (Schlegelmilch et al., 2003). Moreover, they stress the importance of knowing the current rules of the game in the industry thoroughly and being able to completely change their vision of the industry (Cooper and Smith, 1992; Hamel and Prahalad, 1994; Kim and Mauborgne, 1997). However, the emergence of an alternative point of view within an established firm represents a major challenge due to competitive myopia and inability to disrupt the status quo. Thus, the arrival of a new CEO coming from a different industry may facilitate the introduction of a new strategic vision (Markides, 1997). This new CEO brings new cognitive references that may trigger the strategic renewal process within the established company. Porter (1980) illustrated this process with the example of Paramount Pictures in the motion pictures industry during the 1970s. The transfer of two top managers from TV networks to the movie theatre business resulted in new rules of the game such as simultaneous diffusion and pre-sales of films.

Managing the disruption

The literature review helped to identify four elements influencing the firm's performance throughout the disruption process. The first one is the speed of diffusion of new rules of the game, which can be related to the literature about first-mover advantages. When a firm introduces a disruption, this firm can implement the new rules of the game faster than early imitators in order to achieve a pre-emption of the industry renewal (Nault and Van Den Bosch, 1996; Ilinitch et al., 1996; Kim and Mauborgne, 1997; Hamel, 1998). The advantage lies in the fact that a market disruption is associated with high profits rewarding the risks taken by the pioneering firm (Lieberman and Montgomery, 1988).

The second element that is to be taken into consideration is the impact of the disruption on the established firms' positions. Here, the literature suggests that the firm disrupting the status quo should employ a self-cannibalization strategy (Nault and Van Den Bosch, 1996), namely, disrupting its own market positions based on the old business model. The aim of the self-cannibalization strategy is to avoid the situation where a competitor introduces new equipment before the firm. Even if the process of self-cannibalization is hard to implement, it appears as a necessity for an established firm willing to protect its market positions. Besides, in the case of a fast imitation from competitors, this strategy helps reduce the competitive rivalry within the regenerated industry as long as competitors are respecting their mutual territories.

A third element can be derived from the two previous ones and concerns the transition from the old to the new business model. I believe that a fast business model substitution is a key success factor of a disruptive strategy (Gilbert, 2003). In other words, the established company should concentrate its efforts on the new business model and proceed to a complete and fast regeneration of its market positions. The resources dedicated to the old business model must be progressively transferred to the new model. The activity associated with the old business model is condemned to become marginal due to the adoption of new rules of the game by all stakeholders (competitors, customers, suppliers, and so on).

Lastly, the literature suggests that a high level of competitive aggressiveness may be helpful in the process. Since the 1990s, some research has demonstrated that there is a positive relationship between the level of a firm's aggressiveness and its market performance (D'Aveni, 1994; Smith et al., 2001; Ferrier, 2001). According to these authors, a firm's performance is related to its ability to be competitively active, namely introducing more competitive actions than its competitors in order to destabilize them. Thus, this research has developed multi-criteria measures of competitive aggressiveness, namely the volume of competitive actions, the heterogeneity of these actions (price, marketing, services, signal, capacity, etc.) and their impact on competitive dynamics. In light of this view of competition, an established company introducing a disruption should be very aggressive in order to accelerate its market pre-emption.

Taking advantage of the disruption

The literature about disruption also investigates the consequences of this strategy both for the market and for firms' performances. Among traditional effects, an industry regeneration driven by new rules of the game is usually observed (Baden-Fuller and Stopford, 1992). Indeed, a disruptive strategy often leads to an increase of the whole industry turnover and to a market extension (Kim and Mauborgne, 1997). An industry regeneration is especially important for established firms as it implies new perspectives of growth and the opportunity to achieve a pre-emption of the new demand.

The second impact of the disruption concerns the competitive game. Most of the time, a disruptive strategy leads to a polarization of competitors. Two types of competitor emerge within the process of industry renewal: those adopting new rules of the game and those refusing or unable to adopt them (Thomas, 1996; Ilinitch et al., 1996). This implies an increase of the gap in terms of performance between the two types of firm. Besides, the weakest competitors may be the first victims of the disruption. Their lack of competitive resources often justifies their eviction from the market (D'Aveni, 1994; Nault and Van Den Bosch, 1996). This effect allows the rule breakers to improve their market share and their control over the industry. The type of competition may also be altered by the disruptive strategy including the emergence of new key success factors.

The last effect of a disruptive strategy concerns the vertical dimension and precisely the way the value created downstream is divided between different actors in the industry. Research has not fully explored this kind of consequence but most publications suggest that changing the rules of the game in an industry should lead to the redefinition of the amount of value that a firm is able to capture. This is related to the redefinition of the entire business model (Kim and Mauborgne, 1997).

2.   RESEARCH METHODS

This research is based on a single case study: the transformation of the film exhibition sector in France since the beginning of the 1990s. Throughout this process, the introduction of multiplex-type theatres illustrates a disruptive strategy. Indeed, this new equipment offers a new value proposition to customers including a larger capacity, an extended choice of movies, some additional services and products, a brand new type of location (away from city centres compared to traditional theatre locations), parking facilities and so on. In France, multiplexes were introduced and mainly diffused during the 1990s by the three dominant domestic firms (Pathé, Gaumont and UGC). Therefore, the selected case study offers the opportunity to explore the specific role played by established firms in a disruption process.

In terms of data collection, I tackled the case with three different sources of data. First, 40 semi-structured interviews were conducted with top managers and various stakeholders in the industry in order to precisely understand the industry's transformations over the period of time studied. The aim of this first method was to gather different points of view about the industry's evolution. Therefore, I interviewed top managers from the three dominant companies, as well as their competitors, their suppliers and different kinds of industry stakeholders (public authorities, trade unions, etc.). The transcription and analysis of these data helped me to build my own understanding of the disruption, its characteristics and the specific role played by each actor. Interviewing 40 managers from different companies and organizations helped me build a holistic comprehension of the phenomenon and also helped reduce the subjectivity of my analysis. Besides, these qualitative data offer the opportunity to obtain some verbatim research results and to bring an empirical basis to the theoretical discussion.

Secondly, in order to build a detailed analysis of competitive moves during the period, I achieved a structured content analysis of main firms' competitive actions and reactions from 1990 to 2004. Based on a weekly trade publication (*Le Film Français*), this second analysis was very useful in obtaining a precise understanding of the nature of competition during the disruption process. Inspired by the method of Smith et al. (1992), the analysis consisted in identifying every competitive move as related by the professional publication. Eight different types of competitive move were distinguished: price, marketing, capacity, signals, financial, alliances and acquisitions, vertical moves and miscellaneous. This second method was specifically required for the discussion about the link between competitive aggressiveness and market performances. It helped identify differences between firms in terms of competitive behaviours and the emergence of a new type of competitive game.

Lastly, I built a database gathering main characteristics of all French multiplexes. These secondary and quantitative data were at the core of my empirical study. The transformation of the French market needed to be as detailed as possible. Therefore, it required the collection and synthesis of quantitative data related to topics such as the investments engaged by

companies, types of location, sizes of new theatres, chronology of multiplex openings and so on. Also, the construction of this database aimed at
bringing some objective and quantitative data in order to reinforce inter-
pretations based on primary qualitative data (interviews). In other words,
this database was a way of limiting the multiple biases attached to the qualitative material. Table 6.1 offers a synthesis of the method triangulation at
the core of this research.

3.   MAIN RESULTS

Introduction of Multiplex Theatres

Concerning the French market, the domestic firm Pathé introduced the
first multiplex theatre in June 1993. This strategic move took place in a
context of structural crisis. The fall of the demand curve (down by 42.5
per cent between 1982 and 1992) was then a direct and major threat for
the three dominant companies (Gaumont, Pathé and UGC). The analysis of both primary and secondary data revealed that the decline of the
sector stimulated the emergence of a disruptive strategy, in this case for
two main reasons. The first one was defensive and related to the fall of
demand and its implications for established firms. Indeed, in the early
1990s, the multiplex-type theatre offered the opportunity to introduce new
perspectives of growth for the French sector and represented a convincing
solution to the increasing threat of substitutes such as cable TV and VCR.
The second reason was proactive and lay in the capacity of dominant firms
to succeed in introducing a disruptive strategy due to their market and
institutional power. The case study illustrates the argument suggesting that
industry maturity is less a fatality than an illustration of firms' inability
to stimulate demand (Baden-Fuller and Stopford, 1992; Bettis and Hitt,
1995).

   In this case, the strategic intent of Pathé's CEO lies in his will to improve
the relative position of the firm within the French oligopoly (see Table 6.2).
Indeed, data treatment reveals that Pathé was a dominant firm on the
French market in 1992 but a challenger within the oligopoly, compared to
UGC and Gaumont. Therefore, it suggests that Pathé was the most likely
to disrupt the competitive status quo (D'Aveni, 1994; Hamel, 1998; Ferrier,
2001). Pathé possessed both the advantages of a dominant firm (large
amount of resources and competences, market power, established network
of relationships in the industry, etc.) and was subject to fewer risks associated with a disruption compared to Gaumont and UGC. Here, the risk is
mainly expressed in terms of cannibalization between the new (multiplex)

Table 6.1 Method triangulation

	Method No. 1 Interviews	Method No. 2 Structured Content Analysis	Method No. 3 Database
Data Type	Primary Qualitative	Secondary Qualitative	Secondary Quantitative
Material	40 semi-structured interviews with top managers of industry's stakeholders	244 competitive moves between 1990 and 2004 were identified from a review of 780 issues of the publication *Le Film Français*	Characteristics of 127 French multiplexes (date of creation, size, owner, location, investment, etc.)
Treatment	Thematic analysis (Miles and Huberman, 1994)	Codification of competitive moves (following Smith et al., 1992)	Statistics (averages per company)
Focus	Motivations and effects of strategic moves	Competitive aggressiveness	Impacts of strategies, time- and spatial-interactions
Method Advantages	Data directly related to the phenomenon	Exhaustivity of competitive moves, longitudinal analysis	Improves research validity
Method Limits	Bias due to data interpretation, limited sample	Bias due to journalists' vocabulary	Difficulties to define the concept of multiplex

Table 6.2   Situation of the oligopoly in 1992

	Market share (in terms of admissions)	Volume of screens in France	Profit/Loss
UGC	14.8%	228	15 M€
Gaumont	11.4%	208	15 M€
Pathé	7.3%	128	−5M€

and the old types of theatre. Changing the rules of the game appeared as an opportunity for Pathé to improve both its level of performance and its relative position within the oligopoly.

Beyond the competitive characteristics of Pathé, another element played a major role in the introduction of the disruption. An international and diversified group named Chargeurs acquired Pathé in 1990. Among the consequences of this acquisition was the arrival of a new CEO (Jérôme Seydoux) who was characterized by a managerial background acquired in very different industries (textile and airline industries). According to the literature (Schlegelmilch et al., 2003), this new actor brought new cognitive scripts to the motion pictures industry such as an industrial vision of the business, the introduction of marketing techniques and modern management tools and the necessity of benchmarking foreign markets (especially the North American market). In other words, he had an alternative vision of the industry far from the traditional and dominant culture of the business. Jérôme Seydoux acted as an entrepreneur and a rule-breaker, as related by a top manager from a direct competitor (UGC):

> Pathé played a major part in these evolutions. The fact that it was bought by a businessman such as Jérôme Seydoux had consequences because of his experiences acquired in very different and non-cultural industries. In the airline or wool industries you must monitor the price of raw materials, you have to take a look at international markets, etc. Therefore, when he bought a cinema company like Pathé, he wondered what were the business practices, what were the key success factors, what were the new innovations, etc. This new vision of the business stimulated us by creating a new kind of competition on the French market (interview, Paris, July 2004).

Such a cultural change led to the introduction of new key success factors concerning the type of theatre location (from downtown to peripheral areas), new price strategies and new sources of profit (beverages, confectionery, video games, etc.). Indisputably, the cognitive disruption that took place in an established firm accelerated the introduction of the multiplex in the French market (Markides, 1997; Schlegelmilch et al., 2003).

The Process of Market Regeneration

Between 1993 and 2004, Pathé, followed by UGC and Gaumont, managed to pre-empt the French multiplex market. At the end of this period, the three firms owned almost 60 per cent of the market and the best positions in largest cities. The high-velocity diffusion of multiplex theatres (127 openings in ten years) allowed them to lock-in the market and to deter new entrants (especially foreign competitors) from penetrating the market. After Pathé's strategic move in 1993, rapid imitations by UGC (within 17 months) and Gaumont (within 21 months) are observed, illustrating the determination of these two followers not to let Pathé monopolize advantage on the new market. These competitive reactions as well as public authority regulations did not allow Pathé to achieve a solo pre-emption of the market. However, this strategic renewal helped Pathé to improve its competitive position and to become the leader on the French market after merging with Gaumont in 2001 (see Table 6.3).

Data treatment also sheds light on the technique of self-cannibalization, namely the practice of introducing a multiplex in an area where the firm already possesses a traditional theatre. Here, the three dominant firms followed similar strategies. Before conquering new territories, the first action of dominant firms consisted in protecting their historical local positions. This protective strategy revealed a desire to consolidate their competitive advantage by bringing their equipment up to date (Nault and Van Den Bosch, 1996). The analysis of firms' performances over this period of time showed that the firm that took the longest time to update its equipment (Gaumont) experienced a relative drop in its competitive position. Conversely, the most protectionist firm (UGC) greatly improved its relative competitive position in particular by achieving a lock-in of the highly strategic Parisian market.

The direct consequence of the pre-emption and self-cannibalization strategies is a fast transition between the two business models. Indeed, this

Table 6.3   Evolution of competitive positions

	1992	1999	2004
Admissions in France (millions)	116	153.6	194.8
Competitive position and market share	1. UGC 14.8% 2. Gaumont 11.4% 3. Pathé 7.3%	1. UGC 17.6% 2. Gaumont 13.8% 3. Pathé 11.7%	1. EuroPalaces 22%[a] 2. UGC 16.5% 3. CGR 9%

Note: a.   EuroPalaces is the result of the merger between Pathé and Gaumont.

Table 6.4   The share of the multiplexes in dominant firms' theatres portfolio

	1993		1999		2004	
	Volume of screens	% of multiplexes	Volume of screens	% of multiplexes	Volume of screens	% of multiplexes
Gaumont	208	0	358	169 (47%)		
Pathé	128	28 (8%)	201	106 (53%)	596	447 (75%)
UGC	228	0	343	152 (44%)	370	217 (59%)

research confirms the fact that established firms should carry out such a transition rapidly when new rules of the game are introduced in their industry (Gilbert, 2003). In this case study, oligopoly members understood early the necessity to adopt the new business model associated with the multiplex and to substitute its rules for those associated with the traditional business. Therefore, the three firms achieved a process of rationalization of their assets by progressively selling their traditional theatres and creating a new portfolio of theatres focused on multiplexes. During this process, Pathé achieved a faster refocusing move due to a limited stock of assets associated with the old type of theatres compared to Gaumont and UGC (see Table 6.4).

The study of the regeneration process finally led us to tackle the degree of firms' aggressiveness during this period of time. I used three measures of competitive aggressiveness: the volume of actions, their heterogeneity and their impact on the competitive dynamics. Data treatment illustrates that aggressiveness is a key success factor for established firms diffusing new rules of the game (D'Aveni, 1994; Smith et al., 2001). In this study, the ranking in terms of aggressiveness is the same as the ranking in terms of relative performance. Pathé is simultaneously the most aggressive firm[1] and the winner in terms of relative performance improvement. On the other hand, Gaumont was the least aggressive firm and showed a decline of its relative performance both in financial and competitive terms. This result may be explained by the fact that Gaumont was clearly a follower throughout the industry renewal compared to Pathé (introducer of the multiplex disruption in 1993) and UGC (introducer of a second disruption: an unlimited access card in 2000). This result is illustrated by the delay between Gaumont's competitive moves and moves from its direct competitors Pathé and UGC (see Figure 6.1). Industry stakeholders all agree on the fact that Gaumont did not manage to take advantage of the disruption because of an inability to adopt a more industrial vision of the business.

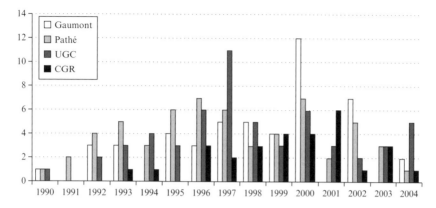

Figure 6.1   Competitive aggressiveness (volume of competitive moves)

The Impact of the Multiplex

Between 1993 and 2004, multiplex development on the French market had many impacts on both competitive dynamics and industry structures. The most notable impact probably lay in the industry regeneration as suggested by the literature (Baden-Fuller and Stopford, 1992; Kim and Mauborgne, 1997). Specifically, it is located in an impressive rise in the volume of admissions (up by 67.9 per cent), a deep modernization of the infrastructures (1.5 billion euros invested), an increasing volume of film production (up by 43 per cent), an increase in the average profit per admission (up by 12.4 per cent) and a doubling of the global industry turnover. Figure 6.2 illustrates the relationship between the volume of multiplexes and the demand curve on the French market. As the main drivers of these evolutions, the three dominant firms were the first winners of this industry renewal. Transition to the multiplex area helped them to build new growth perspectives, to pre-empt the benefits and to increase the dependence of the French motion pictures industry on them.

Another series of impacts concerns the competitive game. First, the disruption increased the gap between strategic groups, which led to a more polarized market structure (Thomas, 1996; Ilinitch et al., 1996). After the regeneration, the market is indeed characterized by two very different types of competitors: on the one side, dominant firms and a few challengers that adopted the multiplex model, and on the other side small firms unable to update their equipment because of limited financial resources. Secondly, the multiplex revolution was accompanied by an eviction effect for the weakest competitors (Nault and Van Den Bosch, 1996). However, in France this effect was limited by the major role played by

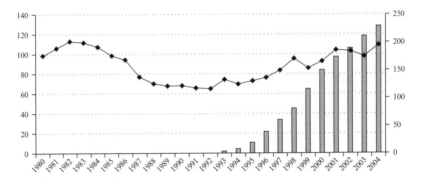

Note: Left scale represents volume of multiplexes and right scale represents admissions in millions.

Figure 6.2   Market regeneration and multiplex development

public authorities in the motion pictures industry, namely the importance of subsidies given to small theatres in order to promote art-house cinematography. The third impact on the competitive game lay in the emergence of a new kind of competition and new key success factors (Schlegelmilch et al., 2003). Competition between firms became more focused on the theatre itself and less on film selection. This means that multiplexes introduced competition mostly based on elements such as the size of the theatre (number of screens, number of seats), parking facilities, services, marketing campaigns and so on. The launch of an unlimited access card by UGC in 2000 perfectly illustrates this new type of inter-firm competition. Thus, multiplex introduction led to the reactivation of both location competition and price competition in this industry. In such a competitive game, the three dominant firms have the competitive resources required to outclass small firms and to deter new entrants from penetrating the French market.

Finally, the disruptive strategy also impacted vertical relationships in the industry. This case study shows that the emergence of a new business model allows dominant firms to renegotiate the way economic value created downstream is divided among an industry's stakeholders (Kim and Mauborgne, 1997). The new value chain associated with the multiplex led to an increase in the exhibition profitability due to a higher volume of activity and a diversification of revenue sources. In addition, an evolution of inter-sector relations within the industry can be observed: the exhibition sector increased its relative power compared to upstream sectors (distribution and production). Upstream sectors became more and more dependent on the multiplex owners as they represent a major and unavoidable source of revenue. This fact also implied increasing bargaining power for the owners of the multiplexes towards distributors in terms of film-renting rates. The updated and increased control of the industry's downstream stages led to a major renegotiation of value-sharing terms and conditions.

4. CONCLUSION

To conclude, the disruptive strategy led to a redefinition of the industrial model by altering its frontiers, its structures, its dynamics and firms' performances. For established firms, the disruption process offered the opportunity to reinforce both their market power and their role within the industry. These firms increased industry stakeholders' dependence on them. Thus, this research demonstrates that such a strategy is not only available to new entrants but can also be a powerful way to consolidate an existing competitive advantage. The detailed study of disruption effects on the French market shows that it had a major impact on the admissions curve, the volume and type of film productions, key success factors within the exhibition sector and also upstream in the value chain, firms' competitive practices and cultural elements. These virtues of disruption helped established firms to consolidate their market power and prepare themselves for the next round of the industry's transformations (digital cinema, 3D cinema, etc.).

If these research results are limited by the fact that they are attached to a single-industry study, I believe that disruptive strategy and its implications require both more conceptual deepening and more empirical work. Changing the rules of the game appears as a rewarding strategy for a company willing to find new sources of competitive advantage in a more and more challenging environment. New research perspectives may include investigations about the motivations, the conditions of success/failure as well as the different natures of disruption. Recent and current transformations taking place in cultural industries such as film, photography or television are offering many opportunities for researchers willing to explore these areas. New empirical contributions are required to expand the knowledge about disruption both for practitioners and academics.

NOTE

1. Between 1990 and 2004, Pathé conducted 22 per cent of the competitive actions (compared to 21 per cent for UGC and 18 per cent for Gaumont), used 8 types of competitive actions (compared to 6 for both UGC and Gaumont) and introduced 6 of the 9 pioneering actions that took place during that period of time.

REFERENCES

Baden-Fuller, C. and Stopford, J. (1992). *Rejuvenating the mature business, the competitive challenge*. Routledge.

Bettis, R.A. and Hitt, M.A. (1995). The new competitive landscape. *Strategic Management Journal*, 16, 7–19.

Christensen, C.M. (2000). *The innovator's dilemma*. Harper Business.

Cooper, A.C. and Smith, C.G. (1992). How established firms respond to threatening technologies. *Academy of Management Executive*, 6(2), 55–70.

D'Aveni, R. (1994). *Hypercompetition*. Free Press.

Ferrier, W. (2001). Navigating the competitive landscape: The drivers and consequences of competitive aggressiveness. *Academy of Management Journal*, 44(4), 858–77.

Gilbert, C. (2003). The disruption opportunity. *Sloan Management Review*, 44(4), 27–32.

Hamel, G. (1998). Strategy innovation and the quest for value. *Sloan Management Review*, 39(2), 7–14.

Hamel, G. and Prahalad, C.K. (1994). *Competing for the future*. Harvard Business School Press.

Ilinitch, A., D'Aveni, R. and Lewin, A. (1996). New organizational forms and strategies for managing in hypercompetitive environments. *Organization Science*, 7(3), 211–20.

Kim, W.C. and Mauborgne, R. (1997). Value innovation: The strategic logic of high growth. *Harvard Business Review*, January–February, 103–12.

Kim, W. and Mauborgne, R. (2005). *Blue ocean strategy*. Harvard Business School Press.

Lieberman, M. and Montgomery, D. (1988). First-mover advantages. *Strategic Management Journal*, 9, 41–58.

Markides, C. (1997). Strategic innovation. *Sloan Management Review*, 38(3), 9–23.

Markides, C. (2008). *Game-changing strategies*. John Wiley & Sons.

McCann, J.E. and Selsky, J. (1984). Hyperturbulence and the emergence of type 5 environments. *Academy of Management Review*, 9, 460–70.

Miles, M.B. and Huberman, A.M. (1994). *Qualitative data analysis*. Sage Publications.

Nault, B.R. and Van Den Bosch, M.B. (1996). Eating your own lunch: Protection through preemption. *Organization Science*, 7(3), 342–58.

Porter, M.E. (1980). *Competitive strategies*. Free Press.

Prahalad, C.K. and Hamel, G. (1994). Strategy as a field of study: Why search for a new paradigm. *Strategic Management Journal*, 15(special issue), 5–16.

Schlegelmilch, B., Diamantopoulos, A. and Kreuz, P. (2003). Strategic innovation: The construct, its drivers and its strategic outcomes. *Journal of Strategic Marketing*, 11(2), 117–32.

Smith, K.G., Ferrier, W. and Grimm, C. (2001). King of the hill: Dethroning the industry leader. *Academy of Management Executive*, 15(2), 59–70.

Smith, K.G., Grimm, C.M. and Gannon, M.J. (1992). *Dynamics of competitive strategy*. Sage.

Thomas, L.G. (1996). The two faces of competition: Dynamic resourcefulness and the hypercompetitive shift. *Organization Science*, 7(3), 221–42.

7. Innovation in the film sector: what lessons from the past tell us about Hollywood's digital future – and what that means for Europe[1]

Sophie De Vinck and Sven Lindmark

1. INTRODUCTION

The film industry is undergoing a profound process of transformation as digital methods of film production, distribution and consumption are impacting business and audience relationships. The revolutionary or evolutionary character of these changes has been widely debated in a variety of analyses at academic, press and policy level. One of the recurring discussions centres on the potential of digital technologies in terms of offering opportunities for smaller industry players and/or new market entrants. This is inherently linked to the impact of digital evolutions on the firms constituting the Hollywood oligopoly,[2] which have been on top of the global film market for many decades. It is unclear to what extent the future shape of the film sector will affect existing market power relations, and whether such a digital film ecosystem will increase the margins for manoeuvre of European films and firms.

One way to attempt to get a better understanding of future evolutions is to look back in order to situate current events within longer-term historical trends. This is not the first time technological change has been introduced in the film sector. By situating events and (r)evolutions in their historical context, we can better understand their origins and the way they build upon, or differ from, similar events in the past. They also may help us to discern trends that span different periods of innovation. This may in turn give us clues to the shape of the future global film sector.

In this chapter, we therefore compare current debates and evolutions with other time periods in the past when the sector was confronted with innovations that were potentially 'disruptive'. On top of that, we aim to explore the complexities behind the notion of 'disruptive innovation' itself, and the different ways in which it may manifest itself. Our case study approach is therefore framed within existing theoretical insights on the disruptive force of innovation, building upon the pioneering work of Schumpeter (1942) and more recent works on disruptive innovation (popularized by Christensen, 1997).

The key question is whether the audience reach of European films may be enlarged in a digital context. Posing this question has two consequences. First of all, rather than focusing on one stage of the film value chain, we are interested in the global picture arising at the level of the value *network*.[3] Do the various innovations have an impact on the overall (power) position of the Hollywood studios or do they create room for challengers, in this case European film producers and distributors? Secondly, in particular we will be looking for clues to how the introduction of new technologies has affected the delivery of film to the audience, including the level and type of choice the consumer has. The assumption here is that the introduction of new channels for watching films increases the potential for audiences to access films, and that this in turn increases the potential for European films and firms to reach this audience.

The chapter begins with a discussion of the theoretical concepts that help us to understand what drives disruptive innovation and how it impacts value network configurations. Next, we draw lessons from the introduction of television and home video in Hollywood, including insights into the nature of evolving Europe–Hollywood relations. We chose the introduction of television and home video as they are examples of the introduction of new film distribution 'windows', and as such may be more informative in view of the current introduction of digital delivery of films than other past innovations in film that did not directly affect the delivery phase (e.g. sound, colour). In the last section of this chapter, we bring theory and history together in a preliminary assessment of what the digital future, with its introduction of dematerialized film distribution and consumption, holds in store for Hollywood and its European challengers.

A historical perspective is crucial to our approach, but this does not mean that this chapter contains a complete historical analysis of the periods we selected. Due to the scope and purpose of this chapter the full complexity of the cinema's history cannot be unveiled. Instead, we focus our attention on the key issues we identified, namely the (dominant) position taken up by Hollywood studios, the potential room for manoeuvre created for European producers and distributors and, ultimately, the evolving position of the audience in the broader film value network. We have drawn from a variety of authors writing on the subject, including European (e.g. Jäckel) and US perspectives (e.g. Gomery), broad oversight works (e.g. Maltby) and studies of a specific period (e.g. Anderson, 1994), technology-oriented works (e.g. Enticknap) as well as business perspectives (e.g. Puttnam). Overall, we do not look at the history of film from a cultural content perspective but focus on the evolution of industry and audience relationships.

2.   DISRUPTIVE INNOVATION AND VALUE NETWORKS: LESSONS FROM THE LITERATURE

A classic theoretical starting point is that innovation transforms industries in processes of 'creative destruction' (Schumpeter, 1942). On the one hand, it allows for new entrepreneurial companies to enter the market and for existing ones to grow and enhance their competitive positions. On the other hand, it challenges incumbent players, sometimes in a disruptive way destroying companies and entire industries. Well-known historical examples include the shift from natural to artificial ice-making, from sailing ships to steam ships, from typewriters to word processing on computers, all of which were accompanied by structural change where many leading incumbent firms were not able to maintain their positions (see for example Utterback, 1994). Following these observations, there has been a growing body of literature trying to come to grips with the circumstances under which innovation in general and technological change in particular would have disruptive effects on industry structure. Starting from the simple and common distinction between radical and incremental innovations (referring to changes in the underlying technology of products), research has tried to specify further under what circumstances technological change has a disruptive effect on industry structure[4] (see Ehrnberg, 1995 for an overview). Radical innovations (that is, in some sense large changes in technology) were usually claimed to be more likely to have a disruptive effect on market structure than incremental innovations.[5]

However, the radical character of technological change was found not to sufficiently explain and predict disruption. Tushman and Anderson (1986) added the dimension of *enhancing* vs. *destroying competence*, where competence-destroying discontinuities tend to have more disruptive effects since they would lower entry barriers and give incentives for new firms to invade the industry. Incumbents, on the other hand, are faced with a disadvantage because of organizational inertia and rigidities – their core competences also become core rigidities (Leonard-Barton, 1992).

Throughout such analyses, however, the focus is often on structural change in rather narrow parts of the value chain. In the film sector for instance, the introduction of sound films and the related demise of silent film production can be seen as an example of such creative destruction.

In a digital context, the use of digital cameras instead of 35 mm cameras forms another example of how disruptive innovation may replace one element of a sector's value chain by new technology. The leading companies in these parts of the chain, for example Kodak in the case of the move from 35 mm to digital, often have difficulties in responding to these changes. Yet other ways of looking at innovation have emerged and have taken up a broader perspective. Rosenbloom and Christensen (1994, and a series of related articles and books) have been crucial with their argument for a *value network* dimension to fully explain why some incumbents fail to survive technological discontinuities. Incumbent firms are likely to ignore new technologies introduced in value networks where customers value product or service attributes differently from those in the old mainstream networks, since they concentrate on what the mainstream customers in their old value networks demand. Incumbents' disadvantages are therefore associated with their inability to change strategies (Christensen and Rosenbloom, 1995; Christensen, 1997) and are also related to demand patterns of customers. The works of Christensen et al., in particular the *Innovator's Dilemma* (Christensen, 1997), popularized a stream of research that we may label as Disruptive Innovation Theory (Yu and Hang, 2009). Numerous subsequent studies have been conducted on the topic of disruptiveness (reviewed by, among others, Danneels (2004), Yu and Hang (2009) and Sandström (2010)) in the process of refining the theory and attempting to provide guidelines for new players and incumbents. Christensen himself asserts that disruptive innovation should be viewed as a business model problem rather than a technology problem and that the most disruptive innovations are the ones that are incompatible with incumbent firms' business models (Christensen, 2006).

In the film sector, initially centred on the public projection of films, the introduction of channels and devices to watch films in a non-theatrical environment (the television, the video cassette, the Internet) seems to be an example of such broader innovation processes. Rather than replacing or changing the way one film delivery activity takes shape, these innovations more fundamentally question existing business models affecting the supply and consumption of films. A key issue is then whether and how incumbent players react to the introduction of such types of innovation that challenge their existing business and audience relationships. Does the 'old guard' indeed try to resist innovations, losing out in the process? Or is a wait-and-see approach crucial for balancing short-term existing benefits and long-term innovative potential, often resulting in re-established leadership at the end of the process? Applied to our case, we are particularly interested to know if these types of changes, in the past and/or today, have had an impact on Hollywood's global film sector leadership. Have they opened up opportunities for non-Hollywood (European) firms and films to become more visible to global audiences, and if so, does this occur at the level of supply and/or consumption?

The particularities of the film sector and its digital transformation make it necessary to introduce two more elements to this debate. They offer some arguments that add to, but at the same time nuance, the potential opportunities to challenge the incumbent players in a context of (digital) change. First, the notion of Hollywood versus European competition introduces a geographical element to this area of study. Some students of disruptive technologies have indeed argued that similar innovation mechanisms can be discerned beyond the firm level. In the literature on regions and clusters, advantages of geographical proximity are stressed (e.g. Krugman, 1991; Porter, 1990). Hollywood is a prime example of such a cluster. While shared links to advanced customers, technology-supplying institutions, and favourable regulation can be a source of competitive advantage, a firm's vision of the future and its ability to respond to technological change is also often developed in exchange with its regional environment (see, for example, Ehrnberg and Jacobsson, 1997). Clustering can delay innovation in a way that is harmful in the long term. Regional industrial clusters like Hollywood are to some extent locked into a path-dependent process. Changes to their basic technological and market tenets therefore result in crises of adjustment as the group as a whole creates rigidities that prevent the adoption of innovation. If they do not pursue change, other, more dynamic competitors may prevail in the long term (Scott, 2005; Porter, 2008). Yet cluster membership can also lead to the early recognition of new technological and other innovative possibilities as well as enhancing the flexibility and capacity with which to react to them. A conservative reaction to innovation by the firms within a cluster may moreover have less disruptive consequences. Cluster members may be able to delay commitments to new innovations until they are more assured that they will be successful. Large companies in a cluster are also able to develop close links with smaller, more nimble entities, profiting from their more innovative approach (possibly even acquiring them in the end) (Porter, 2008).

Secondly, while the reasons for Hollywood's emergence are complex (see Thompson, 1985 and Trumpbour, 2002 for an overview of the rise of Hollywood in the first half of the twentieth century), the strength of its distribution and marketing arm has been key in its continued dominance (Scott, 2005). In contrast, the European film production and distribution industry consists mostly of smaller, non-integrated entities that are fragmented along territory lines. Throughout our discussion of the different cases, we will pay attention to the modalities of this competitive strength and its possible evolution over time. Crucially, the introduction of digital

technologies in the film value network opens up possibilities for demate-
rialization of activities in the value network, which in turn allows for disintermediation. The importance of the intermediary distribution role may
thus be lessened. This process of eliminating activities in the value chain
forms an added challenge for incumbent players (Hawkins et al., 1999), in
our case the Hollywood studios. In contrast, the potential opening up of
the market for films, in particular the control over distribution and marketing, offers opportunities for European films and firms. The possibilities
of reaching an audience outside of the Hollywood distribution machinery
increase. This increased access in turn may translate into a stronger economic viability of such non-mainstream offers. This boils down to the
'long tail theory', that argues that the digital economy increases the potential to offer and consume niche and catalogue content, which are situated
in the long 'tail' of available content (Anderson, 2006).

However, Hawkins et al. point towards a number of elements that may
result in a continued dominance of the larger incumbent players (in our
case: Hollywood). Not only may they try to off-set the disintermediation
process, but business players may prefer the stability of existing business
relationships over the loose ties of new, disintermediated, business structures (Hawkins et al., 1999). Moreover, value chain control may not evapo-
rate but instead shift to different players in a process of re-intermediation
(Bustamante, 2004; Hawkins et al., 1999). Finally, the material and
immaterial world remain linked, which may lead to media conglomerates
(which the Hollywood studios are parts of) exploiting different (online and
offline) offers under one brand name and associated marketing push. As
such, even if they are not first movers, they may remain the most successful
in the long term (Hawkins et al., 1999).

In summary, we retain three lessons from this review of the literature.
First of all, disruptive innovation seems useful as a concept to apply to
the film sector, and theorists have pointed to the impact such processes of
creative destruction may have on incumbent players.

Second, it is clear that we need a broader value network perspective
to fully assess the notion of change in the film sector and its impact on
Hollywood's and European film industries' relation to the audience.
Following from both, we may expect Hollywood studios to be challenged
in their dominance if they tend to hold on to existing business relationships that are incompatible with new relationships built around innovative
delivery channels to the audience.

Third, however, the specifics of the film sector offer elements that both
add to and nuance the potential challenge to existing Hollywood–Europe
imbalances in the face of innovative change. On the one hand, the strength
of Hollywood's cluster ties may enable it to take on a wait-and-see

approach and still come out stronger at the end. Even if their position of control may shift towards other parts of the value network and/or may rely upon an existing brand name, they are not fundamentally challenged in the long term. On the other hand, a cluster dynamic may increase the importance of business rigidities, resulting in group conservatism. In a context of disintermediation, the lower market entry barriers for smaller players and the introduction of new audience relationships may in turn strengthen the position of challenging (European) production and distribution.

Overall, our discussion of the literature shows the complexities of the processes accompanying the introduction of innovations. An evolutionary rather than revolutionary perspective thus seems appropriate. As stated before, we therefore turn to periods of innovation in the past, in order to better understand and situate current digital changes. In the next section we look at the introduction of television and home video and its impact on the film industry. We have selected two innovations that introduced important alternatives to watching films on the big cinema screen. The first period of transition discussed centres on the introduction of television, as it introduced film consumption in a context and place very different from the public screening of films: the home. The second period we will discuss is that of the introduction of home video. Not only did audiences now have the choice to watch a film outside or inside the home, they could also decide when to watch a film, by taping, buying or renting it on a physical carrier – first VHS, then DVD. We will describe the introduction of these new delivery channels to the audience from a value network perspective, looking at the long-term consequences they had on the Hollywood oligopoly as well as on the European production and distribution sector. Have European firms been able to challenge Hollywood throughout these periods of change, and if so, did this have a more fundamental impact on the supply of and demand for European films in the longer term?

3.   LOOKING BACK: THE HOLLYWOOD–EUROPE RELATIONSHIP THROUGHOUT THE INTRODUCTION OF TELEVISION AND HOME VIDEO

3.1   The Introduction of Television in the Post-war Era

When television was introduced to the masses shortly after World War II (Enticknap, 2005), the film sector was already an important leisure industry, in which a number of integrated companies had taken the global lead. Hollywood was the physical location that had become synonymous with the power of the 'Big Five' (Warner Bros, Paramount, Loew's/Metro-Goldwyn-Mayer, Fox/20th Century Fox, Radio-Keith-Orpheum), who together with the 'Little Three' (Universal, Columbia and United Artists) dominated not only the US market, but also the European film territories (see Gomery, 2005).

The introduction of television posed an important challenge to theatrical screenings, which had until then been the dominant form of film distribution. At first sight, the confrontation between cinema and television had disastrous results for movie theatres: their audiences dropped and over 5000 US theatres went out of business between 1946 and 1953 (Belton, 2005; Sedgwick, 2002). Yet a closer look reveals that, in terms of the evolution of both audience and business relationships, the reality was more complex than that and has to be situated in broader evolutions. As such, the introduction of television was at once a symptom and result of the fundamental move towards a leisure society. For the 'leisured masses' (Belton, 2005, p. 306), television became an important alternative to traditional cinema outlets for the audience's leisure time and entertainment spending. At once it provided a new window for screening Hollywood movies, and a new competitor for Hollywood movies in the form of made-for-television content. Crucially, however, the public screening of films in movie theatres decreased in importance, but never disappeared. A new balance emerged between the theatrical public screening of films and the viewing of audio-visual content (not limited to films) in the home environment.

This evolution in terms of audio-visual consumption evidently had an impact on evolutions on the business side, and vice versa. Hollywood studios seem to have recognized the potential of television early on. The fact that Walt Disney decided in 1936 not to renew its distribution contract with United Artists because of a conflict over television rights, is an example of this foresight (Anderson, 1994). Yet Hollywood became increasingly hostile when it failed to achieve control over this new distribution and exhibition outlet for films on its own terms (Anderson, 1994; Wasser, 2001). The Hollywood studios wished to include television in their classic integrated system and were unwilling to produce television content as long as the networks were controlled by other parties[6] (Anderson, 1994). In short, the incumbents did not deny the innovation and its potential, but the existing value network relations they had built did hamper their willingness to embrace it. They wished to control non-theatrical exhibition in the same way as they had controlled theatrical exhibition. By focusing on copying their set of (theatrical) business rules to a television setting, opportunity was created for challenging parties who were not hampered by these concerns.

Indeed, smaller studios and independent producers soon found refuge in the television world for content that had difficulties reaching the audience in face of the studios' dominance of the theatrical screen. As a number of more established – but not the largest – players in production also became involved in television series production, the potential of this new channel came even more to the fore. Walt Disney's success was instrumental in showing even the top majors that this new outlet could be profitable to them despite the lack of control they had over TV stations and networks (Anderson, 1994). They became involved in television production, increasingly used television as a marketing tool for their cinema releases, but also started selling the rights to their feature film back catalogue (Wasser, 2001; Anderson, 1994; Kirsner, 2008).

It would be a simplification to view this evolution from hostility to cooperation as smooth: conflicts were manifold and were linked for instance to issues of licensing, division of revenues (e.g. with the actors and screenwriters), and ownership restrictions (cf. Anderson, 1994; Wasser, 2001; Kirsner, 2008; Gomery, 2005). Crucially, however, by 1960 some of the majors raked in nearly half of their yearly income from television (Meza, 2007, p. 91). As the dust settled, Hollywood content had conquered the television screen to much of the same extent as it dominated theatrical screens. Independent producers and smaller studios had been pushed aside by the incumbents (Kirsner, 2008, p. 48).

This does not mean that the value network and Hollywood studios' position in it had not changed throughout the process. The introduction of television, together with other factors such as the 1948 Paramount Decision (via which US anti-trust authorities separated theatrical exhibition from the interests of production and distribution studios; Maltby, 2003, p. 129) and the emergence of new leisure patterns of the audience, all played a role in the gradual move towards a new Hollywood 'system'. It is in this period that the first signs of the blockbuster pattern became visible, with profits increasingly centred on a limited number of titles (Anderson, 1994; Maltby, 2003; Paul, 2002). Most importantly, this is the time when distribution became the nexus of power, while production increasingly involved outside players on a contractual basis (Sedgwick, 2002). On top of this, as a result of a late 1960s merger and acquisition wave, the Hollywood studios became subsidiaries of transnational media conglomerates,[7] thus building up strong multi-sector competitive positions (Anderson, 1994; Maltby, 2003).

Throughout all of this, the Hollywood–Europe relationships do not seem to have fundamentally changed. The early 1960s were the period of the French 'Nouvelle Vague', when innovative directors like Claude Chabrol, Jean-Luc Godard and others (followed by film-makers from other European countries such as Federico Fellini and Ingmar Bergman) achieved critical success in their home countries and abroad (Segrave, 2004; Puttnam, 1997). Yet at the same time, in the post-war period of recovery, Europe became increasingly important for US movie players and Hollywood films (Jäckel, 2003; Segrave, 2004; Thompson, 1985). The Nouvelle Vague could not alter this, nor did the ascent of television in Europe seem to offer particular opportunities to challenge Hollywood.

In fact, European film producers and distributors do not seem to have been more embracing of television as a new delivery channel to the audience. The diffusion of television sets among households was slower to take off in European markets (e.g. in 1956 only 2 per cent of French homes possessed a television; Noël, 1995, p.176; Puttnam, 1997, pp.190–92), but by the 1960s, it was spreading quickly while box office admissions dropped all over Europe (Gimello-Mesplomb, 2006; Ogan, 1990). The market of film library sales only slowly opened up as a result (Garçon, 2006; Puttnam, 1997). Just as in the US, the relationships between film professionals and new television players gradually normalized, but the newly established business relations were of a different nature, as were the broadcasters themselves. Most of the television broadcasters in Europe were publicly funded, with a monopoly position in the market and a focus on in-house production (Puttnam, 1997; Wyver, 1989). Thus the potential of television for external film producers and distributors was different. From the 1970s on, television would take on a more important role in the film sector by starting to participate in the financing of European film productions. Whereas in the US, television became an important 'secondary' market for the Hollywood studios, in Europe broadcasters would more directly influence the financing of European film production. The value network relations between television and film industry players thus were of a very different nature. Between Europe and Hollywood, however, the overall relationship remained one of competitive imbalance.

3.2   The Introduction of Home Video (1970s–1980s)

As a new Hollywood system was taking shape and European industry players were shifting into a post-Nouvelle Vague reality, another technological upheaval was waiting around the corner. Different consortia had been working on various types of video systems for the home, when two main variants came to the fore in a decisive format war in the mid-1970s. Whereas some of the earlier systems focused on video play-only, the 'killer app' driving video's take-off turned out to be the time-shifting potential of a video recording system. With audience lifestyles increasingly fragmented, they were particularly attracted to a system that not only offered more choice in terms of available content, but also offered the choice of when to watch this content (Enticknap, 2005; Meza, 2007; Wasser, 2001; Wyver, 1989). In the format war that ensued, JVC's VHS video cassette recorder (VCR) system soon took the lead over Sony's Betamax (Wasser, 2001). Yet convincing Hollywood of the merits of video would prove harder than convincing the audience. Indeed, Motion Picture Association of America's chief Jack Valenti famously stated that 'the VCR is to the American film producer and the American public as the Boston strangler is to a woman home alone' (1982, quoted in Meza, 2007, p. 84).

While Meza simply calls them short-sighted (Meza, 2007, p. 67), Wasser lists other reasons for this initial reluctance of the Hollywood majors. Executives were unsure what the effect of home video would be on the audiences for movies in cinemas or on television (the cannibalization effect). This is not too different from the fear of television's impact on theatrical exhibition some decades earlier. Moreover, the studios were afraid of illegal consumption, i.e. piracy (Wasser, 2001), made possible by the recording function of video. Universal Studios and Disney even took the lead in a court battle against Sony, the advertising agency behind the Betamax campaign, several retailers and one individual user (Wasser, 2001). After a long battle, the studios lost the case in the US Supreme Court in 1984, but, more importantly perhaps, in the meantime the attitude of Hollywood studios had shifted as well. In fact, the sale of pre-recorded tapes turned out to have such a positive impact on the film entertainment industry that it overshadowed the risks associated with time-shifting and illegal film consumption (Wasser, 2001). The benefits of home video rental, which had also sprung up, were less clear to the studios at first. Once again, they were struggling to secure an income from this new market on their own terms. Smaller, independent entities took the lead, but as the rental business took off, the majors again followed suit (Wasser, 2001).

From an overall and longer-term perspective, we see thus confirmation of a number of elements that have been brought to the fore in theory. The incumbent players' responsiveness to this innovation was slow, and the cluster dynamics clearly played a role, for instance in the joint legal battle waged by some of the studios against video. At the same time, however, the incumbents' position did shift once business relationships were clarified and the potential of the new exhibition channel was tried and tested. The first ones to recognize the potential of this innovation indeed turned out to be smaller, independent producers and distributors as well as new companies.

At the same time, with video, audiences' access to and choice of films had expanded again, which in turn led to a renewed interest in independently produced content, sometimes made especially for the video markets (Wasser, 2001). Expectations for the European film sector also soared as the larger shelves of the home video store seemed to offer possibilities for non-mainstream content that were not present in the theatrical market or on television (Segrave, 2004).

However, it became clear over time that non-theatrical revenue could be linked to the theatrical performance of the film. In the theatrical market, the majors continued to rake in most of the box office income through a more limited number of titles, which negatively impacted the potential for independent titles' performance in the non-theatrical marketplace. The majors moreover inserted the extra income from the video market into increasing budgets and expensive advertising campaigns – with which the independent players could not compete (Maltby, 2003; Paul, 2002; Wasser, 2001).

In other words: marketing and distribution prowess became an even bigger component of Hollywood's global competitive position. More generally, the studios moved even further away from the classic studio system in this period (Wasser, 2001). A new round of mergers and acquisitions occurred in the 1980s, now sometimes even combining hardware and software/content interests, for example with Sony acquiring Columbia Pictures in 1989 (Wasser, 2001; Wyver, 1989). The mainstream global movie marketplace also became increasingly international, with European and Japanese media companies becoming more involved in Hollywood during the 1980s and 1990s. Yet these companies were equally focused on mainstream Hollywood content (Puttnam, 1997). A 'New Hollywood' now fully emerged, centred on new distribution and marketing mechanisms. Home video's dependable audience revenues contributed to the consolidation of the blockbuster trend. Big-budget movies were branded profusely in campaigns geared towards quick recognition, in order to facilitate both cinema theatre attendance and subsequent sales of all associated commodities such as home videos and merchandise (Wasser, 2001). The different markets became organized in an elaborate 'release windows system', with revenues from each release version accumulating to a total revenue that was far more profitable than the theatrical revenues achieved in the classic Hollywood system (Maltby, 2003). While these different windows stood in competition with each other, the organization of the windows on a basis of exclusive access, with time holdbacks separating each from the other, resulted in a set of relatively stable business relationships.

Meanwhile, in Europe, the theatrical market was in decline in the 1980s: box-office and admission levels dropped and many cinemas closed in this period. Television deregulation, the rise of pay television and the boom of home video were all blamed. The initial response to home video was in other words not necessarily more positive than in Europe, resulting in an uneven adoption process throughout the continent. When the theatrical market recovered somewhat, it was by following the multiplex model, which in turn programmed more and more US blockbusters (Puttnam, 1997; Wasser, 2001). With the monopoly of public service broadcasting broken down in Europe, commercial television channels filled their programming slots with a lot of Hollywood content – which was also popular in the video market (Wasser, 2001). Once again, neither the increase of choice and the introduction of new delivery channels for films, nor the transition period itself that comes with the adoption of an innovation, led to a larger audience reach for European films.

4.   ANYTIME, ANYPLACE. . .ANYHOW? THE DIGITAL FUTURE FOR HOLLYWOOD AND EUROPE

So far, we have seen that the introduction of new delivery channels for film has typically been met with reluctance by the incumbent players in the global film marketplace, that is the Hollywood studios. Yet going against what one might expect based on some of the theories on innovation, these periods of disruptive change did not fundamentally challenge the dominant competitive position of these players. In the long run, Hollywood successfully reconfigured its business relationships every time, in turn capturing the largest audiences both in theatres and at home. This somewhat contradicts the clearly expanding choice for audiences. With the introduction of first television and then home video, they now have greater flexibility in terms of when and where they want to access films. The larger number of screens and shelf space seemingly did not impact the actual success of European films among audiences, however. It goes beyond the scope of this chapter to fully capture the reasons for this, but cluster dynamics may play a role. Furthermore, the Hollywood studios are the ones that successfully transformed their classic studio system into a 'New Hollywood' that is centred on a core distribution and marketing strength and the integration of film divisions in larger, international media conglomerates.

With these observations in mind, we turn to the digital innovation phase that the industry is currently facing with low expectations as the potential to structurally challenge Hollywood's competitive strength seems limited. Yet just as the previous periods of transition were not completely similar, the current evolutions of course have their own set of unique characteristics. Could digital distribution lead to disintermediation and, in turn, translate to new opportunities for European films and firms?

It is in the 1990s that the film sector started this new transformation process that is still ongoing. Sometimes depicted as a digital revolution, sometimes as an evolution, it has impacted the foundations of the analogue film sector based on celluloid film. The contemporary film sector is increasingly based on immaterial formats, such as the replacement of 35 mm reels with digital files. As such, the transformation has a cumulative effect on all traditional aspects of the film sector's value chain, both in direct and indirect ways.

The delivery of films to the audience is thus also affected by this evolution. In a first stage, the introduction of digital technology in this area was more akin to 'narrow value chain replacement' such as the Digital Versatile Disc (DVD) replacing the home video cassette. Put to market in the mid-1990s, the Hollywood majors were eager to expand on the now booming home video market. DVDs provided a better picture and sound quality, durability, easier navigation and the potential to add additional material or 'extras' (Gillespie, 2007; McDonald, 2007; Maltby, 2003). Perhaps due to its rapid adoption leading to considerable profits for the film industry (McDonald, 2007), the overall image of the introduction of DVD technology is one of a smooth transition. In a narrow sense, it replaced the VHS rapidly and almost completely, but it did not affect the stability of the existing value network in a broader sense. In a next phase, however, after the turn of the millennium, digital technology-driven innovations surfaced that centred on delivery of films to the audience and impacted the film sector as a whole in a more profound way.

The introduction of television and home video had introduced new 'screens' for filmed entertainment, and, by expanding choice, made inroads into the popularity of existing screens (notably the cinema theatre) – even if never fully replacing it. The introduction of what can be called non-material or online film delivery adds to this, and thus increases the complexity of the value network even more. Crucially, the rise of the Internet has created a new window for films that is multifaceted and essentially 'mobile'. The audience can now access films at any time, any place, and on any device it wants – both established ones (the cinema screen, the television screen) and new ones (the tablet, the smartphone). On top of that, the consumer no longer needs access to physical copies (whether they be home video tapes, DVDs, or – the latest format – Blu-ray) to watch a film.

As in previous periods of transition, the effect this may have on existing delivery channels is the topic of debate. In particular a fear of the possible end of the profitable home entertainment market has contributed to the initial reluctance of Hollywood and other film players to embrace digital possibilities (for more on this, see, for example, Currah, 2007). We noted that, despite the introduction of new delivery channels, existing channels – especially the theatrical market – in the past never disappeared completely.

Given that attending a public screening of a film still constitutes a different experience from watching a film on demand at home, we do not expect digitization to fundamentally challenge the theatrical model. Whether the physical disk home experience can constitute a distinct pillar alongside digital alternatives is less certain. DVD retail and rental markets are already in decline, but the market is still in full evolution. It is not certain whether they will disappear altogether nor to what extent – and for how long – Blu-ray will be able to compensate for current losses.[8] Probably the most direct victim of digital is expected to be the classic video rental store, which offers similar services but with less convenience (McDonald, 2007).

In any case, the development of Video on Demand services brings old questions regarding the competitive position of Hollywood versus European players to the fore again. Most importantly, some of the answers also remind us of earlier periods of transition.

First, we can see that the reaction of Hollywood majors to these new avenues to some extent reflects their earlier response to television and home video. While they were early to investigate the possibilities of the digital marketplace,[9] they have been eager to fit digital into their analogue business and audience relationships, rather than to adapt their own business and audience strategies to the digital opportunities. More concerned with sustaining acquired markets, Currah noted in 2007 that Hollywood was mostly eager 'to transform the networked environment into a secure, predictable and 'well-mannered' marketplace' (Currah, 2007, p. 360). European rights holders were not particularly proactive either, and took on an initially reluctant approach with regard to putting new films online (NPA Conseil, 2008).

Just as independent or smaller Hollywood players were the first ones to explore television and home video markets, the tipping point of digital film delivery was instigated by players from outside the core Hollywood cluster – but again, not in Europe. The start of video download sales in the Apple Store and the introduction of new video download services by various big names from the Internet industry (Google Video, Amazon Unbox) make 2006 a tipping point in the establishment of the online film market, says Ulin (2010, p. 305). After this date, Hollywood slowly but surely started to consider usability factors that are crucial to win over the audience, for instance through the creation of the digital security format UltraViolet, which aims for interoperability between devices (Siegler, 2010). A key question then is whether they will manage to adapt their business and audience relationships to the changed realities in time. For now, they are still struggling with inter-industry balances, for instance with regard to the system of release windows that we outlined earlier (cf. KEA and MINES, 2010).

While such a rebalancing of release windows and, more generally, old and new business relationships, is not new, the context within which this occurs has however fundamentally altered with digital. The fact that a parallel 'sharing economy' has successfully ignored the constraints associated with finding a balance between different delivery channels, associated windows and players, adds pressure to the issue at hand. Indeed, the benefits that come with working digital (cost-efficiencies, consistent quality and so on) have not remained limited to the legal area. In a sense the delivery of films to the audience in illegal ways is a form of disintermediation, as it creates a direct form of access for the consumer.

The potential impact of piracy is still under debate, sometimes with doom and gloom, and exaggerations on both sides. Overall, both sides disagree with each other on three issues, namely: (1) the size of the damage done to rights holders by illegal downloading; (2) the potential positive effects of illegal consumption on legal sales; and (3) a broader debate on the societal and economic impact of piracy (Schermer and Wubben, 2011). What is clear, however, is that piracy poses a challenge, both in terms of direct economic loss and in a more indirect way, as current 'democratized' piracy menaces the basic premises of copyright. It creates a consumer who increasingly expects films whenever, wherever, and free of charge. The profit-maximizing strategies behind the release window system enhance the attractiveness of pirated versions, which do not adhere to similar time holdbacks and thus fulfil an audience's demand to view films before their official release in different markets (Currah, 2007). As a result, the fight against piracy has become a main attention point for Hollywood. Yet as the past shows, the outcome of this issue centres to a large extent on the take-off of legal alternatives that acknowledge the shifted characteristics of the audience. As Ulin notes, once the online legal market is mature enough and legitimate use has become common, piracy may continue to be a threat, but not a killer (2010, p. 301).

Yet disintermediation trends are also visible in the legal parts of the digital film value network. Digital technology in particular creates cost-efficiencies in film production and distribution, with lower market entry barriers as a result. Film productions can be made cheaper and be easily disseminated on the Internet, thus potentially reaching a global audience. This extends to user-generated content or amateur film producers, but – interesting in view of our focus – may also bring with it opportunities for European players. According to some, this evolution may even lead to a disappearing of the distributor's role altogether (Eliashberg et al., 2006; Zhu, 2001). While some independent film-makers have embraced the idea that they could directly deal with traditional exhibitors or even the audience (Doyle, 2002), we have seen that behind disintermediation may lie new forms of re-intermediation. In a digital context, distributors may take on new roles and/or new players may take on intermediary positions.

Both can be applied to the Video on Demand market (VoD). In theory, VoD increases the 'shelf space' for films and thus leads to a better and more immediate match between audience demand and the supply of films. We have already discussed how earlier innovations, in particular home video, introduced the notion of increased choice and, in particular, the potential larger audience reach of European films.

In a digital context, the long tail theory, as put forward by Anderson (2006), builds further upon this. It centres on three notions: (1) that the 'tail' of the offer of films is longer than expected; (2) that this tail now comes within (economic) reach; and (3) that the aggregation of niche markets can sum up to a market of significant size. One might imagine the emergence of pan-European communities for a given European film, crossing traditional language and culture borders and aggregating small 'fan bases' in a feasible new business proposition (see Gubbins, 2012). The long tail theory moreover predicts that as people get access to a quasi-unlimited selection of (movie) titles, 'they wander farther from the beaten path, they discover their taste is not as mainstream as they thought (or as they had been led to believe by marketing, a hit-centric culture, and simply a lack of alternatives)' (Anderson, 2006, p. 16).

As a result, some of the analogue European film sector (distribution) weaknesses may be offset by these digital possibilities. However, this proliferation of choice and digital shelf space has also been nuanced, with Anderson himself acknowledging that demand is not automatically shifted to niche content (Anderson, 2006). Narrowness of consumption thus remains an issue even in the face of abundance (Hesmondhalgh, 2007). As a result, the role of the distributor may shift towards a stronger focus on marketing. In this area as well, social networks, recommendation tools and so on (see, for example, Eliashberg et al., 2006; Vickery and Hawkins, 2008; Ulin, 2010), offer new possibilities to target audiences in a more cost-efficient, hands-on way. While this seems promising for European players, we must remember that the brand is one crucial competitive asset that firmly remains in the hands of the Hollywood majors. Especially in a context of abundance, they may be best placed to translate offline branding power into online dominance.

While it is still early days, according to the limited data at hand, the online market is so far not more diverse than the analogue one, in terms of both supply and demand for European films (cf. Peacefulfish & Media Consulting Group, 2008; KEA and MINES, 2010).

Perhaps even more important is the second manner in which re-intermediation can be said to occur. Even if the long tail becomes more important, its economic benefits are not so much reaped by the producers and distributors of the films, but rather by the aggregators, that is the VoD platforms. With VoD income fragmented over an ever-increasing number of titles, control may be shifted to the owners of the platform – not to European players.

5.   CONCLUSIONS

In this chapter, we have aimed to increase our understanding of the evolution of the competitive relationship between Hollywood and Europe's film industries. We did this by looking back at two earlier instances of innovative change in the film industry: the introduction of television in the post-war era and the emergence of the home video market in the 1970s–1980s.

We found that various insights from disruptive innovation theories helped us to frame our analysis. First of all, a broader value network perspective proved crucial. At first sight, it shows us a persistent dominance of Hollywood players throughout successive periods of change. However, such an assessment fails to capture the full complexity of how innovation was introduced and adopted in the film sector. Second, we observed that incumbent sector players, both in Hollywood and in Europe, typically reacted with reluctance to new technological possibilities and the introduction of new delivery channels to the audience. This was particularly the case when they perceived that the innovation would affect their controlling position (in the case of Hollywood) or more generally, their existing business and audience relationships (also for European players). As a result, thirdly there has always been a transition period that seemed particularly open in terms of new players and non-mainstream film supply. This coincides with the recurring expectation that the introduction of new channels will lead to increased audience demand for European films, ultimately strengthening the competitiveness of the European industry. In a digital context, the long tail theory has been the most prominent translation of such hopes, but we identified similar expectations when home video was first introduced. Yet fourthly, despite these periods of change and potential, the overall evolutions have up until now been to the advantage of Hollywood. The specifics of the film industry that we initially identified may play a role in this. We noted how cluster dynamics seem to influence Hollywood studios' reaction to innovations. As such, some smaller players within the broader cluster may pave the way for the big studios, as was the case with Disney when television was introduced. The specifics of the film sector's value network organization have been important throughout from a more general point of view as well. We noted how control over distribution became more important in the television era and has continued to be a key factor in the continuous dominance of Hollywood in the global film marketplace.

It is therefore particularly significant that distribution is one of the key areas in which digital change is coming to the fore. Disintermediation trends could make control over distribution less important and thus create new opportunities for European players and films.

Yet perhaps the most important observation is one that is visible in the long term, overarching the different periods we studied. It is at the level of the audience that we identify the most fundamental shift over time. In the long term, it is clear that the move towards abundance and choice has been a long time coming. Throughout the different phases of innovation, the autonomy and choice of the audience has continuously increased. Mostly, the introduction of new delivery channels has not made other channels disappear, but has instead increased the complexity and multiplied the potential relations between film supply and demand, including dis- and re-intermediation trends. The rise of an illegal circuit for films adds to this. Today, the position of the audience within the film value network thus has become so crucial that it affects the capacity of players to reproduce old business relationships in a transformed value network.

In the face of this, albeit for different reasons, the key challenge for both Hollywood and European players is to translate increased access and audience fragmentation into revenues and a viable industry eco-system. The outcome of this is not yet clear, but the branding prowess of Hollywood appears to give it a continued competitive edge when tackling this challenge.

NOTES

1. This chapter reflects Sophie De Vinck's personal opinions and does not necessarily reflect the views of the European Commission and/or its DG Competition.
2. An oligopoly is an advanced form of horizontal concentration, with firms integrating across the same sector in order to reduce competition. If taken even further, this results in the creation of a monopoly (Creton, 2008, p. 89). The characteristic structure of the cultural industries consists of a mixture of three types of firms: the oligopolistic groups, the medium-sized firms and the independents (Flichy, 1980, p. 151). Creton describes the film industry's structure as 'un oligopole à franges', or an oligopoly of major studios with 'fringes' where smaller and medium-sized companies gravitate (Creton, 2008, p. 93).
3. The notion of a value network, instead of the more traditional 'value chain' structuring model, in our view better captures the complex and non-linear relationships currently visible in the film sector. The value chain moreover is better suited to describe the activities surrounding one individual company, whereas the value network refers to the larger surrounding system of suppliers, distributors, buyers and so on (each with their own individual value chain) (see also Porter's discussion of the 'value system', 1990: 41–3).
4. Industry structure is then most often explicitly or implicitly treated in terms of changes in

the population of firms acting as sellers on a market, typically taking market shares into consideration.

5. Cooper and Schendel (1976), Abernathy and Utterback (1978) and Foster (1986) made early contributions with a strategic management perspective.

6. This became a particularly important factor after the Federal Communications Commission (FCC) declared a freeze on TV station licensing until 1952, which effectively excluded major film studios from owning television stations (Anderson, 1994; Wasser, 2001).

7. Paramount was purchased by Gulf and Western (1966), United Artists by Transamerica (1967), MGM by real estate mogul Kirk Kerkorian (1969) and Warner Bros. by Kinney National Services (1969) (Anderson, 1994, p. 291; Belton, 2005, p. 86), signs of a move towards multi-sector concentration.

8. According to the European Audiovisual Observatory, DVD retail transactions across 17 European markets (AT, BE, CZ, DE, DK, ES, FI, FR, GB, GR, HU, IE, IT, NL, PL, PT, SE) fell from 663 million in 2007 to 525 million in 2011. Blu-ray retail grew in those same markets and years from 2 million to 57 million. Rental transactions dropped more dramatically in European markets between 2007 and 2011, even when Blu-ray and DVD are counted together. In the US, it is remarkable to see that DVD rental transactions went down from over 2.1 billion in 2007 to little over 1.6 billion in 2011. Yet with Blu-ray rentals of over 500 million, the total number of rental transactions remains somewhat stable for now (cf. European Audiovisual Observatory, 2013).

9. Early Hollywood-driven initiatives were, for example, Movielink, set up in 2001 by a consortium of Sony, Universal, MGM, Paramount and Warner. It offered movies to download for a period of 30 days, during which they could be watched once over a 24-hour period. The Hollywood majors also started to offer licences to other VoD players such as Cinema Now (set up in 1999, first Hollywood deals signed in 2002) (McDonald, 2007, pp. 172–3; Ulin, 2010, p. 303). Gradually, Hollywood majors began to make their films available in download-to-own and/or download-to-burn models, but usage options remained limited, which hampered the uptake of these offers (McDonald, 2007).

REFERENCES

Abernathy, W. and Utterback, J. (1978). Patterns of industrial innovation, *Technology Review*, Vol. 80, No. 7, pp. 40–47.

Acland, C. (2008). Theatrical exhibition: accelerated cinema. In P. McDonald and J. Wasko (eds), *The Contemporary Hollywood Film Industry* (pp. 83–105). Malden/Oxford/Carlton: Blackwell Publishing.

Anderson, C. (1994). *Hollywood TV: The Studio System in the Fifties.* Austin: University of Texas Press.

Anderson, C. (2006). *The Long Tail. How Endless Choice is Creating Unlimited Demand.* London: Random House Business Books.

Ballon, P. (2007). Business modelling revisited: The configuration of control and value, *Journal of Policy, Regulation and Strategy for Telecommunications, Information and Media*, Vol. 9, No. 5, pp. 6–19.

Belton, J. (2005). *American Cinema/American Culture* (2nd edn). New York: McGraw-Hill.

Bresnahan, T. and Greenstein, S. (1999). Technological competition and the structure of the computer industry, *The Journal of Industrial Economics*, Vol. XLVII, pp. 1–40.

Bustamante, E. (2004). Cultural industries in the digital age: Some provisional conclusions. *Media, Culture & Society*, Vol. 26, No. 6, pp. 803–20.

Chantepie, P. and Le Diberder, A. (2005). *Révolution Numérique et Industries Culturelles*. Paris: La Découverte.

Christensen, C. (1997). *The Innovator's Dilemma: When New Technologies Cause Great Firms to Fail*. Boston, MA: Harvard Business School Press.

Christensen, C.M. (2006). The ongoing process of building a theory of disruption, *Journal of Product Innovation Management*, Vol. 23, No. 1, pp. 39–55.

Christensen, C. and Rosenbloom, R. (1995). Explaining the attacker's advantage: Technological paradigms, organizational dynamics, and the value network, *Research Policy*, Vol. 24, pp. 233–57.

Cooper, A. and Schendel, D. (1976). Strategic Responses to Technological Threats, *Business Horizons*, February, pp. 61–9.

Creton, L. (2008). *L'économie du Cinéma en 50 Fiches* (2nd edn). Paris: Armand Colin.

Cunningham, S., Silver, J. and McDonnell, J. (2010). Rates of change: Online distribution as disruptive technology in the film industry, *Media International Australia*, No. 136, pp. 119–32.

Currah, A. (2007). Hollywood, the Internet and the world: a geography of disruptive innovation, *Industry and Innovation*, Vol. 14, No. 4, pp. 359–84.

Danneels, E. (2004). Disruptive technology reconsidered: A critique and research agenda, *Journal of Product Innovation Management*, Vol. 2004, No. 21, pp. 246–58.

Doyle, G. (2002). *Understanding Media Economics*. London: Sage.

Ehrnberg, E. (1995). On the definition and measurement of technological discontinuities, *Technovation*, Vol. 15, No. 7, pp. 437–52.

Ehrnberg, E. and Jacobsson, S. (1997). Technological Discontinuities and Incumbents' Performance – An Analytical Framework, in C. Edquist (ed.) *Systems of Innovation: Technologies, Institutions and Organizations*. London: Pinter.

Eliashberg, J., Elberse, A. and Leenders, M.A.A.M. (2006). The motion picture industry: Critical issues in practice, current research, and new research directions, *Marketing Science*, Vol. 25, No. 6, pp. 638–61.

Enticknap, L. (2005). *Moving Image Technology. From Zoetrope to Digital*. London/New York: Wallflower Press.

European Audiovisual Observatory (2013). *Yearbook 2012. Online Premium Service*. Accessed online (29 April) at www.obs.coe.int.

Finney, A. (2010). *The International Film Business: A Market Guide Beyond Hollywood*. London/New York: Routledge.

Flichy, P. (1980). *Les Industries de l'Imaginaire. Pour une Analyse Economique des Media*. Grenoble: Presses Universitaires de Grenoble/Institut National de l'Audiovisuel.

Foster, R. (1986). *Innovation: the Attacker's Advantage*, New York: Summit Books.

Garçon, F. (2006). *La Distribution Cinématographique en France (1907–1957)*. Paris: CNRS Editions.

Gillespie, T. (2007). *Wired Shut: Copyright and the Shape of Digital Culture*. Cambridge/London: The MIT Press.

Gimello-Mesplomb, F. (2006). 'The economy of 1950s popular French cinema', *Studies in French Cinema Journal*, Vol. 6, No. 2, pp. 141–50.

Gomery, D. (2005). *The Hollywood Studio System: A History*. London: British Film Institute.

Guback, T. (1987). 'The evolution of the motion picture theatre business in the 1980s', *Journal of Communication*, Vol. 37, No. 2, pp. 60–77.

Gubbins, M. (2012). *Digital Revolution. The active audience: reach - experience - engagement. A Cine-Regio report in collaboration with Shareplay.* Cine-Regio.

Hawkins, R., Mansell, R. and Steinmueller, W.E. (1999). Toward digital intermediation in the information society, *Journal of Economic Issues*, Vol. 33, No. 2, pp. 383–91.

Henderson, R and Clark, K. (1990). Architectural innovation: The reconfiguration of existing product technologies and the failure of established firms, *Administrative Science Quarterly*, Vol. 35, pp. 9–30.

Hesmondhalgh, D. (2007). *The Cultural Industries.* 2nd edn. London: Sage Publications.

Jäckel, A. (2003). *European Film Industries.* London: British Film Institute.

KEA European Affairs and MINES ParisTech Cerna (2010). *Multi-territory Licensing of Audiovisual Works in the European Union.* Brussels: European Union.

Kirsner, S. (2008). *Inventing the Movies. Hollywood's Epic Battle between Innovation and the Status Quo, from Thomas Edison to Steve Jobs.* CinemaTech Books.

Krugman, P. (1991). *Geography and Trade.* Cambridge: MIT Press.

Leonard-Barton, D. (1992). Core capabilities and core rigidities, a paradox in managing new product development, *Strategic Management Journal*, Vol. 13, pp. 111–25.

Maltby, R. (2003). *Hollywood Cinema* (2nd edn). Malden/Oxford/Carlton: Blackwell Publishing.

McDonald, P. (2007). *Video and DVD Industries.* London: British Film Institute.

Meza, P.E. (2007). *Coming Attractions? Hollywood, High Tech, and the Future of Entertainment.* Stanford: Stanford University Press.

Moore, James F. (1996). *The Death of Competition: Leadership & Strategy in the Age of Business Ecosystems.* New York: HarperBusiness.

Noël, B. (1995). *L'histoire du Cinéma Couleur.* Croissy-sur-Seine: Editions Press Communication.

NPA Conseil (2008). *Vidéo à la Demande en Europe: Second Recensement des Services de VoD.* Paris: DDM/OEA.

Ogan, C. (1990). The audience for foreign film in the United States, *Journal of Communication*, Vol. 40, No. 4, pp. 58–77.

Paul, W. (2002). The K-Mart audience at the mall movies. In G.A. Waller (ed.), *Moviegoing in America* (pp. 282–95). Malden/Oxford: Blackwell Publishers.

Peacefulfish & Media Consulting Group (2008). Study on the role of SMEs and European audiovisual works in the context of the fast changing and converging home entertainment sector (PayTV, Homevideo, Video on Demand, video games, Internet, etc). SMART 2007/0004. Final Report. Peacefulfish/MCG.

Porter, M. (1990). *The Competitive Advantage of Nations.* London: Macmillan.

Porter, M.E. (2008). *On Competition.* Updated and expanded edn. Boston: Harvard Business Press.

Puttnam, D. (1997). *Movies and Money.* New York: Vintage Books.

Rosenbloom, R. and Christensen, C. (1994). Technological discontinuities, organizational capabilities, and strategic commitments, *Industrial and Corporate Change*, Vol. 3, No. 3, pp. 655–83.

Sandström, C. (2010). A revised perspective on disruptive innovation: exploring value, networks, and business models. Doctoral Thesis, Dept. of Technology Management and Economics, Chalmers University of Technology, Gothenburg, Sweden.

Schermer, B.W. and Wubben, M. (2011). *Feiten om te delen. Digitale Contentdistributie in Nederland.* Amsterdam: Considerati.

Schumpeter, J. (1942). *Capitalism, Socialism and Democracy.* New York: Harper and Brothers.

Scott, A.J. (2005). *On Hollywood: The Place, the Industry.* Princeton/Oxford: Princeton University Press.

Sedgwick, J. (2002). Product differentiation at the movies: Hollywood, 1946 to 1965, *The Journal of Economic History*, Vol. 62, No. 3, pp. 676–705.

Segrave, K. (2004). *Foreign Films in America: A History.* Jefferson/London: McFarland & Company.

Siegler, M. (2010). With DECE's UltraViolet, we're about to see just how powerful Apple really is. *TechCrunch*, 20 July. Retrieved from http://techcrunch.com/2010/07/20/dece-ultravioletapple/.

Thompson, K. (1985). *Exporting Entertainment: America in the World Film Market 1907–34.* London: British Film Institute.

Trumpbour, J. (2002). *Selling Hollywood to the World: U.S. and European Struggles for Mastery of the Global Film Industry, 1920–1950.* Cambridge: Cambridge University Press.

Tushman, M. and Anderson, P. (1986). Technological Discontinuities and Organizational Environments, *Administrative Science Quarterly*, Vol. 31, pp. 439–65.

Ulin, J.C. (2010). *The Business of Media Distribution: Monetizing Film, TV and Video Content in an Online World.* Burlington/Oxford: Focal Press.

Utterback, J. (1994). *Mastering the Dynamics of Innovation: How Companies can seize Opportunities in the Face of Technological Change.* Boston: Harvard Business School Press.

Vickery, G. and Hawkins, R. (2008). *Remaking the Movies: Digital Content and the Evolution of the Film and Video Industries.* Paris: OECD.

Wasser, F. (2001). *Veni, Vidi, Video. The Hollywood Empire and the VCR.* Austin: University of Texas Press.

Wyver, J. (1989). *The Moving Image: An International History of Film, Television & Video.* Oxford/London: Basil Blackwell/BFI.

Yu, D. and Hang, C.C. (2009). A reflective review of disruptive innovation theory, *International Journal of Management Reviews*, Vol. 12, No. 4, December, pp. 435–52.

Zhu, K. (2001). Internet-based distribution of digital videos: The economic impacts of digitization on the motion picture industry, *Electronic Markets*, Vol. 11, No. 4, pp. 273–80.

8. The creative destruction of the United States' Audio-Visual Media Ecosystem

Sergio Sparviero

INTRODUCTION

The evolution of media industries is certainly dependent on a large variety of processes of change and societal dimensions. These include, for example, changes in the technological, cultural, institutional, economic and/or political spheres. As a result, when the most standard business and economic theories are applied to the study of how media activities operate, perform or change, they need to be somehow refocused and customized. Picard (2005), for example, defined the field of *media economics* as 'a specific application of economic laws and theories to media industries and firms' (p. 23) and stressed the need to understand how regulation and financial pressure exercise an influence on these activities and the markets in which they operate. Alternatively, Stoneman (2010) focused on creative industries and on the role of soft innovations, which are 'primarily concerned with changes in products (and perhaps processes) of an aesthetic or intellectual nature, that has largely been ignored in the study of innovation prevalent in economics' (p. 1).

The arguments presented in this chapter follow the same tradition; they support and illustrate that disruption is a feature affecting the activities engaged in the production of feature films and other audio-visual products; yet they maintain that, not only technical, but also many institutional innovations have played an important role in forcing incumbent stakeholders to adapt and formulate new business strategies that marked a departure from the past. Institutions are understood here as 'systems of established and prevalent social rules that structure social interactions' (Hodgson, 2006, p. 2): therefore, institutional innovations include regulatory changes and related policy objectives, but also changes to less formal 'norms of behaviour and social conventions' (Hodgson, 2006, p. 3). Hence, mainstream theories and discourses that underpin policy objectives and regulatory changes are also included.

The main object of this analysis is the United States' Audio-Visual Media Ecosystem (AVME), described here as the interrelated activities that contribute to generate audio-visual media content and to provide end users with the opportunity to experience it in different forms. In order to persuade the reader about the potential for disruption of institutional innovations, it is argued here that these have played a major role in shaping the evolution of the AVME in the United States in different phases, each marked by a dominant business logic shared by the main stakeholders, related organizational principles, and by the emergence of different activities and specific relationships between organizations. These three phases are: the Golden Age of the Hollywood studios (from the 1920s to the 1940s); the emergence of specialized audio-visual media services (1950s to 1985); and the rise of global info-entertainment conglomerates (mid-1980s to the present day).

The theoretical framework provides an understanding of disruption and informs the analysis by explaining the relationship between techno-economic and socio-institutional innovations. This also describes the long waves of development affecting all market economies, and not only the different phases of the AVME in the United States. Moreover, given that this account focuses on the largest info-entertainment conglomerates, which nowadays have a global reach, scholars interested in the evolution of the AVME outside the United States should also find this account informative. A description of each of the phases of the AVME composes the core of this chapter while the conclusion, in addition to summarizing the main arguments, also reflects on the fitness of the current regulatory framework and its compliance with the innovation drivers of the AVME. Beforehand, the following section introduces and explains the theoretical framework, that is an institutional analysis of long waves of development.

DISRUPTION AND GREAT SURGES OF DEVELOPMENT

According to some innovation and institutional economists (e.g. Perez, 2010; Freeman and Louçã, 2001) the second part of a 'techno-economic paradigm' or 'Great Surge of Development' (GSD) is a period of important social transformations. In order to understand the dynamic of these long waves, which are both more articulated and modern notions of a 'Kondratieff wave' or an 'economic revolution', these alternative economists divide innovations into two families: techno-economic and socio-institutional. The former type of innovation, which is driven by business initiatives, tends to be more radical and dominant in the *installation period*, or the first part of a long wave of economic development. In fact, in the initial chapters of a new GSD, a new generation of innovators emerges and introduces new pervasive technologies, which then provide the basis for more complex technological systems and service activities. These technologies are diffused by the 'model enterprises' of the new industries, which redefine the same concept of innovation and bring prosperity to the economies that incubate, develop and adopt them.

During this period techno-economic change unfolds at a fast pace, while institutions, which depend on complex systems of negotiations between many stakeholders, resist major changes. Moreover, during the installation period, venture capital plays a crucial role as it supports the industries that produce these new technologies and technological systems (Perez, 2004; 2009). Therefore, de-regulation and innovations in the financial sector are characteristics of this phase, and they are favoured by the positive economic momentum, the growing power of financial institutions and the availability of quick and large profits. The availability of capital coupled with prospects of short-term gains, the extreme confidence in the new ventures exploiting new technologies, when, however, these have reached the maturity stage, is at the origin of a major technology and liquidity bubble. It is the collapse of this bubble (or bubbles, if the first is not severe enough for the establishment of the appropriate radical changes) that marks the beginning of the second stage of a GSD (Perez, 2004; 2009).

According to these innovation economists, Information and Communication Technologies (ICTs) are at the origin of the current and fifth GSD. This long wave of economic development was generated by the introduction of semiconductors (the motive branch), it developed and grew through the expansion of the computer, telecommunication and software industries (the carrier branches). Schumpeter's process of creative destruction takes place during this first phase or installation period (Perez, 2010): technical and social innovations generate new industries and new production processes that replace older industries and force 'old ways of making things' into retirement. Certain jobs become obsolete and redundant, and some investments in old technologies do not bring the expected returns, but from the viewpoint of society, the benefits are larger than the losses. Therefore, the *digitalization* of the economy (and therefore, also of the AVME) can be understood as the comprehensive and pervasive process of disruptive transformation led by the emerging industries of the fifth GSD. However, the rapid growth of the induced branches, which are the last generation of the newly emerged industries (in the case of the current GSD these are companies such as Amazon, Google and Facebook), should be indeed a sign that the first part of a long wave of economic development is reaching maturity and that the radical-technological-driven phase of the process of digitalization of the economy is mostly completed. Indeed, if on the one hand the first part of a GSD is mainly fuelled by technical innovations, on the other hand this last generation of new companies is not responsible for introducing new radical technologies. These companies rather grow and innovate very quickly because they introduce new business ideas and other social innovations that build on the technologies introduced by the motive and carrier branches and that have triggered and sustained the long wave.

This theoretical approach also explains that during the second or 'deployment' period of a long wave of economic development, governmental agencies regain more weight in the economic sphere, and socio-institutional changes become essential for driving investments from short-term to long-term opportunities, from the financial sphere to the world of production, for reaping the benefits of technical innovations, and, as a result, for bringing economic and social well-being (Perez, 2004; 2010). This is also referred to as the period of *creative construction* (Perez, 2010) and can be understood as a period of disruptive innovations that are mostly institutional. The last and fully completed of these deployment periods marked the end of the fourth GSD, that is the age of oil, automobile and mass production (Perez, 2010). The deployment period of this long wave of economic development was triggered by the crisis of the 1930s and was indeed characterized by the establishment of strong states (Perez, 2004). The next deployment period is assumed to be shaping as a result of the burst of the technology and financial bubbles of the last decade and the consequent periods of crisis, that is in the next 20 to 30 years.

THE GOLDEN AGE OF THE HOLLYWOOD STUDIOS: FROM THE 1920s TO THE 1940s

This theory of long waves of development provides an explanation of the drivers and the logic of innovation at the highest level of the industrial apparatus and, therefore, of the economic and social contexts in which the AVME developed. Therefore, the first two stages of the development of the AVME mostly took place during the deployment period of the fourth GSD, which Perez (2009) places between the 1930s and the beginning of the 1970s, when the oil and automobile industries represented the model that innovators in other sectors wanted to emulate. Consequently, the successful and innovative enterprise of the time was large, vertically integrated and produced standardized goods of mass consumption. However, because these two phases of the AVME unfolded in the deployment period of a GSD, the cluster of innovations that shaped the current wave were reaching the maturity stage, while the radical socio-institutional innovations were gaining momentum. As a result, also in the communication and media sector, the regulator (in a broad sense, i.e. composed of different institutions having an influence on the AVME) played a rather active role and, as argued, was responsible for disruptive institutional innovations that forced the AVME's established stakeholders to radically transform the core values and business principles guiding their activities. More specifically, new rules were introduced in order to break the vertical concentration of the studios, to open up different segments of the value chain to competition, and to increase the diversity of services available to final consumers. Moreover, these measures favoured the introduction of important innovations that still feature in the AVME, such as the blockbuster movie format and thematic cable channels.

The Golden Age of the Hollywood studios started in the early 1920s, after what was probably one of the seminal antitrust regulatory acts affecting this sector: the lawsuit involving the Department of Justice and the Motion Picture Patents Company. This was a trust company between owners of the most important motion pictures' patents, which also benefited from the exclusive distribution of the most used raw film or celluloid produced by Eastman-Kodak. This trust company was sued under the antitrust Sherman Act and declared illegal in 1917 (Winston, 1998). At that time, the cinema industry was already an important industrial and commercial reality. Notably, in this period, movie theatres were the only outlets for audio-visual media products and a large majority of films were produced by a few production companies. These Hollywood studios, or 'the Majors', were initially conceived, owned and run by innovators and entrepreneurs who shaped and influenced the early history of this sector (e.g. Marcus Loew or the Warner brothers). These media companies were responsible for the production and distribution of movies and partly for their exhibition as most of these companies owned a sizeable portion of movie theatres. The Majors who did not own theatres were able to secure exhibition of their products by block-booking the venues and/or by other types of tight commercial agreements with theatre owners (De Vany and McMillan, 2004).[1]

Following the innovation model of the fourth GSD, these companies were indeed organized as 'Fordist' industries, and therefore characterized by routinization, task fragmentation and mass production (see Storper, 1989). Actors and writers as well as other employees with less creative tasks were employed by the studios and involved in the production of several movies (DeFillippi and Arthur, 1998). Notably, thanks to the realization of economies of scale and scope, a Fordist organization typically aims at maximizing profits by producing the largest amount of output with the lowest costs possible. As a result, each major studio was producing a larger number of movies and audio-visual material than any production company does today. This was also due to the fact that studios not only produced 'main feature films', but also other types of content including newsreels, slapstick shorts, cliff-hanger serials and 'B features' (Epstein, 2010). Universal, for example, produced more than 250 films in a single year and some studios even sold films by the foot (Hampton, 1970, cited in Rifkin, 2005).

However, the closer an organization is to the Fordist model, the more standard is the output. Therefore, this organizational structure was as peculiar for the cultural industry sector as it was short-lived. The first of two fundamental factors that contributed to the sunset of the Golden Age of the Hollywood studios was the introduction and the diffusion of television broadcasting (see Winston, 1998) as this provided an alternative venue for experiencing audio-visual media products. The second factor was institutional and the result of the Paramount litigation, which was an anti-trust case between the Department of Justice and Paramount that led to a flow of Consent Decrees and decisions, issued and taken between 1949 and 1952, aimed at breaking the vertical integration between film distribution and exhibition. As a result of this litigation the Majors who owned movie theatres were forced to divest (see De Vany and McMillan, 2004).

Moreover, franchises and master contracts governing general terms were dissolved; some forms of contractual arrangements between exhibitors and film distributors, including block booking and forms of 'forward contracting', such as 'blind selling' (exhibition deals signed before the movie was produced) and season contracts (the purchase by an exhibitor of a studio's entire production of a season) were made illegal. In place of these tight contractual arrangements which restricted competition in the movie industry, standard spot contracts or single licences for each individual film, theatre, and play date, became the only admissible form (De Vany and McMillan, 2004). Part of the rationale for the Paramount litigation was to preserve and expand the parallel and smaller independent film industry, which was already present in the Golden Age of the Hollywood studios and differentiated itself from the Majors in many aspects. Already at this time, for example, independent production companies used to create temporary associations and contract employees on a short-term/project basis (DeFillippi and Arthur, 1998). Moreover, independent productions were delivering 'hit or miss' type of projects: on average, independent producers used to spend more on a movie than a Major studio, and their revenue and profit margins were also higher, although more volatile (Robins, 1993).

THE EMERGENCE OF SPECIALIZED AUDIO-VISUAL MEDIA SERVICES (1950s TO 1985)

Many new activities emerged in the AVME during this second phase, including the production of new forms of content and the distribution by cable and satellite television, a development which was also heavily influenced by a new regulatory framework. Moreover, the Paramount litigation started a process of disruption for the Majors as their main focus and core activity became the distribution of audio-visual media content, rather than its production or delivery. Therefore, these stakeholders had an interest in collaborating with, and sometimes hindering the development of, the new distribution systems from the first days of these new ventures.

Moreover, following a general trend in the media sector, the AVME shifted from being run by owners-entrepreneurs to being managed by corporate professionals during this period (Louw, 2001). Indeed, the 1960s were distinguished by a new interest of financial and business corporations in media companies, and they marked the beginning of the complex professional era, characterized by the rise of large public companies led by corporate managers. Furthermore, this period witnessed the introduction of new methods of management, new organizational structures, and the appearance of new, small and medium size companies and of a complex web of inter-firm networking and strategic alliances (Hesmondhalgh, 2002).

The beginning of this phase of the AVME was marked by increased audience selectivity and, more generally, a reduced demand for films. Improved transportation, the baby boom and the arrival of television are some of the factors that contributed to this trend (Robins, 1993). Majors and independent productions, however, were affected by these changing social conditions in contrasting ways: while production costs and revenues both fell significantly over time for the former, both rose considerably for the latter. Thus, contrary to what usually happened before World War II (and the effects of the Paramount litigation) some releases did not reach the break-even point. Given the reduced demand for movies and the more selective audience taste, 'hit films' became the primary source of revenue for the studios while the demand for commodity-like (and more 'standardized') films and other audio-visual media content collapsed (Balio, 1976, cited in Robins, 1993).[2]

Therefore, between the 1950s and the 1970s, and as a consequence of these market trends, the Majors made several attempts to adjust and find a new way forward for popular cinema, a way that had to include combinations of aesthetics and business solutions (Scott, 2004). As a result of this changed environment and in order to provide a viable alternative to the informational and entertainment value of television programmes, the Majors drastically decreased their output and began to invest larger amounts on fewer productions. Therefore, while the more standardized shorts and newsreels were eliminated from production, 'blockbuster' movies became their staple products (Aksoy and Robins, 1992; Brown, 1996; Epstein, 2010).

Furthermore, in order to adapt to this new staple product, the Majors modified their production processes and organizational settings and adopted the business model of independent producers. Therefore, they separated the vertical stages of their production process and started to create temporary/project-based organizations each aimed at the production of one movie. The new type of organization, however, presented a shortcoming: as studios no longer had 'creative' personnel under contract on a long-term basis, for each new project, producers had to bring together writers, directors, stars and support crew (Lampel and Shamsie, 2003). Nonetheless, despite pre-production arrangements becoming more costly, the organization of the production process as a project was more sustainable as it better matched the new type of production.

The Majors also started to finance and/or co-produce movies with independent producers or simply to distribute movies for them in order to diversify and deliver distinctively and qualitatively superior products (Robins, 1993) or, more simply, to generate more revenue and to compensate from the reduced level of in-house production (Aksoy and Robins, 1992). Moreover, by the 1970s, Hollywood studios were not only producing feature films for movie theatres, but also television programmes (Winston, 1998). Therefore, from this period, audio-visual media distribution became the strategic and core activity of the complex networks of business led by the Majors.

Additional disruptive institutional innovations, aimed at increasing competition in the AVME, were also introduced during this phase: financial syndication (fin-syn) rules, for example, adopted in 1970, affected the sector's organizational structure for the following 30 years. As a result of these rules, instead of using their own productions, the national television broadcast networks were forced to purchase all their prime-time programming from a third party, with the exception of news and sports programmes (Bielby and Bielby, 2003; Christopherson, 2006). As a result of the fin-syn rules and mostly to the benefit of the Majors' television subsidiaries and of new (medium size) independent production companies, the demand for media entertainment products was reinvigorated.

Moreover, if broadcast television was the first important new exhibition outlet of this period, the introduction of cable technologies and non-broadcast channels was an important contribution to the increase in the demand for audio-visual media content. Cable television was born in the early 1950s as an ancillary service to terrestrial television. Community Antenna Television (CATV) was the first form of cable television and its main business purpose was to capture local television signals using reception facilities and redistribute them to households using recently developed wideband amplifiers and coaxial cable technologies (Bates and Chambers, 2004; Maule, 2003; Parsons, 2003). Therefore, CATV services exploited the inability of television stations to provide the entire community they served with good reception, by rebroadcasting their signals and collecting monthly fees from their user. This industry was partly regulated by municipalities and local governments to whom they paid fees to buy rights of way (Strover, 2005). However, CATV was not under the Federal Communications Commission's (FCC) jurisdiction as it did not use radio airwaves to broadcast radio signals. Moreover, although initially CATV did not pay any fees for retransmitting radio signals, local terrestrial/over-the-air (OTA) television broadcast channels and national networks had a vested interest in its development as they benefited from the additional revenue they collected from advertisers as a consequence of the extra audience.

The relationship between the OTA television channels and the cable industry changed in 1961 when a San Diego-based cable company started to distribute the signals of four stations in the Los Angeles area in addition to the three local VHF stations (Corn-Revere and Carveth, 2004). This change introduced Multichannel Video Programming Distribution (MVPD) services and the cable industry gradually became an important, more independent media outlet with the ability of creating value-added from content. This change, however, affected OTA television channels which were regulated (and protected) by the FCC. Therefore, in its First Report and Order of 1965, the FCC issued a new institutional change, named Syndicated Exclusivity (or 'Syndex') Rules. These rules forced cable companies not to air programmes already aired by local stations for a period of at least 30 days (Winston, 1998). Additionally, as of 1969, cable television channels were allowed to show only movies that had been in circulation for at least ten years and sporting events that had been in circulation for at least five years (Strover, 2005). Also, as of 1972 and by virtue of the 'must-carry' rule, cable companies were obliged to carry and distribute the signal of the local television stations in the area where they operated (defined as a 50-mile radius) (Kassel, 2005). These regulations, which essentially aimed at preserving the local and rural dimension of the cable industry, also restrained or prohibited television and telephone companies from owning cable companies in the same local area (Strover, 2005).

However, in the 1970s, the cable industry was reinvigorated by the introduction of a new distribution method. As the transmission of television signals through satellite technologies became cheaper, some media entrepreneurs saw an opportunity to launch a new type of television station. This new type of station presented two advantages: first, it did not require a licence from the FCC to use the radio spectrum, and second, it could reach virtually any household in the national territory that was using a (rapidly expanding) cable service. Home Box Office (HBO) is believed to have been the first of the non-broadcast networks. It was conceived by the Sterling Manhattan Cable owner, Charles Dolan, who launched the service in 1972 (Winston, 1998) and distributed it to cable companies by using the American Telephone & Telegraph (AT&T) long-distance network until 1975, when it started to be distributed by satellite communication (Strover, 2005). Another pioneer in the creation of non-broadcast channels was Ted Turner, who started leasing satellite time in 1977 to transmit thematic channels for cable companies (Winston, 1998).

However, although HBO and other non-broadcast networks had the opportunity to expand and to be distributed to hundreds of cable systems over the national territory, they were still severely affected by the restrictions imposed on their choice of audio-visual media content introduced by the FCC in the previous decade. Therefore, in 1977, HBO brought the Commission to Court claiming that, by limiting its programming options, the latter had exceeded its jurisdiction. Finally, the District of Columbia Court of Appeals supported HBO's position and recognized that it deserved greater First Amendment protections because of its new editorial role (Strover, 2005).

Therefore, there is no doubt that an institutional innovation, coupled with the availability of new technologies, was at the origin of a series of new ventures, which destabilized the AVME. Non-broadcast networks differentiated themselves from broadcast networks from the start and, as a consequence, introduced new types of programming formats. These included infomercials, 24-hour news and weather services, music video services, home shopping channels, arts channels, and a host of other narrowly targeted programming formats (Maule, 2003; Strover, 2005). With the increasing number of channels and expanding cable systems, the number of bilateral negotiations and agreements between content providers and deliverers grew exponentially. Therefore, the sector greatly benefited from the standardization of the 'rules of the game' or of the relationship between cable providers and channel distributors that was introduced with the Cable Compulsory License Provisions of the 1976 Copyright Act. This act eliminated the need for bilateral negotiations as it provided a simplified procedure to allow the transaction between the parties involved and it invested the Copyright Office and the Copyright

Royalty Tribunal with the role of interfaces. This law allowed cable systems to retransmit many television broadcast signals containing copyrighted programmes without the express consent of the copyright owners, upon the payment of a statutorily fixed royalty fee (Dobal, 1998).

Moreover, the 1980s introduced a change in the general institutional and regulatory framework that led the AVME into a new phase. Although district courts had overruled some of the FCC interventions, up to the beginning of the 1980s the regulatory changes that were introduced by the Commission aimed at protecting television broadcast networks by limiting the expansion of cable companies and non-broadcast networks. However, Mark Fowler, the Reagan-appointed Chairman of the FCC from 1981 to 1987, supported a marketplace approach to media regulation that essentially put cable on a more equal footing with broadcasting (Strover, 2005). As a result, first, the 1984 Cable Act gave the FCC the authority to regulate the cable industry (Bates and Chambers, 2004), and second, syndicated exclusivity and network non-duplication rules were eliminated (Corn-Revere and Carveth, 2004). More importantly, the Act also deregulated rates so that operators could charge what they wanted for different service tiers as long as there was 'effective competition' to the service. This effective competition was defined not in relation to other cable systems (as they were basically local monopolies) but in relation to the presence of three or more OTA signals. As a result of this definition, over 90 per cent of all cable markets could fix their own prices (Strover, 2005). The last major restriction imposed on cable companies, however, was removed as a consequence of a court decision (see Corn-Revere and Carveth, 2004; Strover, 2005).

THE RISE OF GLOBAL INFO-ENTERTAINMENT CONGLOMERATES (MID-1980s TO THE PRESENT DAY)

The last phase of the evolution of the AVME unfolded during the installation period of the fifth GSD, that is the emergence and the beginning of the maturity stage of modern ICTs. This period was characterized by a new techno-economic paradigm, and by a gradual reduction of the regulator's influence on media markets and businesses in light of the rapid growth and success of the new and unregulated motive, carrier and induced branches (e.g. semiconductor, computer, and some digital telecommunication industries). Furthermore, the process of deregulation was also favoured by the popularization of the neoliberal doctrine, the political philosophy that preached a limitation of state power and the enhancement of a private sphere characterized by free markets and private property (McChesney, 1999). The enterprises that represent nowadays the new and most important success stories of the unfolding GSD are no longer vertically integrated, but they are organized as modular networks: standards have been created so that companies in different areas of the communication industries can indirectly collaborate and autonomously innovate. Moreover, this organizational setting enables mass-customization, which is 'the use of flexible processes and organizational structures to produce varied and often individually customized products and services at the price of standardized, mass produced alternatives' (Hart and Taylor, 1996, cited in Peters and Saidin, 2000, p.104).

However, even though during this phase new activities emerged, such as the rental and sale of videotapes and then DVDs, and later the distribution of audio-visual media content through the Internet, instead of creating joint ventures and partnerships following the example of new model enterprises, in most cases the Majors still embraced the model of the previous GSD and mostly attempted to adapt to the new environment by vertically integrating new ventures with mergers and takeovers (see Jin, 2013).

To a large extent, the wave of deregulatory changes introduced in this period reversed the effects of the institutional innovations introduced in the previous phases: in the early 1980s the consequences of the Paramount decisions were offset and feature film distributors were allowed to own movie theatres (Christopherson, 2006). On another front, the process of dismantling the fin-syn rules was initiated in 1991, when the FCC was prompted to change these rules due to three factors. First, a study by the National Institute of Statistical Sciences (NISS) concluded that despite 20 years of fin-syn rules, diversity or competition in the programme supply market had not increased. Second, the Justice Department and the Federal Trade Commission stated that there was no sound evidence that the fin-syn rules were limiting the television broadcast networks' market power. Finally, as suggested by the same FCC chairman, the video marketplace of the early 1990s was very different from the time when the rules were originally adopted and the rationale of the introduction of the rules no longer applied (Christian, 1995).

The FCC chairman's suggestion referred to, and fed into, a more general and diffused opinion about new technologies and the changing video marketplace. According to this popular argument, new media technologies made deregulation possible, as the increased number of media outlets reduced the importance of the scarcity of airwaves and the need for an intervention from the central authority (see Louw, 2001).[3] Therefore, the FCC argued that the national broadcast networks were no longer in the position of monopolizing the production of audio-visual media content and, as a consequence, the rationale for the fin-syn rules was dismissed. Thus, given the FCC's position, these rules were further relaxed in 1993 and finally eliminated with the changes brought about by the comprehensive revisions of the regulations governing the information sector imposed by the 1996 Telecommunication Act.[4]

However, if on one hand the fin-syn rules seemingly failed to increase competition in the production of programmes, their elimination clearly favoured the AVME's concentration. During this phase, the largest owners and producers of audio-visual media content (i.e. the Majors) bought the main television broadcasting networks and created an oligopoly of distribution of television content. They managed to do so because they had a competitive advantage over smaller players, as they could afford to exploit expensive studios in order to produce a higher-quality output, and because they owned the rights of television programmes (see Ferguson, 2004).

Moreover, the new regulatory paradigm did not affect only OTA television, but also the cable industry. In 1985, or one year after Congress officially invested the FCC with regulatory power over the cable industry, the Commission adopted, as part of its Cable Act, a 'three-signal standard'. According to this rule, any cable television company serving customers in an area covered by at least three OTA television signals (the case of the large majority of them) was considered to be in 'effective competition', as well as constituting a local monopoly of the specific service of cable television provision. As a consequence of the existence of effective competition as defined by the Act, a cable company was freed from any regulation regarding the price of its basic tier (Corn-Revere and Carveth, 2004).

As the cable industry moved towards saturation and the availability of new markets shrank, cable companies tried to exploit economies of scale by investing in horizontal integrations. Therefore, they started to look into 'clustering' or regional consolidation (Parsons, 2003). By this process, companies would buy out or exchange systems in order to group them and take advantage of scale economies, not only in areas such as personnel, marketing and advertising sales, but also in emerging technologies such as fibre ring topologies and digital servers. As a result, the total number of cable systems in the United States fell between 1994 and 1999 from about 11 200 to about 10 500 (National Cable Telecommunications Association, 2001, cited in Parsons, 2003).

This new trend of regulatory changes, which was further fostered by the 1996 Telecommunication Act and the 1997 World Trade Organization (WTO) agreement, facilitated both vertical and horizontal integrations in the AVME (Jin, 2013). It relied on the assumption that, because of the convergence to digital formats and the interoperability of networks, more systems could provide substitute services and compete against each other.

Therefore, with this Act, Congress established the basis for the enlargement of the audio-visual content media services by establishing the Open Video System (OVS) framework. This allowed the local telephone companies to benefit from a different regime from cable providers and to provide video services in their own area (FCC Media Bureau, 2006). In addition, it modified the current media concentration rules and allowed any single company or network to own TV stations that reached as many as 35 per cent (as opposed to the previous 25 per cent) of the nation's television households (Corn-Revere and Carveth, 2004). As a result of the many regulatory changes favouring the integration of the different activities (not only audio-visual, but media in general), the once-family-run film production companies that evolved into the Hollywood Majors are nowadays part of large media information and entertainment conglomerates.

CONCLUSION

Informed by theories of long waves of development, the chapter essentially argues that institutional innovations played a major role in shaping the behaviour of the main stakeholders of the AVME in the United States. Indeed, three different phases can be identified, each supported by important institutional changes and characterized by a dominant business logic, related organizational principles, and the emergence of various activities and specific relationships between different types of organization. Indeed, the account provided explains that in the Golden Age of the Hollywood studios, the main stakeholders of the AVME in the United States were vertically integrated and followed the model of Fordist organizations. However, the transition to a new phase started in the early 1940s, when a variety of factors, including many technical innovations, forced these incumbent players to change their core values and the scope of their activities. As this phase of the AVME's transformation took place during the deployment period of a GSD, or during a phase in which economic intervention and regulatory changes are also responsible for the transformation of key economic sectors, change in the AVME also followed this trend and included the following institutional innovations: the antitrust case against Paramount, which forced the company and then the other Majors to become independent from the theatrical exhibition of feature films; the financial-syndication rules, which forced broadcasters to purchase their prime-time programming from third-party companies; and the syndicated-exclusivity rules, which forced cable television providers to create their own sources of content. Moreover, the introduction of these institutional innovations strongly influenced the emergence of thematic cable channels and of the blockbuster movie format, which are still features of the AVME today.

Alternatively, the current and still unfolding phase of the evolution of the AVME takes place during the installation phase of the fifth GSD, therefore concurrently with the emergence of a new techno-economic paradigm established and supported by the ICT sector. In the installation phase, the private enterprises defining the new techno-economic paradigm drive the process of change, and institutions tend to be facilitators rather than active stakeholders. Therefore, the general trend in policy design that emerged in that period, characterized by deregulation, also affected the AVME: indeed, during this phase the FCC dismantled the rules which were introduced in the previous phase in order to increase the number and variety of independent stakeholders in the sector. Also, the FCC embraced the viewpoint that the concentration of assets in the communication sector supports innovation, because it helps to build the financial capital necessary to take risky investments (see FCC, 2001). Therefore, as M&As complied with its policy objectives, during the last 20 years, the FCC has had a tendency to be rather in favour than against them. As a result, M&As became a popular way for the legacy media enterprises to embrace the new paradigm by joining forces with (or acquiring knowledge from) the 'new' media enterprises.[5] Although M&As notably also took place in order to simply gain market power, they were mostly justified as responses to the emerging *media convergence* environment, that is the increased availability of new possibilities of disseminating media content through different platforms, as a result of the digitalization of the media and communication industries (see Jin, 2013).

However, this innovation and media convergence model shared by the main players of the AVME, which links technical convergence and the digitalization of media with the vertical and horizontal integration of organizations, is in contrast to the innovation model designed by the enterprises that support the techno-economic paradigm of the current long wave. In fact, one could argue that it is the *modularization* of technological systems and of organizations, rather than their *integration*, which are prominent features of convergence during the fifth GSD. Technologies are modular when open interfaces are established so that different producers can create components for a complex system, independently and without having to test the outcome of their work with other producers (see Baldwin and Clark, 2000; Sanchez and Mahoney, 1996). Furthermore, the organizational setting that produces modular technologies is realized when the value chain is composed of different activities or of companies that collaborate through the establishment of agreements that function as technical interfaces and minimize the need of coordination or continuous negotiations. Technological systems, on the other hand, are integrated when all the components are designed by one producer and therefore do not require open interfaces. While at the level of the organization, *integration* is the result of prioritizing the creation of value by combining activities within the value chain of a merged company, that is the creation of synergies.

Examples of technological convergence by modularization include the personal computer, which merged audio, text and graphics by combining parts made by different companies (Campbell-Kelly and Aspray, 2004). Also mobile phone devices providing Internet access outside of 'walled gardens' or giving access to a wide range of applications developed by third-party companies are complex modular systems. Also, distribution of music in digital format is an example of convergence by modularization, as traditional media content is delivered to end users through a value chain composed of interdependent – not integrated – activities (e.g. musician – music distributor – digital music provider – Internet provider) (Rogers and Sparviero, 2011). Furthermore, the diffusion of ICTs contributed to the reduction of those transaction costs that make joint ventures less attractive, and the increased use of outsourcing partnerships for service activities, which are indeed modularizations of the value chain through the establishment of contract-'interfaces', is an illustration of this change.

As a result, the emergence of a media convergence model that promotes the concentration of capital and the consequent integration of the value chain is somehow anachronistic and potentially hinders faster and more radical changes in this sector. This happens because processes of change in modular network organizations are fostered by simultaneous efforts to innovate, which are carried out by the different module makers, each specialized in their own domain. Vertically integrated industries, on the other hand, have fewer opportunities to benefit from innovation by other companies as they are focused on, if not limited to, producing synergies within their own value chain, that is the activities that they own and control.

Moreover, as Jin dal Yong documented (2013), the AOL-Time Warner is the most famous example of a large wave of de-mergers, split-offs and spin-offs, which have started to occur since the early years of the twenty-first century and are increasingly characterizing the media industries, but also the ICT sector. Calling it 'de-convergence', as the author does, one could argue it illustrates the decline of the convergence-by-concentration model. Therefore, as the business world is already embracing mass-customization, modular organizations and network structures, regulatory bodies should consider adapting, and facilitate or enforce these features where possible. Radical institutional changes introduced during the last deployment phase of a GSD, as this chapter suggested, led to important innovations that reinvigorated the AVME. Therefore, the objective of policies and regulations should not be to bring back the Golden Age of the integrated Hollywood studios, but to facilitate the golden ages of modular information and entertainment activities.

NOTES

1. By the late 1940s the major companies that owned movie theatres were Metro-Goldwyn-Mayer (Loew), RKO, 20th Century Fox, Warner Bros and Paramount. On the other hand, United Artists, Columbia and Universal did not own theatres (De Vany and McMillan, 2004).
2. Confirming Balio's observations is the data collected by Robins (1993), as it shows an increased concentration of revenue per film.
3. Louw also explains that, however, other and new forms of interventions were needed to allow the expansion of the new technologies, such as regulations regarding satellite orbital spots (Louw, 2001).
4. In 1993, the FCC had to redefine the rules to include the following points: (1) Network Acquisition of Back-End Rights; (2) Network Syndication of Off-Network Programming; (3) Network Participation in the First-Run Programming Market; (4) Entities that Qualify as a Network; and (5) Reporting Requirements Imposed on Networks (Christian, 1995).
5. However, as the Commission is also aware of the negative consequences from the concentration of activities, in some cases it attempts to limit them with further regulations. For example, specific sets of rules prevent any single broadcasting company or network from reaching more than 35 per cent of the nation's households (Corn-Revere and Carveth, 2004).

REFERENCES

Aksoy, A. and Robins, K. (1992), 'Hollywood for the 21st century: Global competition for critical mass in image markets', *Cambridge Journal of Economics* 16: 1–22.

Baldwin, C.Y. and Clark, K.B. (2000), *Design Rules: The Power of Modularity*. Cambridge, MA: MIT Press.

Balio, T. (1976), 'Retrenchment, reappraisal and reorganization'. In T. Balio (ed.), *The American Film Industry* (pp. 315–31). Madison: University of Wisconsin Press.

Bates, B.J. and Chambers, T. (2004), 'The economics of the cable industry'. In A. Alexander, J. Owers, R. Carveth, A.C. Hollifield and A.C. Greco (eds), *Media Economics: Theory and Practice* (3rd edn). Mahwah: Lawrence Erlbaum.

Bielby, W.T. and Bielby, D.D. (2003), 'Controlling prime-time: Organizational concentration and network television programming strategies', *Journal of Broadcasting & Electronic Media* 47(4): 573–96.

Brown, A. (1996), 'Economics, public service broadcasting and social values', *Journal of Media Economics* 9(1): 3–15.

Campbell-Kelly, M. and Aspray, W. (2004), *Computer: A History of the Information Machine*, 2nd edn. Boulder, Colorado: Westview Press.

Christian, T. (1995), 'The financial interest and syndication rules – take two', *CommLaw Conspectus* 3: 107–20.

Christopherson, S. (2006), 'Behind the scenes: How transnational firms are constructing a new international division of labor in media work', *Geoforum* 37: 739–51.

Corn-Revere, R. and Carveth, R. (2004), 'Economics and media regulation'. In A. Alexander, J. Owers, R. Carveth, A.C. Hollifield and A.N. Greco (eds), *Media Economics: Theory and Practice* (3rd edn). Mahwah: Lawrence Erlbaum.

De Vany, A. and McMillan, H. (2004), 'Was the antitrust action that broke up the movie studios good for the movies? Evidence from the stock market', *American Economic and Law Review* 6(1): 135–53.

DeFillippi, R.J. and Arthur, M.B. (1998), 'Paradox in project-based enterprise: The case of film making', *California Management Review* 40(2): 125–39.

Dobal, C.H. (1998), 'A proposal to amend the cable compulsory license provisions of the 1976 copyright act', *Southern California Law Review* 61: 699–732.

Epstein, E.J. (2010), *The Hollywood Economist: The Hidden Financial Reality Behind the Movies*. Hoboken, New Jersey: Melville House.

Federal Communication Commission (FCC) Media Bureau (2006), 'Twelfth MVPD Competition Report'. MB docket, 05–255. (Online). Available from: http://www.fcc.gov (Accessed January 2007).

Federal Communications Commission (FCC) (2001), 'Memorandum Opinion and Order. Applications for Consent to the Transfer of Control of Licenses and Section 214 Authorizations by Time Warner Inc. and America Online, Inc., Transferors, to AOL Time Warner Inc., Transferee'. CS Docket No. 00–30. (Online). Available from: http://www.fcc.gov (Accessed September 2008).

Ferguson, D.A. (2004), 'The broadcast television networks'. In A. Alexander, J. Owers, R. Carveth, A.C. Hollifield and A.N. Greco (eds), *Media Economics: Theory and Practice* (3rd edn, pp. 149–71). Mahwah: Lawrence Erlbaum.

Freeman, C. and Louçã, F. (2001), *As Time Goes By – From Industrial Revolutions to the Information Revolution*. Oxford and New York: Oxford University Press.

Hampton, B.B. (1970), *History of the American Film Industry: From its Beginning to 1931*. New York: Dover.

Hart, C.W. and Taylor, J.R. (1996), 'Value creation through mass customization. Achieving competitive advantage through mass customization'. Paper presented at the University of Michigan Business School seminar.

Hesmondhalgh, D. (2002), *The Cultural Industries*. Oxford: Sage Publications.

Hodgson, G.M. (2006), 'What are institutions?' *Journal of Economic Issues* 40(1): 1–25.

Jin, D.Y. (2013), *De-Convergence of Global Media Industries*. New York, USA and Abingdon, Oxon, UK: Routledge.

Kassel, M.B. (2005), 'Must carry rule'. The Museum of Broadcast Communications, March 2007. Available from: http://www.museum.tv/home.php (Accessed March 2007).

Lampel, J. and Shamsie, J. (2003), 'Capabilities in motion: New organizational forms and the reshaping of the Hollywood movie industry', *Journal of Management Studies* 40(8): 2189–210.

Louw, E. (2001), *The Media and Cultural Production*. Oxford: Sage Publications.

Maule, C. (2003), 'Television'. In R. Towse (ed.), *A Handbook of Cultural Economics* (pp. 458–75). Cheltenham, UK and Northampton, MA, USA: Edward Elgar.

McChesney, R.W. (1999), 'Introduction'. In N. Chomsky (ed.), *Profit over People: Neoliberalism and Global Order*, (pp. 7–16). New York: Seven Stories Press.

National Cable Telecommunications Association (NCTA) (2001), 'Cable television developments'. Washington, DC.

Parsons, P.R. (2003), 'Horizontal integration in the cable television industry: History and context', *The Journal of Media Economics* 16(1): 23–40.

Perez, C. (2004), 'Technological revolutions, paradigm shifts and socio-institutional change'. In E. Reinart (ed.), *Globalization, Economic Development and Inequality: An Alternative Perspective* (pp. 217–42). Cheltenham, UK and Northampton, MA, USA: Edward Elgar.

Perez, C. (2009), 'The double bubble at the turn of the century: Technological roots and structural implications', *Cambridge Journal of Economics* 33(4): 779–805.

Perez, C. (2010), 'The financial crisis and the future of innovation: A view of technical change with the aid of history', The Other Canon Foundation and Tallinn University of Technology Working Papers in Technology Governance and Economic Dynamics: pp. 1–42.

Peters, L. and Saidin, H. (2000), 'IT and the mass customization of services: The challenge of implementation', *International Journal of Information Management* 20(2): 103–19.

Picard, R.G. (2005), 'Unique characteristics and business dynamics of media products', *Journal of Media Business Studies* 2(2): 61–9.

Rifkin, J. (2005), 'When markets give way to networks. . . everything is a service'. In J. Hartley (ed.), *Creative Industries* (pp. 361–73). Oxford: Basil Blackwell.

Robins, J.A. (1993), 'Organization as strategy: Restructuring production in the film industry', *Strategic Management Journal*, 14(Special Issue: Corporate Restructuring), 103–18.

Rogers, J. and Sparviero, S. (2011), 'Same tune, different words: The creative destruction of the music industry', *Observatorio* (*OBS**), 5(4), 1–30.

Sanchez, R. and Mahoney, J.Y. (1996), 'Modularity, flexibility and knowledge management in product and organisation design', *Strategic Management Journal* 17(Winter Special Issue): 63–76.

Scott, A.J. (2004), 'Hollywood and the world: The geography of motion-picture distribution and marketing', *Review of International Political Economy* 11(1): 33–61.

Stoneman, P. (2010), *Soft Innovation: Economics, Product Aesthetics, and the Creative Industries.* Oxford: Oxford University Press.

Storper, M. (1989), 'The transition to flexible specialisation in the US film industry: External economies, the division of labour, and the crossing of industrial divides', *Cambridge Journal of Economics* 13(2): 273–305.

Strover, S. (2005), 'United States: Cable television', March 2007. Available from: http://www.museum.tv/home.php. (Accessed March 2007).

Winston, B. (1998), Media Technology and Society. A History: From the Telegraph to the Internet. London & New York: Routledge.

PART II

Co-creation, crowd-funding and crowd-sourcing

9. Modes, flows and networks: the promise of crowdfunding in documentary filmmaking and audience development[1]

Mary Elizabeth Luka

In a media business world swept up by the potentially extraordinary benefits of crowdsourcing and crowdfunding, can crowdfunding help a filmmaker get to production, distribution and beyond? In this environment, media producers must ask themselves: am I the next Veronica Mars? (Thomas, 2013).[2] If you are an established documentary filmmaker operating with minimal staff or financial resources outside the three main urban production centres in Canada (Toronto, Montreal and Vancouver), it's unlikely that this could happen. Having an existing connection to the American market, however, helps, as does an extensive professional and personal network. If you are a well-established non-profit organization based in one of those three centres, promoting the industry with an existing support base and networks of volunteers, staff and members, it's quite likely you will succeed. This chapter draws from five case studies where crowdfunding has been used to fund modestly-sized projects and generate core audience commitment and growth. Three of the case studies are based in Halifax, Nova Scotia, two with significant partnerships to the US market. A fourth case study is international with clear links to the United States; the fifth is based in Vancouver, BC, targeted to a Canadian-only market.

It's evident from these case studies and metrics available from crowdfunding websites that crowdfunding easily inserts itself into the leveraging processes already in place in the screen-based industries. This does not necessarily increase the overall pools of funding available, but demonstrates to potential investors that each project has an audience and compelling creative vision. For documentary projects in particular, this has the potential to help ameliorate the relative, ongoing loss of development and production funding. The strategies and execution details required to be successful bear a significant resemblance to traditional fundraising strategies in the voluntary and non-profit industries. (For a comprehensive overview of such strategies in North America, see for example, resources and publications available at Imagine Canada (http://www.imaginecanada.ca/), Giving USA (http://www.givingusareports.org/) and the Lilly Family School of Philanthropy at Indiana University-Purdue University Indianapolis (http://www.philanthropy.iupui.edu/research-and-news); also see Broadbent and Omidvar, 2011).) All the filmmakers and project leaders involved in this study are reasonably well-established, award-winning professionals whose work draws audiences and traditional funding. Was crowdfunding worth the effort required? It seems evident that crowdfunding compels filmmakers and non-profit organizations to act as temporary but also fragile nodes of activity around which programming, funding and audiences are constellated in integrated ways.

RESEARCH METHODS AND SOURCES OF DATA

For this study, I drew on my own 15 years of experience as a television and internet producer-director, video-artist, and broadcasting programmer, as well as ten years of experience in non-profit management including fundraising. Extensive original research was generated through a mixed-methods approach, incorporating open-ended discussions, emails and interview-based case studies (Yin, 2009) to focus on the experience of five veteran filmmakers (Walter Forsyth, Connie Littlefield, Johanna Lunn, Conteh Ngardy and Scott Simpson) and the experience of a Canadian film promotion club director (Anita Adams), complemented by industry metrics including funding raised, audience data and media attention. Two high-profile crowdfunding websites – Kickstarter (www.Kickstarter.com) and IndieGoGo (www.IndieGoGo.com) – were studied, with additional information gathered from the emerging specialty music crowdfunding site PledgeMusic (www.pledgemusic.com). Each interviewee addressed the support structures and key components involved in their crowdfunded projects, and each assessed the significance, advantages and drawbacks of the process.

The research responded to the following working hypotheses:

> *Funding for film production and distribution can be generated through crowdfunding.* Metrics related to types of projects, funding logistics and results, and the creators involved in Kickstarter and IndieGoGo provide indicators of this, as does media attention received.
> *Success in crowdfunding media and arts production is realized mainly by drawing on support from an already-existing network of supporters, using a proven format.* This would be remarkably similar to traditional methods of non-profit fun-

draising and, to some degree, media financing. Analyses of specific projects contextualize the aggregated data.[3]

MEDIA LANDSCAPE AND DISCUSSION FRAMEWORK

Media and arts production in Canada and the United States continues to be in flux, through corporate consolidations, decreased commissioning funds at the national and international levels, and tightly competitive production and advertising markets. More recently, it has become evident that the way in which advertising funding circulates in the industry differs from before, including how people are employed in media production, and what kind of programming is made. At the same time, profits continue to rise, particularly for those companies that are finding ways to monetize digital production and distribution (CRTC, 2011, 2013a, 2013b; EY Canada, 2013; Statistics Canada, 2011). Since 2010, celebrity projects aside (see, for example, Chen et al., 2013; Hayden, 2013),[4] crowdfunding has been embraced as a viable funding option for small creative projects to undertake specific tasks (e.g. pre-sales of DVDs and books to develop a demo recording or to offset costs to install creative work in a specific environment). However, it is not yet formally recognized as a component of the complex *equity financing* structure required for making media in Canada today. In the spring of 2013, the Canada Media Fund (CMF), Canada's primary media financing organization, launched a dedicated web space for crowdfunding resources for the professional media production sector (Canada Media Fund, 2013). The website offers a few case studies and best practice observations, plus interpreted data generated by US-based Massolution (for details, see Massolution, 2013), a company that tracks crowdfunding data through industry surveys. The site provides high-level insights into the possibility of future equity investment potential (the core business of the CMF), and a list of crowdfunding instruments available to Canadian producers.

The definition of crowdfunding emerges from both scholarly and corporate environments, including Don Tapscott and Anthony D. Williams' (2008) research on crowdsourced educational and collaborative activity such as wikis. Douglas Rushkoff's (2003; 2010) studies of the Internet and other digital technologies enumerate the potential for mobilizing democratic political actions. More plainly, Paul Belleflamme, Thomas Lambert and Armin Schwienbacher (2011 [2010]) define crowdfunding as the application of crowdsourced tactics to revenue generation in an entrepreneurial (often for-profit) environment. They express interest in its mathematical formulations in a business context, rather than for non-profit uses. Extrapolating from these working definitions, in my research crowdfunding refers to internet- and digital-technology-based crowdsourced funding operations: the creation and growth of specific virtual social networks ('assemblages') of people who provide resources for cultural production.

Incorporating digital media production and distribution complicates business practices, particularly when projects are born digital. The encounter with digital technology holds the promise of generating a new way to mobilize resources available for creative labour and production processes. This helps reshape what Benjamin Lee and Edward LiPuma (2002) term 'cultures of circulation' concerning the mobilization of flows of community, capital, risk and labour in media production and dissemination,[5] with a profound impact on creativity in North America. Scrutinizing the case studies through a mobility studies lens inflected by political economy analysis offers a useful analytical approach to understand the articulation of crowdsourced funding to creative projects and production resources in filmmaking.

UNPACKING NODES AND NETWORKS: IMAGINING THE CIRCULATION OF FINANCING

My analysis explores how a preliminary mapping of project creators and funders as nodes offers an understanding of crowdfunding as aggregations of modes of production, flows of financing and networks of investors. The pathways engendered (for example, the movement of resources, risks, supporter relations and 'perks') within short timeframes suggest temporary trajectories within cultures of circulation that align with recent considerations of how the *imagined circulation of financing* itself can constitute meaning. The schematic I have developed to reflect crowdfunding is shown in Figure 9.1. Such relationships can also be understood in terms that describe interpretive communities as 'in' the Internet:

> Interpretive communities [. . .] set the protocols for interpretation by inventing forms, recognizing practices, founding institutions, and demarcating boundaries based primarily on their own internal dynamics [. . .]. This ethnography of forms [. . .] can be carried out only within a set of circulatory fields populated by myriad forms. (Gaonkar and Povinelli, 2003, p. 391)

UNPACKING NODES AND NETWORKS

Node type 1 is the crowdfunding project creator who has one or more projects they wish to have funded or otherwise supported. What makes this

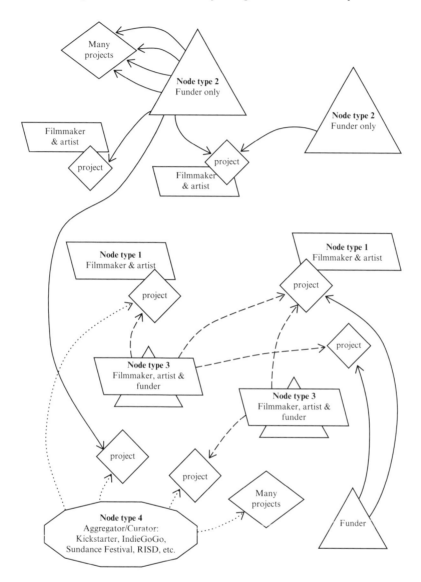

Notes:
Diamonds = projects to fund
Triangles = Funder or Node Type No. 2 Quadrilateral = Filmmaker/Artist or Node Type No. 1
12-sided polygon = Curatorial Node Type No. 2 Quadrilateral + Triangle = Filmmaker/Artist/Funder or Node Type No. 3

Figure 9.1   Crowdfunding nodes, flows and networks

node mobile is the changing composition of the funding network attracted to each new project and the short-term nature of each project. Each new campaign highlights the potential to reform the personal networks of each individual, their project(s) *and the crowdfunding sites themselves*. This is the creation of a culture of circulation based on a social imaginary articulated as (a) mobile global culture (sector). The ongoing nature of the seemingly transparent relationships configured in the public space of the website is integral to the formation of the mobile node.

Node type 2 is composed of a small group of funders who support multiple projects, suggesting that these individuals move beyond personal networks or single causes into a visibly philanthropic mode. In these cases, the category or a specific cause predominates in the selection of projects. This is consistent with the use of social media marketing for media production in general, as Julie Giles (2011) has shown. Generating a trajectory of support for complementary projects is the task here. All project leaders understood the importance of speaking to 'fans' or demographics with proven interest in the purpose of their project. Emphasizing category, cause and popular perks are also promotional strategies employed by crowdfunding websites themselves. All interviewees spoke of the considerable personal efforts required to generate interest and expand their networks of supporters. Success in attracting leading multiple-project funders plays a determining role in the overall success rate.

Node type 3 is an intriguing combination of project-leader *networks* and funder *trajectories*. These are project creators who fund and support projects other than their own. Showing support through cross-promotion of other films allows all the projects concerned to gain more attention. Discussions with the Nova Scotia-based project leaders emphasized the sharing culture assumed to operate in the Canadian Atlantic region as a factor in success. These findings are consistent with Tracy Zhang's discussion of cooperative filmmaking in the Maritimes (2009). Likewise, the Vancouver-based project leader emphasized the significant support realized from the close-knit Vancouver and Atlantic film-going connoisseur communities, as do reviews of the funder lists for all projects in relation to their specific fan or demographic communities.

A final node presents itself as curatorial aggregator of projects. For example, in July 2010, a film festival was hosted and curated by some of the founders of Kickstarter, who have themselves funded several projects (Ryzik, 2010). Additional curated or aggregated sections on the Kickstarter website include those of the New Museum in New York, City of Portland, Rhode Island School of Design (RISD), and a dozen others. These sections feature or commission Kickstarter projects that have an association with the respective curator or aggregator (Luka, 2012).

IndieGoGo favours partnerships over curated zones or pages. Their work with the entrepreneurial-oriented Startup America Partnership headed up by United States President Barack Obama is one example (IndieGoGo, 2011). Each of the node number 4 examples can be understood as adding value through the reputation of the organization or individual involved in endorsing or curating the project. This is a *performance of value* rather than the direct provision of funding. Such a performance helps to open new pathways or trajectories for funding.

Provocative questions are generated about the roles of the artist-creator or producer, the (culture) patron, and the curator-aggregator in this context. Are these groups creative stewards, fundraising staff or business managers, or all three? According to data generated from a 2013 industry report by Massolution, 'there are over 580 active crowdfunding platforms worldwide as of April 2012, the majority of which are located in Western Europe and North America' (as cited in Canada Media Fund, 2013). Remarkably, Canada was tied with the United States, United Kingdom, the Netherlands, Germany and Spain for the number of crowdfunding platforms (45 according to Massolution data, up from 17 in 2012) and now is estimated to have 52 (National Crowdfunding Association of Canada, NCFACanada.org, 26 June, 2013), though its population is much smaller than most of those other countries. North America boasts the largest proportion of crowdfunding participation, though it is worth noting 'worldwide crowdfunding volumes reached $2.66 billion in 2012, up from $1.47 billion the previous year' (MacLellan, 2013).[6] Given the international emphasis of much crowdfunding activity, specific iterations of crowdfunding assemblages and flows can be considered a series of globalized cultures of circulation that engender value and meaning, potentially indicating the formation of a new social imaginary concerned with creative business practices based on social values. The use of 'social imaginary' in this context is based on Charles Taylor's configuration of how each society or nation-state is comprised of (more-or-less) agreed-upon civic social relations, including business or market-based exchanges, the sharing of social values throughout a society, and how individuals and groups interact and take responsibility for the functioning of society (Taylor, 2004).[7]

MOBILIZING SOCIAL RELATIONS: THEORETICAL PERSPECTIVES

My research draws from how the concept of 'assemblages' is mobilized by Stephen B. Crofts Wiley, Daniel M. Sutko and Tabita Moreno Becerra (2010) in their discussion of fieldwork conducted on personal networks in Chile. Wiley et al. map the articulation of people to overlapping social groups and the evolving spaces of social relations as assemblages. The authors trace the intersections of social relations to local, national, global and cultural spaces, by delineating the day-to-day experiences of each interviewee. Building on this rhythm analysis (Lefebvre, 1992), they extrapolate an assessment of primarily urban flows and mobilities that parallels Saskia Sassen's research on interventions in urban public spheres (2006). Similarly, it is useful to understand crowdfunding platforms as public spheres within which the relationships of one project to another can happen through connections among one or many creator-producers and a series of funders. Further, Stephen B. Crofts Wiley and Jeremy Packer (2010) suggest that the highly customizable nature of 'the production of social space' is critical (p. 264). Research from locative mobility studies (for example, Galloway and Ward, 2006; Wilken, 2010) would further suggest that crowdsourced funding is more akin to the production of *mobile* social space and *mobile* interactions. Drawing on Adriana de Souza e Silva and Jordan Frith's (2010) research on users of mobile devices in urban spaces as 'nodes' of activity, my research maps temporary connectivity in crowdfunding as a frequently shifting mobile assemblage comprised of nodes and support networks connecting within a specific culture of circulation. Furthermore, conceiving of crowdfunding as cultural production in its own right activates the intersection of personal/professional networks with social and economic systems. In other words, crowdfunding practices are understood as philanthropy, as business investment *and* as social relations. A robust theoretical framework incorporates the ideas of value(s)-based cultures of circulation and connects them to creative modes, creator nodes and their assemblages.

The cultures of circulation model helps analyse how media production is financially generative, by allowing observations of how crowdfunding networks of filmmakers grow and shrink over time. These actions and systems are bound together in the creation of new social imaginaries (i.e. of the political and economic organizations called nation-states), building on day-to-day business, cultural and communication practices – as Benedict Anderson has suggested must happen in order to imagine a nation into being (2006[1983]). Significant performances of community-building and fund-raising processes are visibly induced together in practices of crowdfunding. By comparatively considering how these nodes, networks and flows work in the context of cultural production initiated in relation to crowdfunding, the 'do-it-with-others' ethos and the advantages of crowdfunding websites can be better understood.

That filmmakers and artists attract highly diffused groups of funders to creative projects speaks to a complex set of social relations, the fluidity of the projects and their networked assemblages of supporters. Georgina Born theorizes in recent work (2010) that the social relations involved in the management of aesthetics and creative labour in cultural economy terms are critically and helpfully interlocked in five important thematic ways. These include: 'aesthetics and cultural object[s]; the place of institutions; agency and subjectivity; questions of history, temporality and change; and problems of value and judgment' (Born, 2010, p. 172). Likewise, the mission statements and non-profit rhetoric found on crowdfunding websites seem to depend on the mobilization of affect through an ambiguous, hybrid combination of commercial and public service production practices and aesthetics. This results in a 'participatory' (aka funding) appeal based on a sophisticated combination of entertainment value, philanthropic mores, and the display of strategic marketing savvy. Such an appeal bolsters the illusion that there is no institution behind the projects, and that artistic values and individual agency are structurally paramount for the project creators, funders and supporters. As the crowdfunding business matures, this becomes more obvious.

THEORETICAL AFFILIATIONS IN RELATION TO BEST PRACTICES

Grouping nodes of activity (e.g. the virtual producer-patrons, funders, curators, aggregators and/or partners) can also be configured as Bourdieuvian[8] cultural intermediaries in the marketplace. Intermediaries are not nodes of their own – the concept of the node is meant to suggest individuals around whom activity constellates at a particular point in time. Rather, the idea of cultural intermediaries is useful as a way to point to structural power relations and production patterns that can be incorporated into theories of circulation and the construction of social capital (value). Cultural intermediaries have been usefully implicated elsewhere in a complex and relational class- and education-based system involving taste-making cultural workers, including artists, television producers, graphic designers, architects and fashion models (Soar, 2002; Stevens, 1998; Wissinger, 2009). Sean Nixon and Paul du Gay (2002) critique the lack of precision and over-determination of Bourdieuvian cultural intermediaries in order to make explicit their too-broad conceptual boundaries. In my research, complicating this concept with that of precarity (for example, Neilson and Rossiter, 2008) allows a more nuanced understanding of creative workers and supporters to emerge. A Bourdieuvian approach suggests that little agency is available to creative industry participants as individuals – each must be confined within the available position and parameters. In the case of crowdfunding, this is made explicit through the many 'how to' and 'best practices' documents and analyses, including the requirement to present a compelling video, specific timelines, all-or-nothing funding options and so on. Scholars studying the precarious nature of employment in the creative field focus on the dynamic between individual workers and the employers or projects to which they temporarily 'belong'. For example, in media production, an intense relationship develops among crew and above-the-line producers for the duration of each project. Creative participants can feel that they belong – and contribute – to the particular project but also to their profession (Christopherson, 2008; Deuze et al., 2007; 2010; Terranova, 2000). The core contribution to be made from the literature around affective, emotional or immaterial labour is the acknowledgement of a deep emotional connection to and ownership over creative work. Often couched as entrepreneurial or independent work, the upside of economic instability in the cultural industries is precisely the individual's sense of commitment to and control over their art (McRobbie, 2002).[9] Such an intense affiliation is consistent with the tantalizing promise of crowdfunding and the experience of crucial crowdfunding participants. Reflecting on such desires and configurations with the interview subjects is congruent with my own industry knowledge and can be triangulated with crowdfunding metrics.

THE METRICS OF CROWDFUNDING DATA

The crowdfunding market has grown extremely quickly in its first five years, with hundreds of websites and thousands of media and blog articles, opinion pieces and 'how to' guides now available. Kickstarter and IndieGoGo remain industry leaders. Substantial metrics are freely available directly from crowdfunding sites themselves, as well as from industry websites such as Alexa Graphs, VentureBeatProfiles and W3snoop. com. As of June 2012, Kickstarter began aggregating and updating key measures on a daily basis ('Kickstarter Stats', 2013b). As an industry leader that makes data available, Kickstarter is used here as a baseline. Before then, they provided round-ups on their blog on 28 April, 2011, the anniversary of their second year in operation, and on 9 January, 2012, at 2011's year-end (Luka, 2012). The typical user at Kickstarter is disproportionately 18–34 years old, which has dropped down from 2011–12, when the demographic tended to reach up to 45 years. IndieGoGo also tends to draw 18–34 year-olds. Kickstarter attracts more males than females, with the opposite case for IndieGoGo (Alexa Graphs, 2011a, 2011b, 2012, 2013). A 2012–13 comparison of unique visitors on Kickstarter versus

IndieGoGo shows a reversal of the patterns of 2011–12. The numbers fluctuate dramatically for IndieGoGo, with 200000 in May 2012; 1 million in December 2012; 400000 in February 2013, and 600000 in May 2013. This contrasts with about 100000 consistently in 2010, and 200000 by the end of 2011. For Kickstarter, the numbers remain consistent at about 1 million through 2012 and into the first half of 2013, peaking at 1.2 million in August 2012 and May 2013. Compare this to fluctuations ranging from 300000 to 500000 in any given month in 2010, and between 375000 and 800000 throughout 2011 (VentureBeatProfiles, 28 April 2011; 6 March 2012; W3Snoop, 29 June 2013).

In terms of success rates, Kickstarter has launched 104548 projects, of which 44089 (42 per cent) met their goals, raising $584 million. Of these, fully 10525 (24 per cent) of successful projects were for film and video with 62 per cent of those (6475) raising $1000–9999, and another 16 per cent (1638) raising $10000–19999. Interestingly, only two film and video projects have raised over $1 million, while 22 games projects have done so, even though only 1892 games projects altogether have been successful (Kickstarter, 2013b). IndieGoGo does not publish aggregated data, but occasionally provides information to journalists. In its release of information for 2012, social media business website Mashable reported on the financial metrics provided:

> Campaigns appear to have garnered more support in 2012, raising an average of 20 per cent more than projects did in 2011; . . .the most successful campaign, 'Let's Build a Goddamn Tesla Museum,' raised an IndieGoGo record of $1,370,461 in total funding; . . .core campaigns ran an average of 49 days, as opposed to 60 in 2011, and successful campaigns ran for an average of 39 days (Petronzio, 2013).

IndieGoGo claims to be the largest crowdfunding operation in the world, though a scan of their website shows only 26946 projects listed (4491 pages × 6 projects per page), including thousands that didn't reach their goals (2013a). IndieGoGo develops blog posts with 'tips' and 'tricks', and shares modest pieces of data about those that are consistent with the experience of the creators I spoke to, and with the 'how to' manuals on the market (for example, Ideavibes, 2011; Youngdale, 2012). For example, a recent IndieGoGo post noted that most of the funding is raised at the beginning and the end of each project, including 20 per cent of the funds in the first 1/10 of the campaign, and 25 per cent in the last 1/10 (IndieGoGo 'Winning the middle game', 2012a). By now, supporters are used to this pattern and may time their contributions accordingly as early supporters or last-minute saviours. Finally, IndieGoGo offers 'top 12' lists at the end of the year, which do not include any contextual information, such as how many projects exist in each category, and how the decisions are made to select the 'top' projects. Many simply earn lots of money (IndieGoGo 'Top 12', 2012b).

PROJECT CREATORS AND THEIR PROJECTS

To deepen understanding about the implications of industry-based metrics, five case studies based in the Canadian media market were examined. To begin, consider a creatively integrated example of standard crowdfunding strategies. Filmmaker Scott Simpson designed the PledgeMusic crowdfunding music video project 'Give A Little' to closely mirror the creative process it will fund. The project's web page focuses on how the song story and the concept for the music video are reflected in the choice of artists whose work will appear in the video and are available as perks for the crowdfunding experience itself. From a house concert by musician Erin Costello to visiting the set – 'a superb example of contemporary architecture' (Give a Little, 2013) – to being a background participant or sporting fashion and jewellery items to be featured in the video itself: these perks place the funders into the project before, during and after production. The very title of the song, 'Give a Little', prompts participants to the specific action required to successfully fund the creative project. This is a deliberately holistic *creative experience* for the funding supporters.

The project raised $15 000 in just under ten weeks, with the last 25 per cent coming in during the final week (itself an extension of the original deadline). The basic crowdfunding formula upon which this and the other projects studied (below) were based is compelling. Working through standardized website-based mechanisms that enable affective appeals to specific audiences in a compressed time period is a proven traditional fundraising method. It also homogenizes the projects more than the crowdfunding websites' promotional stances might suggest. I am interested in how the emphasis on the artistic individuality of projects on leading crowdfunding sites such as Kickstarter and IndieGoGo therefore depends on setting up each project creator as a crucial centre (node) of activity. The other four projects analysed explicitly situate project creators in this way.

Filmmaker Connie Littlefield, from Halifax, Nova Scotia, experimented early with crowdfunding on both Kickstarter and IndieGoGo, realizing success in March 2011. Littlefield secured $15 091 from 25 funders against a $15 000 goal on Kickstarter to undertake development for her newest documentary, *Better Living Through Chemistry*, about the history of LSD in the United States and Canada. Littlefield maintains a Facebook page about this project and runs her own production company, Concepta Film (http://www.conceptafilm.com/). A campaign the previous year did not succeed on IndieGoGo for *Life After Hate*, a documentary exploring the peace activist efforts of former Nazi skinheads. Littlefield has produced and directed four feature-length documentary films dealing with health, adolescents, drugs and mental illness over the past decade, while also working in the television industry as an episode director for children's and youth programmes. This combination of personal projects and director-for-hire is typical in the Canadian media industry and is reflected in the professional history of all the filmmakers.

Director Ngardy Conteh and her team have leveraged their experience on Kickstarter for their *Leone Stars* project in several ways. Conteh's team raised $20175 against their $20000 goal on Kickstarter. The project features amputee survivors of the 1990s Sierra Leone civil war whose redemption is found in soccer: 'The team is their family, and their fans their admirers. Soccer has turned these amputees from victims into champions' (Conteh, 2011). An active presence is maintained on the Leone Stars blog (http://leonestars.blogspot.com/) and Facebook page (https://www.facebook.com/LeoneStarsDocumentary). Conteh herself has directed two short documentaries, three music videos and dozens of episodes of reality programming focused on lifestyle and music, telling stories from culturally underrepresented points of view (Conteh, 2012). Along with Conteh, erstwhile producer Walter Forsyth was interviewed for this project. His credits include seven short films, six music videos and four long-form documentaries about personal relationships, art and cooperative film-making over the past decade (Gorgeous Mistake, 2013). The Leone Stars production team is transnational: Conteh is Canadian, born in Sierra Leone and co-located in Barbuda (near Antigua) and Toronto; Forsyth is in Halifax, Nova Scotia; Conteh's co-director Allan Tong is Canadian and located in Toronto; so is executive producer Jerry McIntosh. Another producer (Fiona Aboud) is in New York; and since the initial research period, Forsyth has moved on to other projects and a Montreal-based producer came on board: Katarina Soukup of Catbird Productions (personal communications with Conteh, 9 April 2011, 12 June 2012). As well, musician K'Naan lent a song to the project, and is based in Toronto. Like Littlefield, Conteh and Forsyth articulated complex understandings of how they used Kickstarter. Leone Stars mobilized the momentum of the crowdfunding experience to complete production of the half-hour 'demo' funded by Kickstarter, and leveraged that success into securing development support for a feature film-length version of the story. In September 2011, the Leone Stars feature film project won the 'Pitch This!' competition at the intensely competitive Toronto International Film Festival – the first documentary to do so (Leone Stars, 2011; TIFF, 2011). In November 2011, the project secured support through the prestigious Sundance Institute Documentary Program (2011) – the only Canadian project in a list of 29 – and in January 2012, co-directors Allan Tong and Ngardy Conteh were invited to attend Sundance as one of ten teams in the Sundance Documentary Fellows' Program. Forsyth credits the Kickstarter campaign as a strategic early step in generating profile and support for the project, enough to propel them firmly towards significant industry markers of success (email communication with Forsyth, 27 February 2012).

In the summer of 2012, award-winning documentary filmmaker Johanna Lunn and her producing partner James Hoagland raised $7215 towards a $15 000 goal from 103 donors for the documentary film *An Uncommon King* on IndieGoGo, an intimate look at Tibetan spiritual king Sakyong Mipham Rinpoche. The funding was targeted in three stages: to create a digital cinema master for the film, then a DVD master, and finally to pay for the technical requirements to release it on iTunes. Enough funding was secured to support the first two tasks. The documentary itself was a labour of love, pulling together 17 years of footage. Both Lunn and Hoagland have long careers in the industry, and have been at the helm of many successful projects. Lunn has received three Gemini awards, worked as an in-house executive producer for CTV and director of programming for Alliance Atlantis, and helped to launch IFC Canada as well as independent companies Wild East Productions and Centre East Media. She won best documentary at Hot Docs International Film Festival for her film, *Forgiveness: Stories for Our Time*. Hoagland has worked for over 30 years as a producer, camera operator, sound recordist and editor, including on archives and educational projects. His film credits include *The Lion's Roar* about the life of His Holiness the 16th Gyalwa Karmapa and *Living Peace*, about an award given to His Holiness the Dalai Lama at The Great Stupa of Dharmakaya in Colorado. Their IndieGoGo campaign featured many carefully designed perks, several video teasers from the documentary, and the capacity for US tax receipts to be issued by non-profit organization From the Heart Productions.

In 2010, First Weekend Club (FWC) began formally exploring the possibility of setting up a subscription-based streaming service for Canadian films, around the time that the American service Netflix entered the Canadian market (CTV News, 2010). Through a six-week IndieGoGo campaign in late 2011, FWC raised $22 718 on a $20 000 goal from 216 funders to provide seed dollars towards its establishment. The full service is expected late in 2013. Executive Director Anita Adams was able to leverage the funding raised in the IndieGoGo campaign to persuade several industry organizations to participate. Since 2003, FWC has encouraged supporters of Canadian filmmaking to help build word-of-mouth attendance for Canadian films by purchasing tickets during the first weekend of a feature film release in theatres. The box office receipts realized during that first weekend determine how long and where a theatre run will be. FWC began as an email list-serve in Vancouver and now involves 15 000 members via email, their website and Facebook (personal communication with Executive Director Anita Adams, 19 December, 2011).

GLOBALIZED CROWDFUNDING REVENUE-GENERATING STRATEGIES

A comparative analysis among Kickstarter.com, IndieGoGo.com and PledgeMusic.com suggests the importance of the project creator as a hub or node of activity. The financial and administrative mechanics used to generate a consistent approach and logistics on each site are revealing, as are the visual presentations and language. Mechanics include how each mobilizes the blog format, payment systems and database structure. Until 2012, for most non-Americans, there was an important caveat to using Kickstarter; it required an American bank account and residency. In November 2012, a UK version of the site opened (Strickler and Benenson, 2012), and in August 2013, the Canadian iteration got underway (Dingman, 2013). For Canadians, these initial requirements were a significant challenge, notwithstanding co-production histories and agreements between the two countries. The cases studied inventively accommodated the Kickstarter limits: the Leone Stars team included American members, while Littlefield mobilized the support of an American organization through which funding could be channelled. The determination to make use of Kickstarter is notable. As one filmmaker put it, 'It's like the difference between Coke and Pepsi. . . Coke is at 100 per cent [desirability and market reach] and Pepsi is 70 per cent' (personal communication with Forsyth, 17 April, 2011). Lunn secured an agreement with an American organization for the issuing of tax receipts to American participants, though her IndieGoGo project was targeted to both Canadian and American supporters. Although IndieGoGo correctly touts its international reach and ability to collect funds on behalf of projects around the world as an advantage in comparison to other crowdfunding websites, all funds are secured in American dollars, and participants are subject to American laws by virtue of participating on an American website. For a specifically Canadian project like First Weekend Club's video-on-demand service, the inability to contribute in Canadian dollars proved to be a crucial deterrent to a few potential funders (personal communication with Adams, 2011). For most participants, however, this is simply how business is conducted in a global cultural context.

Most crowdfunding websites are similar in their presentation formats. Kickstarter.com, PledgeMusic.com and IndieGoGo.com use visually rich imagery and not-for-profit marketing rhetoric. They are promoted as sites for creative networks of mostly urbanized cultural supporters, incorporating particular beliefs, values and economic exchange practices regarding art and culture that transcend nation-state boundaries. The wealthier, higher-profile website, Kickstarter, has received a great deal of attention in the popular press, including *Wired, The New York Times, Social Times* and several blogs. IndieGoGo is also a favourite in blogs (see, for example: Adler, 2011; Baughan, 2011; Martin, 2010; Mills, 2011; Ryzik, 2010). According to the list of media coverage on their website, IndieGoGo enjoys accelerating coverage: 101 media items were identified during the 12-month period of March 2011 to February 2012, then 122 more in half the time, from January to June 2013 (IndieGoGo, 2013b). Like other member-based websites (not just crowdfunding sites), members can join as observers-only. Additionally, members can be 'funders' (IndieGoGo), 'backers' (Kickstarter) or 'fans' (PledgeMusic) or generate content ('projects' or 'campaigns'). Members know up-front that they will never get a direct financial return,[10] but will be rewarded by gradations of material benefits known as 'incentives' or 'perks', often temporal (e.g. the first to. . .). The objective is to pledge together with others to share in the creation and early consumption of culture by directly funding projects. Kickstarter, PledgeMusic and IndieGoGo employ straightforward processes for signing members up, and making pledges or payments, through Amazon, PayPal and credit card options. This makes it logistically easy for potential backers to support creative production by matching themselves to creators with specific types of projects on offer.

There are two main investment risk models in crowdfunding. Kickstarter started as a no-risk proposition for backers pledging to projects on the site. If a project does not reach its goal on Kickstarter, no money changes hands but the value of participation is publicly recognized. Everyone involved performs their participation in the creation of value, but Kickstarter collects no fees, the creator collects no funds, and the backer doesn't hand over money pledged to the project. In 2012, IndieGoGo also introduced an 'all-or-nothing' or 'fixed funding' fee system, as well as the original structure that saw the creator keeping the funds raised whether or not a project made its goal. Significantly, a fee is always charged on IndieGoGo – indeed, higher percentages (9 per cent) of funds raised are charged if the goal is not met (versus 4 per cent if the goal is met on IndieGoGo, or 5 per cent on Kickstarter). Value is created and circulated even in this riskier proposition. IndieGoGo projects represented a higher financial risk for the funder and provided an assurance of at least partial 'success' for project leaders. Each of the interviewees addressed this important difference in positioning their relationships with funders. Some filmmakers expressed a preference for the all-or-nothing model, seeing it as a way to convey urgency in appeals while maximizing the chance of financial success 'without risk' to funders. FWC and Lunn decisively preferred IndieGoGo for its transnational philanthropic stance. In the early days of culture crowdfunding (2008–11), funders and project leaders may have preferred the all-or-nothing approach to minimize risk *and* to still be seen as early adopters. With more experience in this kind of financing, the behaviour of participants and project leaders alike has become even more of a performance.

TWO DEGREES OF SEPARATION

Cultural crowdfunding success draws on two degrees of separation[11] from already-existing networks. This was particularly evident in the case of the First Weekend Club, which mobilized the equivalent of 1.45 per cent (216 backers) of its 15 000-strong membership, most of whom were already voluntary FWC members (personal communication with Adams, 19 December, 2011). It was evident in the demographic enlisted to support *Uncommon King* (103), many of whom were already members of the spiritual community reflected in the film. It was also palpable in the intensely engaged personal networks for *Give a Little* (137 backers), *Leone Stars* (125) and *Better Living Through Chemistry* (25).[12] Generally, more than two-thirds of supporters for each project included those with significant personal connections to the project leaders, often no more than two degrees of separation. The second, smaller group of crowdfunders included a small proportion of new contacts for the project creator, almost always involved in other projects on the same crowdfunding site. Funder types include those represented in Table 9.1.

The particular combination of supporters for each project grew the networks of each project creator slightly as well as populating the trajectory of funding for each project. Each project leader incrementally grew the number of overall crowd-funders by attracting new backers to the websites. Since visitors to the sites can trace which projects each funder supports, those who supported at least one other project increased the likelihood of growing their own interest in crowdfunding and attracting additional funders to their first-supported projects. This is strikingly similar to effective non-profit fundraising strategies. In the cases of Leone Stars and FWC, the success of the crowdfunding campaigns enabled them to leverage funding and resources from much larger investors. Typically, this is also an important outcome for a successful fundraising campaign.

Table 9.1 Funder types for crowdsourcing projects

Funder type	Funder description	No. of projects funded	Degrees of separation	Project of their own?	No. of genres or categories
1	One-time funder	1	1–2 mostly	No	1
2A	Friend funder	1–3	1–2 mostly	No	1
2B	Artist/leader friend funder	1–3	1–2 mostly	Yes	1
3A	Genre funder	4+	1–3 mostly	No	1 (mostly)
3B	Artist/leader genre funder	4+	1–3 mostly	Yes	1 (mostly)
4A	Culture funder	4+	1–3 mostly	No	2–3 (mostly)
4B	Artist/leader culture funder	4+	1–3 mostly	Yes	2–3 (mostly)
5A	Culture sector funder	4+	2–3 mostly	No	Multiple
5B	Artist/leader culture funder	4+	2–4 mostly	Yes – often also a curatorial role	Multiple

Notes: Type 'A's in this table are funders who are not filmmakers or artists. Type 'B's noted in the table are funders who are also filmmakers or artists with projects in the respective crowdfunding websites. Note that the numbers reflect the analysis conducted on three out of five projects: Better Living Through Chemistry; First Weekend Club; and Leone Stars. Through preliminary reviews of the funding lists of the other two projects (Give a Little; Uncommon King), it is evident that the proportions are similar. Both reflect a more highly personalized and targeted group of supporters than the original three.

Source: Based on detailed analyses of the lists of funders on the crowdfunding project web pages.

All the projects capitalized (on) extended personal networks. The *Leone Stars* team confirmed that two-thirds to three-quarters of their 125 backers were personally known or were involved in a target group where at least one filmmaking team member was known by reputation (e.g. the documentary community in Canada). The steady growth in pledges was maintained during the campaign because each team member took turns to solicit support from their own networks. Of the 125 backers, 9 per cent gave to one other project and 8 per cent more gave to two or more other projects.[13] Littlefield's project persuaded 25 backers, including six who gave to one other project, and five who gave to between two and four other projects. Littlefield confirmed that several participants were personally known to her (i.e. one degree of separation); others came from the donor base of the foundation supporting the project (i.e. two degrees of separation). Adams noted that the geographical distribution of donors reflected the distribution of the regular FWC membership list. The statistics bear out the predominance of existing FWC members in this assemblage of support. Of the 216 contributors, 159 have never given to any other project on IndieGoGo (more than three months after the close of the FWC campaign). Of the other 57 who gave to at least one other project, all 57 gave to film-related projects. Of these, 27 were already IndieGoGo supporters, and most of these individuals gave to FWC early in that campaign, enabling momentum.[14]

The creation of an assemblage of support by generating distinct levels of backers funding one-to-many project(s) consistently results in *successful* projects. Even when a project does not raise the full amount desired (such as *Uncommon King*), if it raises something towards the need identified, it generates a new group of active supporters. Interestingly, in crowdfunded media production, the relatively small group of micro-funders becomes a kind of *virtual multi-headed* producer participating in a culture of circulation by performing support and thereby generating momentum. Intuitively prepared for this, some of the project creators explicitly offer producing credits for some projects as a 'perk', depending on the level of financial contribution. This was a source of astonishment for one early project-creator interviewed, a source of interest for later projects, and an expectation of the most recent project leaders. In the North American media industry, a producer is responsible for generating, coordinating and supervising the resources and the creative approach needed to see a project to completion. On larger projects, there are as many producers as required to generate and manage all of the resources required. In collaborative projects, the producer role can be shared among all or most of the creative group involved. This is evident in credit lists, scholarly media production literature, and borne out by my own producing and broadcasting experience in the media production business for the last fifteen years. The crowdfunding virtual producer acts as a micro-investment collective that comes together 'on' the Internet, using technology and software to temporarily assemble with others. Rather than being paid, the virtual producer accesses perks that cost little to the production, and pays for the privilege of contributing the value of their own labour. However, the virtual producer is a producer with no producing authority; each is a passive backer who has more in common with non-profit fundraising 'friends' and 'club members' than with typical North American media and arts finance-seeking producers.

Grappling with the meaning and role of the virtual producer suggests how crowdfunding websites and filmmakers/artists articulate together to generate project support within a culture of circulation. Developing a profile in order to attract funders is a key function of crowdfunding sites. Each recommends a particular configuration of how to profile and promote each project. This includes preparing a short written pitch, developing a list of appropriate incentives or perks, presenting a short video that illustrates something compelling about your project and providing frequent updates. Littlefield participated at a minimal level in this marketing strategy: she provided only a small amount of sample footage and a short list of imaginative incentives to Kickstarter, including 'good karma'. In her opinion, the recommended marketing structure did not have a significant impact on reaching her goal. For FWC, Give a Little, Leone Stars and Uncommon King, on the other hand, developing compelling videos and one-page pitches, combined with original incentives lists grounded in the projects, were critical: each of these organizations sought longer-term relationships for the project *and* for the production teams involved. Project leaders for FWC, Leone Stars and Uncommon King identified extensive lists of incentives that were subsequently modified in order to bring costs down or to appeal to a more geographically widespread audience. In Simpson's project, the artistic concept synthesized and capitalized on the by-now well-known 'how to crowdfund' instruction manuals and coverage that proliferated starting in 2011. Plugging in content to the recommended promotional structure was a significant contribution to success, reinforcing a support relationship that most hope to continue by converting crowdfunders to blog, website or Facebook participants.

CONCLUSION

Crowdfunding for media projects seems to generate committed networks of media industry workers, suggesting that this highly mobile and individuated creative work force (McRobbie, 2002) can provide linked funding hubs for multiple creative projects. Minna Tarkka (2010) proposes that research into creative forms of mobility practices specific to 'space, place, case (or race)' suggests new ways to demand unpaid labour from artists, creators and crews (p. 132). The crowdfunding model seems to rely on convincing artists, creators and crews to take turns funding the projects of those they know and admire. The one or two degrees of personal separation embedded in this process suggests that those already involved in creative labour are more likely to assist each other, whether for profit or for social good. Such an expansion of shared responsibility holds promise and risk as a social phenomenon worth further study. More broadly, the long-term potential of crowdfunding is positive though still somewhat unclear. Though crowdfunding is growing strong roots within the media and arts community as an audience- or fan-building strategy, the relatively modest nature of the financial successes realized by most project leaders relative to the effort required suggests that crowdfunding is developing into a necessary but not significant component of the financing scenario for most projects, particularly more expensive initiatives. There are caveats.

As with the Veronica Mars project mentioned in the introduction and with the First Weekend Club case study, where there is already a large, vocal supporter group, particularly one already engaged through social media, crowdfunding could be a remarkably successful strategy to mobilize particular segments of the financial picture. Moreover, it seems evident that crowdfunding success is gaining traction as a way to demonstrate to other investors with access to larger funds that there is a broad base of the right kind of support behind a project, such as is shown in the leveraging strategies of Leone Stars and First Weekend Club. Lastly, the experience of building pathways or trajectories of support directly to new backers and the way in which crowdfunding aficionados support multiple similar projects suggests that modest long-term growth of dedicated audiences may be possible.

From a theoretical perspective, the nuanced framework presented here pinpoints the specificity of cultural crowdfunding for twenty-first-century media production within a set of power-based, systemic and contingent social, creative and economic relations, as well as in terms of analysing the roles and implications involved. Raising funding for filmmaking and other forms of media production is traditionally a value-based proposition. Similarly, investing in a project with no expectation of financial return but a high expectation of social capital is a patron's prerogative. Crowdfunding project leaders *and* funders seem to be involved in creative stewardship, a civic contribution that goes substantially beyond the funding contribution. The virtual crowd which funds creative projects sorts itself into temporary assemblages that become a stand-in collective patron *as well as* virtual producer, generating flexible trajectories of support that can be made more or less permanent. These mobile hubs of funding activity combine with nodes of filmmakers and artists (as shown in Figure 9.1) to generate financial and leveraging value for the project, reducing the risk of financial failure and mobilizing immaterial or 'free' labour in the process. Each node includes a network of support related to creative production *and* audience engagement. These can be systematically tracked and almost formulaically predicted. In the highly merged, tightly financed North American media industry, cultural media production that leverages technology and supporters using original, contingent strategies and tactics change not just business models but also the way in which social relations develop. Recognizing and enumerating the interchangeability of today's creative and professional roles and relationships as well as the fluid nature of funding and project development, distribution and promotion is inspiring as well as necessary. New questions emerge and research potential grows in both anticipated and surprising ways. Being attentive to trends in the field contextualized through discussion with the networks of industry participants and scholars willing to provoke and enrich these enquiries helps to realize research and creative goals, and helps respond to the challenges of mapping these new mobile sources of funding for creative endeavours as they unfold and evolve.

NOTES

1. A previous version of the analysis and earlier research covered in this chapter was published in Luka (2012).
2. Producers raised over $5 million from 91 585 donors on leading crowdfunding website Kickstarter.com to support the making of a movie based on this popular television programme (Thomas, 2013).
3. Questions were asked concerning how many supporters were known to those seeking funding, how they were found, and what roles they played. Studying how many backers funded multiple projects suggested a more complicated set of relations, including cause- or passion-related potential. The format, standardized measures of success and aesthetics of the case studies on Kickstarter and IndieGoGo add another dimension. I asked interviewees if standardized promotional components had an impact on success. These included: the preparation of descriptions and marketing videos; incentive plans consistent with the project; and networked support through backers supporting more than one project.
4. Kickstarter itself addressed the backlash about hosting celebrity projects by analysing how many other projects Veronica Mars supporters went on to help fund (Chen et al., 2013; Hayden, 2013). Analysing comparable data was a significant part of my original research in 2010, not least because crowdfunding platforms claim that participation in one project generates potential interest in other projects.
5. For example, see Lee and LiPuma's discussion of the post-1973 practice of 'derivatives hedging' in the circulation of global currencies (2002, pp. 206–207). They incorporate a critique of globalized capitalism and the derivatives market based on the juxtposi-

tion of gift exchange social systems and a post-Marxist 'labour as commodity' analysis, including a reconsideration of the separation between economy and culture, the importance of temporality, and the potential impact on citizenship, nation-state (and so on).

6. Kickstarter's figures may or may not be included in the Massolution data quoted, since they appear not to have participated in the survey, according to the Massolution website.

7. Lee and LiPuma (2002) discuss just such a development in general terms in the European and American context over the last quarter of the twentieth century, emerging from sociological, anthropological and political economy investigations of modernism concerning capital and gift exchange (including Pierre Bourdieu and Marcel Mauss, among others), linguistics and performativity (Claude Lévi-Strauss, Emile Beneviste, and others), nation-building through the vernacular (Anderson, 1983) and the modern social imaginary (Taylor, 2004), cultural flows (Appadurai, 1996), and public space (Habermas, 1989).

8. Pierre Bourdieu was an influential French sociologist and philosopher whose work grapples systematically with how to categorize and investigate social, class and power relations in connection to economic concerns. See, for example, Bourdieu (1984), among many other publications.

9. McRobbie also discussed this at some length in a talk given at McMaster University in February 2012. The video of the talk is posted at http://www.youtube.com/watch?v=C-QMaaFITKM.

10. There are some crowdfunding websites that accommodate lending. With the recent passage of legislation in the United States allowing for equity financing and crowd-funded lending, this may shift significantly. *Forbes Magazine* predicts crowd lending will reach $6 billion in 2013: 'LendingClub reached $75+ million per month in debt lending as a crowd funding platform in November 2012. It is the largest US peer-to-peer lender and will hit an additional $1 billion in loans 2013 vis-à-vis the cumulative $1 billion it lent since inception 2007' (Drake, 2012).

11. One degree of separation means that the project leader and the funder know each other personally or professionally. Two degrees of separation mean the project leader is known by reputation or contact through a close joint professional affiliation (such as the Documentary Organization of Canada), or through another crowd-funder who personally knows the project leader. Three degrees of separation indicates a funder who supports a particular genre and four degrees of separation suggests a curatorial or professional knowledge of the filmmaker or project leader. If it was unclear or unknown whether there was an already-existing relationship, funders were placed in one of the latter two groupings.

12. Here, my own professional experience and knowledge of the Canadian media community served the project well. Between my knowledge of the community and that of the filmmakers, we were able to identify most of the project supporters for the count that took place in the table.

13. Eleven gave to one other project (funder type 2), and six to between two and six projects (funder types 2–5). Four frequent backers (funder types 4 or 5) gave to 9, 14, 31 and 103 other projects respectively.

14. Thirty-nine gave to only one other project (of these, 10 gave to projects prior to FWC). Six people gave to two other projects (all before their FWC contribution); six people contributed to three other projects (five before FWC); four people gave to four projects (all before FWC, and with projects of their own); one person each gave to five projects and twelve projects (before and after giving to FWC, and both of whom had projects of their own). This suggests that 27 contributors to FWC were already IndieGoGo project supporters. Of the 216 contributors, 12 had projects of their own. For additional details, please see the FWC campaign on the *Indigogo.com* website, http://www.IndieGoGo.com/First-Weekend-Club (Luka, 2012).

REFERENCES

Adler, C. (2011). Brothers of Invention. *Wired*. April. pp. 108–13. Retrieved from: http://www.wired.com/magazine/2011/03/ff_kickstarter/.
Alexa Graphs (2011a). Kickstarter and IndieGoGo comparative data. 28 April. Retrieved from: http://www.alexa.com/.
Alexa Graphs (2011b). Kickstarter and IndieGoGo comparative data. 1 May. Retrieved from: http://www.alexa.com/.
Alexa Graphs (2012). Kickstarter and IndieGoGo comparative data. 6 March. Retrieved from: http://www.alexa.com/.
Alexa Graphs (2013). Kickstarter and IndieGoGo comparative data. 29 June. Retrieved from: http://www.alexa.com/.
Anderson, Benedict (2006[1983]). *Imagined Communities*. Revised edn. London & New York: Verso.
Appadurai, Arjun (1996). *Modernity at Large*. 8th edn. Minneapolis: University of Minnesota Press.
Baughan, N. (2011). Finance and Funding. *Moviescope*. 26 March. Retrieved from: http://www.moviescopemag.com/24-fps/finance/we-need-to-talk-about-funding/.
Belleflamme, Paul, Lambert, Thomas and Schwienbacher, Armin (2010). Crowdfunding: Tapping the Right Crowd. *SSRN*. 24 March. Retrieved 13 February, 2011 from: http://ssrn.com/abstract=1578175.
Born, G. (2010). The Social and the Aesthetic: For a Post-Bourdieuian Theory of Cultural Production. *Cultural Sociology* 4, 171–208.
Bourdieu, Pierre (1984). *Distinction: A Social Critique of the Judgment of Taste*, trans. Richard Nice. Cambridge, MA: Harvard University Press.
Broadbent, Alan and Omidvar, Ratna (2011). *Five Good Ideas: Practical Strategies for Non-Profit Success*. Toronto: Coach House Books.
Canada Media Fund (2013). Crowdfunding in the Canadian Context. Retrieved from: http://crowd-funding.cmf-fmc.ca/.
Canadian Radio-television and Telecommunications Commission (CRTC) (2011). Report on Profits in Canadian Media in 2010. 2 June. Ottawa: Government of Canada. Retrieved from: http://www.crtc.gc.ca/eng/com100/2011/r110602.htm.
Canadian Radio-television and Telecommunications Commission (CRTC) (2013a). CRTC releases 2012 financial results for Canadian conventional television stations. 13 June. Retrieved from: http://www.crtc.gc.ca/eng/com100/2013/r130613.htm#.UdGiGz771jR.
Canadian Radio-television and Telecommunications Commission (CRTC) (2013b). CRTC releases 2012 financial results for Canadian commercial radio stations. 19 June. Retrieved from: http://www.crtc.gc.ca/eng/com100/2013/r130619.htm#.UdGjPj771jR.
Chen, Perry, Strickler, Yancey and Adler, Charles (2013). Who is Kickstarter For? Kickstarter.com. 9 May. Retrieved from: http://www.kickstarter.com/blog/who-is-kickstarter-for.
Christopherson, S. (2008). Beyond the self-expressive creative worker: An industry perspective on entertainment media. *Theory, Culture, Society* 25, 73–95.
Conteh, Ngardy (2011). Leone Stars: A documentary. *Kickstarter.com*. Retrieved from: http://www.kickstarter.com/projects/973681195/leone-stars-a-documentary.

Conteh, Ngardy (2012). Mattru Media. Retrieved from: http://mattrumedia.com/.

CTV News (2010). Netflix arrives in Canada amid controversy. *CTV.ca.* 22 September. Retrieved from: http://www.ctv.ca/CTVNews/TopStories/20100922/netflix-canada-100922/.

de Souza e Silva, A. and Frith, J. (2010). Locative mobile social networks: Mapping communication and location in urban spaces. *Mobilities* 5(4), 485–505.

Deuze, M., Bowen Martin, C. and Allen, C. (2007). The professional identity of gameworkers. *Convergence* 13, 335–53.

Deuze, M., Elefante, P. and Steward, B. (2010). Media work and the recession. *Popular Communication* 8(3), 226–31.

Dingman, Shane (2013). Kickstarter crowdfunding arrives for Canadian ideas, finally. *The Globe and Mail.* 7 August. Retrieved from: http://www.theglobeandmail.com/technology/tech-news/kickstarter-crowdfunding-arrives-for-canadian-ideas-finally/article13629886/.

Drake, D. (2012). Crowdfunding will make 2013 the year of the gold rush. *Forbes.com.* 27 December. Retrieved from: http://www.forbes.com/sites/groupthink/2012/12/27/crowdfunding-will-make-2013-the-year-of-the-gold-rush/.

EY Canada (2013). Media companies' digital revenues set to overtake traditional by 2015. 19 June. Retrieved from: http://www.ey.com/CA/en/Newsroom/News-releases/2013-Digital-agility-now.

First Weekend Club (2011). *IndieGoGo.com.* Retrieved from: http://www.IndieGoGo.com/First-Weekend-Club.

Galloway, A. and Ward, M. (2006). Locative media as socialising and spatializing practice: Learning from archaeology. *Leonardo E-Journal Archive,* 14(3). Retrieved 23 February, 2011 from: http://leoalmanac.org/journal/vol_14/lea_v14_n03–04/gallowayward.html.

Gaonkar, D.P. and Povinelli, E.A. (2003). Technologies of public forms: Circulation, transfiguration, recognition. *Public Culture* 15(3), 385–97.

Giles, Julie (2011). How to build an audience for your web series: Market, motivate & mobilize. Andra Sheffer (ed.). Toronto: Independent Production Fund. Retrieved from: http://www.ipf.ca/downloads/IPF-MARKETING-GUIDE.pdf.

Give a Little (2013). Retrieved from: http://www.pledgemusic.com/projects/erincostelomusicvideo.

Gorgeous Mistake Productions (2013). Retrieved from: http://www.gorgeous-mistake.com/.

Habermas, J. (1989). *The Structural Transformation of the Public Sphere: An Inquiry into a Category of Bourgeois Society,* translated by Thomas Burger with Frederick Lawrence. Cambridge: MIT Press.

Hayden, Erik (2013). Kickstarter Founders Address Critics of Zach Braff 'Veronica Mars' Projects. Hollywood Reporter. 9 May. Retrieved from: http://www.hollywoodreporter.com/news/kickstarter-founders-address-critics-zach-520236.

Ideavibes (2011). Crowdfunding: How the wisdom of crowds and the power of social media are changing everything we know about fundraising. 9 June. Retrieved from: www.Ideavibes.com.

IndieGoGo (2011). Partners. Retrieved from: http://www.IndieGoGo.com/partners/suap.

IndieGoGo (2012a). Winning the middle game. July. Retrieved from: http://blog.IndieGoGo.com/2012/07/IndieGoGo-insight-winning-the-middle-game.html.

IndieGoGo (2012b). Top 12. December. Retrieved from: http://blog.IndieGoGo.com/2012/12/top12.html.

IndieGoGo (2013a). IndieGoGo. Retrieved from: http://www.IndieGoGo.com.

IndieGoGo (2013b). Press. Retrieved from: http://www.IndieGoGo.com/contact/press.

Kickstarter (2013a). Kickstarter.com. Retrieved from: http://www.kickstarter.com.

Kickstarter (2013b). Stats. Retrieved 20 June, 2013 from: http://www.Kickstarter.com/help/stats.

Lee, Benjamin and LiPuma, Edward (2002). Cultures of circulation: The imaginations of modernity. *Public Culture* 14(1), 191–213.

Lefebvre, H. (1992[2004]). *Rhythmanalysis: Space, Time and Everyday Life*. London: Continuum.

Leone Stars (2011). Leone Stars wins TIFF's Pitch This! as first documentary ever. 14 September. Retrieved from: http://leonestars.blogspot.ca/2011/09/leone-stars-wins-tiffs-pitch-this-and.html.

Littlefield, C. (2011). Better Living Through Chemistry: The documentary. *Kickstarter.com*. Retrieved from: http://www.kickstarter.com/projects/conceptafilm/better-living-through-chemistry-the-documentary.

Luka, M.E. (2012). Media production in flux: Crowdfunding to the rescue. *WI Journal of Mobile Media*, 6(3). Retrieved from: http://wi.mobilities.ca/.

MacLellan, K. (2013). Global crowdfunding volumes rise 81 percent in 2012. Reuters, US edition. 8 April. Retrieved from: http://www.reuters.com/article/2013/04/08/us-crowdfunding-data-idUSBRE9370QY20130408.

Martin, S. (2010). Indiegogo vs. Kickstarter – And the crowdfunding platform winner is. . . 27 September. Retrieved from: http://www.alchemistintraining.com/indiegogo-kickstarter-winner/.

Massolution (2013). 2013 CF: The crowdfunding industry report. *Massolution.com*. Retrieved from: http://www.crowdsourcing.org/research.

McRobbie, A. (2002). Clubs to companies: Notes on the decline of political culture in speeded up creative worlds. *Cultural Studies*, 16(4), 516–31.

Mills, F. (2011). Crowdfunding your film: Kickstarter vs. Indiegogo. Retrieved from: http://www.blog.filmarmy.ca/2011/02/crowdfunding-your-film-kickstarter-vs-indiegogo/.

Neilson, B. and Rossiter, N. (2008). Precarity as a political concept, or, Fordism as exception. *Theory, Culture & Society*, 25(7–8), 51–72.

Nixon, S. and du Gay, P. (2002). Who needs cultural intermediaries? *Cultural Studies*, 16(4), 495–500.

Petronzio, M. (2013). A look back at IndieGoGo's successful year in crowdfunding. *Mashable.com*. 11 January. Retrieved from: http://mashable.com/2013/01/11/IndieGoGo-crowd-funding-2012/.

Rushkoff, D. (2003). *Open Source Democracy*. London: Demos.

Rushkoff, D. (2010). *Program or Be Programmed: Ten Commands for a Digital Age*. New York: OR Books.

Ryzik, M. (2010). For web-financed film projects, a curtain rises. *The New York Times*. 8 July. Retrieved from: http://www.nytimes.com/2010/07/08/movies/08kickstarter.html.

Sassen, S. (2006). Public interventions: the shifting meaning of the urban condition. *Open 11: Hybrid Space – How Wireless Media Mobilize Public Space*. pp. 18–26. Retrieved from: http://classic.skor.nl/2888/en/saskia-sassen-public-interventions-the-shifting.

Soar, M. (2002). The first things first manifesto and the politics of culture jamming: Towards a cultural economy of graphic design and advertising. *Cultural Studies* 16(4), 570–92.

Statistics Canada (2011). The Daily: Television broadcasting. 1 November. Ottawa: Government of Canada. Retrieved from: http://www.statcan.gc.ca/daily-quotidien/111101/dq111101a-eng.htm.

Stevens, G. (1998). *The Favored Circle: The Social Foundations of Architectural Distinction*. Cambridge: MA: The MIT Press.

Strickler, Yancey and Benenson, Fred (2012). Kickstarter in the UK: The first month. Kickstarter.com. 3 December. Retrieved from: http://www.kickstarter.com/blog/kickstarter-in-the-uk-the-first-month.

Sundance Institute (2011). 29 documentaries receive $582,000 in grants from Sundance Institute documentary film program. *Sundance.org*. 22 November. Retrieved from: http://www.sundance.org/press-center/release/29-documentaries-receive-582000-in-grants-from-sundance-institute-documenta/.

Tapscott, D. and Williams, A.D. (2008). *Wikinomics: How Mass Collaboration Changes Everything*. New York: Portfolio.

Tarkka, M. (2010). Labours of location, in B. Crow, M. Longford and K. Sawchuk (eds), *The Wireless Spectrum: the Politics, Practices and Poetics of Mobile Media* (pp. 131–45). Toronto: University of Toronto Press.

Taylor, C. (2004). *Modern Social Imaginaries*. Durham/London: Duke University Press.

Terranova, T. (2000). Free Labour. *Social Text* 18(2), 33–58.

Thomas, Rob (2013). The Veronica Mars movie project. *Kickstarter.com*. Retrieved from: http://www.Kickstarter.com/projects/559914737/the-veronica-mars-movie-project.

Toronto International Film Festival (TIFF) (2011). Toronto International Film Festival announces participants for talent lab, Telefilm Canada PITCH THIS! and producers lab Toronto. Retrieved from: http://tiff.net/press/press releases/2011/toronto-international-film-festival-announces-participants-for-tal ent-lab-telefilm-canada-pitch-this-and-producers-lab-toronto.

Uncommon King, An (2012). *IndieGoGo.com*. Retrieved from: http://www.IndieGoGo.com/projects/an-uncommon-king.

VentureBeatProfiles (2011). Kickstarter and IndieGoGo data. 28 April. Retrieved from: http://venturebeatprofiles.com.

VentureBeatProfiles (2012). Kickstarter and IndieGoGo data. 6 March. Retrieved from: http://venturebeatprofiles.com.

W3Snoop (2013). Kickstarter and IndieGoGo data. 29 June. Retrieved from: http://w3snoop.com.

Wiley, S.B.C. and Packer, J. (2010). Rethinking communications after the mobility turn. *The Communication Review* 13(4), 263–8.

Wiley, S.B.C., Sutko, D.M. and Becerra, T.M. (2010). Assembling social space. *The Communication Review*, 13(4), 340–72.

Wilken, R. (2010). A community of strangers? Mobile media, art, tactility and urban encounters with the other. *Mobilities*, 5(4), 449–68.

Wissinger, E. (2009). Modeling consumption: Fashion modeling work in contemporary society. *Journal of Consumer Culture* 9, 273–96.

Yin, R.K. (2009). *Case Study Research: Design and Methods*. 4th revised edn. Thousand Oaks, CA: Sage Publications.

Youngdale, B. (2012). *Crowdfunding Tips: Knock Your Project Out of the Park*. San Diego: Daily Crowdsource.
Zhang, T. (2009). On the fringe of the 'Canadian State': Grassroots film and video movements in Halifax, 1960s–1980s, in D. Varga (ed.), *Rain, Drizzle, Fog: Film and Television in Atlantic Canada* (pp. 171–98). Calgary: University of Calgary Press.

10. Crowdsourcing in the production of video advertising: the emerging roles of crowdsourcing platforms

Yannig Roth and Rosemary Kimani

> You can call it crowdsourcing, co-creation or open source innovation. The point is, the reality is, advertising will continue to be democratized. With this radical democratization, the structures of advertising organizations are being transformed. Radically.
> John Winsor, co-founder of Victors & Spoils[1]

INTRODUCTION

Advertising has always relied on creativity as the most important resource for inspiration. Defined as any paid form of non-personal communication about an organization, product, service, or idea by an identified sponsor (Belch and Belch, 2003), advertising is one of the many different activities comprised in the so-called creative industries (Howkins, 2004). In spite of global uncertainty, economic troubles in Europe and lackluster conditions in the US, overall global ad spending is still expected to increase in 2013, albeit at a modest rate (IAB-UK, 2012; Vranica, 2012). As it relates to individual categories, TV is expected to rise 2.8 per cent to $63.8 billion, while internet ad spending which includes mobile, search, social and display is expected to grow a whopping 18.1 per cent. Video advertising is seen as a particularly effective way to promote brands and products (Dishmann, 2011; Torng, 2012). Online, the demand of video advertising revenue will even grow faster than that of all other advertising channels, at an annual growth rate of 19.6 per cent globally from 2011 to 2016, increasing from $4.7 billion to $11.4 billion. Furthermore, it seems obvious that the audience for mobile video will rapidly grow as smartphone and tablet adoption becomes standard. There are already 25 million US adults who consume, on average, 4 hours and 20 minutes of mobile video every month (Stutzmann et al., 2011).

One of the key questions for brands and organizations is to find ways to create quality video content at an affordable cost. This chapter deals with this particular application of creative production: namely film and video production for advertising, hereafter called 'video advertising'. Traditionally, the production of video advertising has been – and still is – carried out by the creative services of advertising agencies. As part of its mission to plan and execute advertising programs for its clients, agencies usually handle the video advertising production process, whether it is done internally or with external video production houses. But many argue that this process is too long and costly: one of the suggested solutions is to use crowdsourcing as a way to generate video content for brands (DeJulio, 2012; Winter and Hill, 2009). The 'creative core' of decision-makers in the production of video content are increasingly becoming open to creative input from the outside (Telo et al., 2012), and online creative platforms are becoming a new venue for these creative individuals to create for brands. This chapter argues that the video advertising industry is undergoing a fundamental change with the advent of a new set of intermediaries that we will call creative crowdsourcing platforms.

To explain what role crowdsourcing plays in the contemporary video advertising landscape, we organize this chapter as follows: first, it is important to define crowdsourcing and differentiate it from related concepts like traditional outsourcing, open source projects or user-generated advertising. We then describe how the use of crowdsourcing has evolved over time, shifting away from the initial amateur focus to becoming an integral part of the advertising production process, involving freelance video advertising professionals. Finally, we describe four models that are currently used by crowdsourcing platforms to create video content for brands, illustrating that the crowd can be solicited in different ways in today's production process. We end the present chapter with a discussion of the evolution of creative crowdsourcing platforms over time.

CROWDSOURCING AS A NOVEL WAY TO CREATE VIDEO CONTENT

What is Crowdsourcing?

Coined in February 2006 by venture capitalist Steve Jurvetson and popularized in the June 2006 issue of *Wired* (Brabham, 2013), the term 'crowdsourcing' describes a new way of organizing work. Originally, crowdsourcing was defined by Jeff Howe as 'the act of a company or institution taking a function once performed by employees and outsourcing it to an undefined (and generally large) network of people in the form of an open call' (Howe, 2006). Crowdsourcing is the precise process by which a company posts a problem online, a vast number of individuals offer solutions to the problem, the winning ideas are awarded some form of bounty, and the company uses the output for its own gain (Brabham, 2008; Estellés-Arolas and González-Ladrón-de-Guevara, 2012). Crowdsourcing has grown in popularity so much so that the term was officially added to *Webster's Dictionary* in 2011.[2] Today, crowdsourcing is being used for a variety of tasks, from the execution of simple tasks that have nothing to do with advertising to the generation of creative ideas and/or advertising content for brands, where people are asked to submit more elaborate creative productions (Brabham, 2010; Kleemann et al., 2008; Penin and Burger-Helmchen, 2011; Schenk and Guittard, 2011). This chapter focuses on creative crowdsourcing, which we define as crowdsourcing of tasks that rely primarily on people's creative abilities to be executed, hence falling under the umbrella of creative industries. Creative crowdsourcing is often used by organizations for their innovation and marketing efforts, as the creative output of the crowd allows them to have access to a variety of fresh ideas to use (Erickson et al., 2012; Howe, 2008; Whitla, 2009). This form of crowdsourcing has also been called crowd creation (Howe, 2008), peer-vetted creative production (Brabham, 2010), crowdsourcing of creative tasks (Schenk and Guittard, 2011) or crowdsourcing of inventive activities (Penin and Burger-Helmchen, 2011) in previous academic literature.

What is Crowdsourcing Not?

Hiring a freelancer, whether it is offline or over the Internet, does not constitute crowdsourcing as there is no open call for participation and the individuals who apply are not asked to submit creative ideas; they are just applying to be chosen as a collaborator. Hence, we don't see this type of contracting as crowdsourcing but as a direct collaboration between a firm and an individual (Barley and Kunda, 2006; Malone and Laubacher, 1998). Recent academic work aligns this position, preferring terms like 'online platform for contract labor' (Agrawal et al., 2012) or 'online platform for outsourced contracts' (Ghani et al., 2012) or 'spot labor markets [where] you know what kind of solution you are looking for and what an appropriate solver looks like' (Boudreau and Lakhani, 2013). Crowdsourcing is also different from open source projects, which might be a good setting for software projects, but not suitable for private company processes because they require access to the essential elements of the product (Brabham, 2008). We would also like to differentiate crowdsourcing from user-generated advertising, where amateurs spontaneously create advertisements for brands

(Kleemann et al., 2008). This type of initiative can be described as 'brokering between aspiring amateurs and commercial content firms' (Van Dijck, 2009), but we think it's still different from crowdsourcing, as no individuals or organizations asked for this content originally.

Crowdsourcing of Video Content: from Amateur Participation to Professional Work

Early examples in the literature of the use of crowdsourcing in the production of video advertising include L'Oreal's ad contest on Current TV, Doritos' 'Crash The Super Bowl' contest, Converse's homemade commercial contest on ConverseGallery.com, or Chevrolet's initiative to allow people to customize 30-second spots for the Tahoe vehicle[3] (Brabham, 2008; Lawrence and Fournier, 2010; Wexler, 2011). These examples of crowd-sourced video advertising were not primarily initiated to generate creative content, but mostly to generate buzz and conversation around the brands. 'The success of user-generated campaigns is partly due to their content, sure, but also partly to their novelty,' said Robert Moskowitz, a consultant and author, in an article about video advertising contests (Moskowitz, 2006).

For example, Doritos' first edition of 'Crash The Super Bowl' was primarily managed by integrated communication agency OMD, and supported by the ad agency Goodby, Silverstein & Partners, the media agency TPN as well as the PR agency Ketchum. 'Crash The Super Bowl' exceeded the initial goal of $5 million in PR value by garnering 1 billion media impressions, an estimated ad equivalency of more than $30 million. 'The hidden driver of our program was the public relations campaign,' the brand explained in a statement,[4] 'the strong consumer aspect of Crash the Super Bowl enabled effective PR, while maintaining ongoing mainstream news coverage at each phase.' Early crowdsourcing initiatives were more PR stunts than ways to produce video content to be used for actual advertising. Campaigns were backed by massive budgets to promote video contests beforehand, to manage and handle brand reputation during, and to communicate and air the winners after the contests. 'Even the most well-known brands often spend millions of dollars upfront to get the word out to consumers,' explained the *New York Times* about advertising contests, underlining that they 'have nothing to do with cost savings'.

The Rise of Creative Crowdsourcing Platforms

The early examples described above show anecdotal evidence about the birth of the phenomenon, in which most of the initiatives were managed by traditional agencies. Nowadays, while integrated agencies still remain in control of campaign creation and coordination, brands are also increasingly relying on creative crowdsourcing platforms to generate video content to feed their marketing efforts. Organizing video contests to generate buzz or to revamp a brand image still exists, but we also see the emergence of new types of video advertising contests that are launched to actually produce promotional content for brands.[5]

For marketers, online video contests on crowdsourcing platforms even become a radical differentiation compared to the early examples of video crowdsourcing for advertising. Nowadays, when it comes to crowd-sourced video content production, quality is becoming increasingly important: 'It is unsustainable to believe that a significant volume of high-quality ads will be produced by everyday consumers who are only guaranteed a reward if they win,' explains Calle Sjoenell, creative director at BBH, in Forrester's 'Crowdsourcing Gains Legitimacy for Advertisers' (Stutzmann et al., 2011). According to this report, using crowdsourcing for advertising is quickly becoming a middle-way between consumer-generated advertising and the work of traditional agencies. It allows marketers to get content in a very fast and cost-effective way compared to the traditional production process handled by agencies (Behan, 2012; DeJulio, 2012; Stutzmann et al., 2011; Whitla, 2009). Not only does crowdsourcing lower the costs of generating one advertisement, but a very important aspect is that they get numerous propositions from a variety of actors who all work on the same brand brief, which also allows them to identify new brand insights by seeing how a heterogeneous crowd of creative individuals interprets the same creative brief. About the 'Energizing Refreshment' contest on eYeka, Coca-Cola's Leonardo O'Grady explained that 'we knew we'd have a number of new perspectives on a common brief that we could use to develop our own idea', highlighting that the initiative had a ripple-effect on the way Coca-Cola thinks about the creative process (Moth, 2012).

The rise of creative crowdsourcing platforms is being showcased on an interactive timeline that visualizes how the use of creative crowdsourcing has exploded among brands since the mid-2000s.[6] This timeline features a wide variety of creative crowdsourcing initiatives organized or sponsored by the 100 brands included in Interbrand's Best Global Brands ranking, and shows that the number of video contests has increased significantly since 2006, mostly due to video contests on creative crowdsourcing platforms (Figure 10.1). From that date onwards, the number of advertising contests organized on creative crowdsourcing platforms exploded, with a peak in 2011, while the number of video contests organized independently remained stable.

The objective of the chapter is to present these creative crowdsourcing

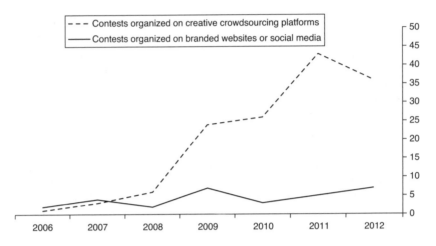

Figure 10.1   Video contests held by the world's most valuable brands since 2006

platforms and to present the role taken in the overall process of video advertising production and distribution. To do that, our chapter will be based on a multiple case study methodology.

Description of our Multiple Case Study Methodology

The case study method allows researchers to explore, describe or explain real-life events such as organizational and managerial changes, or the evolution of particular industries. Case studies are often used when the goal of the research is to relate particular phenomena, like crowdsourcing, to broader contexts, such as the production of video content for advertising (Yin, 2002). This is exactly the aim of this chapter, whereby we want to describe how crowdsourcing-based web platforms are increasingly being used to produce video content for brands and organizations.

The recent phenomenon of crowdsourcing has been described in a variety of contexts, such as innovation tournaments, creative execution or micro-working markets, but we find that the academic field has not addressed this trend in advertising. To our knowledge, the current literature does not go beyond the description of early examples of crowdsourcing, or user-generated video content. Also, and more importantly, no research has been dedicated to crowdsourcing-based video production, a trend that is disrupting the traditional model of agency-controlled video production. This type of work is indeed often initiated and controlled by the creative services of full-service ad agencies, or by specialized creative boutiques such as production houses (Belch and Belch, 2003; Grabher, 2002). To explore this novel set of actors, we chose a multiple case study research design to explore and describe the growing role of creative platforms for the production of video advertising. We focus our research on companies that control web-based platforms on which contributors participate to a variable extent in the production of video content for brands and organizations. Our population comprises 15 creative crowdsourcing platforms that intermediate in the creation of video advertising for brands and organizations (Table 10.1).

We gathered information about these companies using desk research, going further into their precise offerings, analyzing their *modi operandi* to apply crowdsourcing for video production, and by looking closely at what stage of video advertising production are being used. This allowed us to identify the role that the different crowdsourcing platforms take in the production of video content.

ROLES OF CROWDSOURCING PLATFORMS DEDICATED TO VIDEO ADVERTISING

The Traditional Production Process of Video Advertising

In order to understand the role that creative crowdsourcing platforms play in the production of video advertising, we need to look at the way it traditionally gets produced. The creation and distribution of video advertising is often managed by advertising agencies, and particularly their creative services, for the production, and media departments, for the distribution (Belch and Belch, 2003). In some cases, especially in large agencies, a 'traffic department' coordinates all phases of production to see that the ads are completed on time and that all deadlines for submitting the ads to the media are met (Belch and Belch, 2003; Grabher, 2002). These agencies come in all shapes and sizes, from specialists which focus on specific media vehicles to full-service agencies who include strategic planning, project management, media buying as well as creative work (Blattberg, 2011). Once the decision has been taken to use video advertising as part of a brand's communication strategy, the first step of the production process is to find ideas based on this brand's brief, target audience and desired impact.[7] Then, once an idea has been 'sold' by an agency and 'bought' by a client, the next steps of bringing the ideas to life in the production process are usually pre-production (scheduling the shooting, casting the participants etc.), production (directing and shooting the actual spot), and post-production (editing the film, including adding special effects, music

Table 10.1   Creative crowdsourcing platforms encompassed in our study

Name	Origin	Year founded	Tagline	Network size[a]
blur Group	UK	2010	'The Creative Service Exchange'	40 000
Concept Cupboard	UK	2010	'Giving you access to the UK's best young designers'	–
eYeka	France	2006	'The co-creation community'	280 000
Genero	USA	2009	'Video projects'	–
GeniusRocket	USA	2007	'The first curated crowdsourcing company'	500
Mofilm	UK	2009	'The biggest brand video contests and competitions'	65 000
Poptent	USA	2007	'The trusted global source for creative video solutions'	71 000
Production Party	Australia	2012	'Australia's largest video production marketplace'	–
Talenthouse	USA	2009	'Creative collaboration'	–
Tongal	USA	2008	'Where the best ideas find the best filmmakers'	–
Userfarm	Italy	2010	'Viral Video Campaigns through competitions for brands, agencies and publishers'	46 000
Victors and Spoils	USA	2009	'The world's first creative (ad) agency built on crowdsourcing principles'	15 000[b]
Womadz	USA	2012	'Word of mouth advertising'	–
Wooshii	UK	2009	'Professional video production company'	5 000
Zooppa	Italy	2007	'People-powered brand energy'	236 000

Notes:
a.   As of April 2014.
b.   At the time of its acquisition by Havas in April 2012.

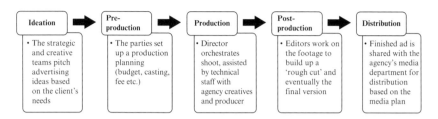

Figure 10.2   The simplified video advertising production process

etc.). The media departments of advertising agencies then take care of the distribution of the produced ads. This results in a five-step process, from ideation to distribution, which is depicted in Figure 10.2. We will now briefly explain each of the steps, describing the nature of the work and the stakeholders that are involved in each of them.

Ideation based on the creative brief
The first step in the production of a video commercial is the creative idea generation phase, which is based on the creative brief. This creative brief is a short document, usually one or two pages, used in agencies to provide guidance in executing creative work on behalf of their clients. It is not provided directly by the client, but by the agencies' strategic teams whose role it is to translate the clients' needs into actionable communication strategies, in which video advertising is often a significant component. A good brief contains information about the market, the product, its positioning, key benefits and differences with the competition. The brief is the most important document that circulates within the agencies, and must be imaginative, concise and yet highly focused. It provides the necessary information and prepares the ground for them to come up with a single-minded campaign idea (Kimani, 1996). It is important that the creative brief is well understood by the creative teams primarily because they actually write the advertisements.

The creative directors should be involved in signing off the creative brief, as their role is to ensure that there is fertile ground in the strategy. The creative team begins the ideation period whereby the art director and copywriter partners start pitching their ideas to each other and when they have enough good ideas they then share them with the creative director. This is an ongoing process where ideas are thrown out, others nurtured and others developed further, where copywriters and art directors work under the direction of creative directors (Wells et al., 2002). During the creative process, agency producers are often consulted to talk about the feasibility of executing certain ideas, but account managers and account planners may also provide input and guidance (Grabher, 2002). Ideas are then presented and explained to the client, using the already approved creative brief as the yardstick to select the ideas that move forward into development.[8]

Pre-production
The first phase of the actual production process brings all the parties together who are needed to bring the video commercial to life. In large agencies, a traffic department is responsible for making sure projects are conducted efficiently and profitably, functioning like project managers where they open up jobs, route approval internally, staff the projects and keep track of timelines and budgets. There are typically three meetings that take place during this pre-production phase: planning is the first meeting, and it establishes what the video is to achieve; the second is the story-boarding of the idea where every shot the audience will see is planned out, which helps reveal any holes in the script and also helps plan time and costs; the final meeting is to gain agreement on the budget. All these meetings aim to bring final agreement on casting, music, production schedule, property and wardrobe recommendations, recommended locations and finally an agreed-upon production quotation/fee. This final agreement is the necessary step before moving into the actual production process of the video footage for the commercial.

Production
Production is when the actual footage for the commercial is being created based on the plans and specifications agreed on in the previous phase. The role of the director is critical in bringing the creative vision of the commercial to life. Based on previous collaborations and the strategic objectives of the advertisement, the director will then choose his creative team to set up a project-based collaboration between in-house creative and external collaborators, who will be commissioned to plan and execute the production of the video commercial (Grabher, 2002). The creative team, managed by a producer, is responsible for creating the ad, with shooting often taking only one or two days. Other key principals involved in the production process include the agency creative team, the casting team and talent, the lighting team and camera crew, all working closely with the director to bring to life his/her ultimate vision of the video content.

Post-production
The post-production phase is where it all starts to come together. This is a critical, yet invisible stage. The editing process begins by going through all the footage to choose the best frames to build up a 'draft' without

voice, music or computer graphics. Once this edit has been approved by the client, the editing process continues and it includes sound mixing, color correction, the incorporation of graphic effects and all necessary elements to create a 'rough cut' for the client. This almost final video allows the client to offer any additional input before completing the project with the final cut. The agency producers manage this process, working closely with the production and editing houses, liaising with the agency teams and the client for approvals throughout the editing process. Once approved, the right formats and right materials get released to media networks for distribution.

Distribution

In a digital world, distribution is critical. The key to airing the most perfect spot is to air it nationally so that the most people can see it and then set up an online presence so people can find it and share it easily. For a traditional TV buy, the finished ad is shared with the agency's media department, which then places the media based on an already approved media plan. The media plan is usually developed concurrently with the creative development and production process. This expertise resides with the agency's media planners and buyers. This team is charged with where to advertise (geography), when to advertise (timing) and what media vehicles to use (media mix) to ensure that the target audience will most likely see the intended advertising. Distribution of advertising consists of the purchasing of advertising space, the broadcasting of the ads and the measurement of their effectiveness. Without a TV buy, it is quite a challenge to distribute online and this is compounded by the millions of videos being uploaded every day on sites like YouTube (Dawson et al., 2011). Very often, online distribution of video content is being amplified by specific service providers whose role it is to push the content to viewers and reach the targeted audience. We represent this five-step process, with production at its center, in Figure 10.3.

Now that we have a basic and common understanding of video advertisement creation, we can describe the different services that creative crowdsourcing platforms can provide, playing significant roles in this process.

Uses of Crowdsourcing in the Creation of Video Advertising

This section explores the different ways crowdsourcing can be used by advertising professionals in the previously presented process. An often used mechanism is that of contests, or competitions, which can be defined as a one- to multiple-round, time-limited competition calling on the general

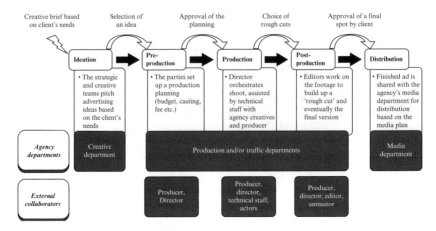

Figure 10.3   The video advertising production process, including external stakeholders

public or a specific target group to make use of their expertise, skills or creativity in order to submit solutions for particular tasks defined by the organizers who strive for a creative solution (Adamczyk et al., 2012). In the space of advertising content creation, we have identified four dominant uses of crowdsourcing in the creation of video advertising: *idea contests* can be used to generate simple ideas, to be used by organizations for the creation of advertisements in a traditional manner; *call for pitches* can be used to identify talented individuals with whom to work and co-create the spots; *simple contests* allow organizations to gather video content after a one-round, traditional competition; and *stage-based contests* allow them to have more control throughout the process by being involved at different stages and channeling the crowd's creativity. We choose to present these four crowdsourcing models in this order as it reflects the growing implication of the crowd along the video production process, from low crowd involvement at the very beginning of the process (*idea contests*) to higher crowd involvement throughout the whole production process (*stage-based contests*).

1.   Crowdsourcing creative inspiration: idea contests

At the beginning of the video advertising creation process is the ideation phase. Crowdsourcing can be used in this phase to find original and creative ideas of advertising spots, thus leveraging the creativity and the diversity of the crowd. Examples of the first type of crowdsourcing initiatives, where only the ideas matter, can be found on eYeka, where the food-products multinational corporation Danone launched several contests with the objective of gathering creative ideas to inspire advertising. In one contest for the Actimel brand,[9] for example, the company was looking for stories of '*how Actimel gives people the inner strength to do the great big things*', requiring members of the crowd to submit their ideas in any form, from pictures and slideshow presentations to storyboards. In another contest for the South African Danone brand Yogi-Sip,[10] the objective was to gather creative ideas to inspire a commercial around the theme of 'the coolest way to keep going', and winning ideas came from countries as diverse as Algeria, Ecuador and Portugal.[11] On another crowdsourcing platform, Userfarm, Microsoft invited the creative individuals registered on the Userfarm platform to 'come up with an idea for a video that will bring the essence of the new Windows Phone to life' for the launch of its Windows phone. Dozens of ideas have been submitted by members of the crowd, allowing the brand to explore a diversity of creative routes to use for its communication.

These examples illustrate the possibility of using crowdsourcing in the idea generation phase, with brands getting a high number of raw ideas to inspire their advertising. In this type of creative crowdsourcing initiative, the value comes from the openness to ideas, wherever they come from and whoever submits them. There is no need to be a copywriter, a screen-writer or a video production professional to participate; only the idea and the story is rewarded (DeJulio, 2012; Whitla, 2009). These contests usually last a couple of weeks and the brands 'walk away' with the ideas without further collaboration with the crowd, using the ideas (or not) to work with their internal communication department and/or advertising agencies.

2.   Crowdsourcing creative talent: call for pitches

Another way to use crowdsourcing is for talent and skill identification. Some creative crowdsourcing platforms indeed use crowdsourcing as a matchmaking mechanism to connect companies to skilled video makers for the execution of specific projects (Lampel et al., 2012). Companies can indeed submit 'briefs' on these websites, along with a budget and a deadline, and participants submit so-called 'pitches' to present their ideas. Here, instead of just gathering creative ideas and using them for internal purposes the companies are looking for both the ideas and the individual to execute these ideas; sourcing ideas and talent. In this model, crowd-sourcing is used in the initial ideation phase and the subsequent produc-tion phases (production and distribution) are not based on crowdsourcing principles, but are executed in the traditional manner, in direct collabora-tion with the chosen creator (Behan, 2012).

Websites such as Blur, Concept Cupboard, Production Party or Wooshii organize calls for pitches targeting small and medium sized enterprises (SMEs) or start-ups. Other platforms also offer a similar service to major corporations for leading brands. GeniusRocket, for example, allows brands to tap into a select group of their most valuable members, among which the client companies can then select the creator(s) with whom to work to produce their video advertisement. In this model, the primary role of the platform is not to organize a contest and to screen incoming entries (whether these are ideas or finished ads) but to select and coordinate the teams who work on project pitches for GeniusRocket's clients. For each video project, the company scans its community for teams and these teams then submit ideas based on the creative brief. The client then chooses the best ideas, rewards them with a prize thus acquiring the intellectual property, and the process moves forward to the creation of storyboards, which can be refined based on quantitative or qualitative research, and the production, which will again be handled by a creative team from the curated community. GeniusRocket pioneered this 'curated crowdsourcing' approach, and other companies have followed. The contest organizers Mofilm offer a service called Mofilm Pro, and Poptent launched a business unit called Poptent Productions, run by the producer Jon Seidman (Behan, 2012). The latter claims to offer a 'faster, more nimble alternative to traditional video production methods' by tapping into its crowd of selected filmmakers. Illustrating this *call for pitches* crowdsourcing model, the *New York Times* reported about the very first Super Bowl ad for Dannon (I used the USA spelling of Danone because it was a US project) which was created by two Poptent community members. Their idea was selected among many others submitted in response to Dannon's creative brief posted mid-2011, and the final spot was produced 'with the advice of Dannon's creative agency of record Y&R New York' (Elliott, 2012). In the *call for pitches* model, the contest takes place at an early stage, and the subsequent stages are based on direct collaboration between the chosen creator and the company.

3. Crowdsourcing finished content: simple contests

The most often encountered use of crowdsourcing in the production of video advertisements through crowdsourcing is still the use of *simple contests*. This is the original, most basic approach to crowdsourcing whereby a company posts a problem online, a vast number of individuals offer solutions to the problem before a specific deadline, the winning ideas are awarded some form of bounty, and the company uses the idea for its own gain (Brabham, 2008). When it comes to video advertising, this type of initiative requires participants to complete all stages needed to come up with an advertisement: ideation (finding the idea); pre-production (preparing the shooting); production (shooting); and post-production (editing the material).

There are numerous web-based companies that allow organizations to tap into their communities to generate video content through one-round contests: leading providers include eYeka, Mofilm, Poptent and Zooppa (Stutzmann et al., 2011), but other companies exist, albeit they have less experience in working with major brands: Genero, Talenthouse, Userfarm and Womadz. These creative crowdsourcing platforms have all organized video contests by which they asked their respective communities of video makers to come up with advertisements for brands. All participants are asked to submit their entries before a predefined date, and they compete within a defined framework which usually includes a creative brief, prize money for the winners, judging criteria and potential participation restrictions linked to the type of product.[12]

Such contests usually last between 4 and 12 weeks and generate dozens of videos coming from members of the crowd. These turnaround times are much shorter than those observed in the traditional process, and allow brands to get a variety of videos, interpreting the same creative brief in different ways. In the simple contest model, the client only provides input by guiding the creative brief at the beginning, selecting winners at the end and supervising its distribution. One of the major setbacks of this type of setting is that there is a high degree of uncertainty about the output from the crowd, and ultimately the success of the creative crowdsourcing initiative (Blattberg, 2011). Additionally, participants don't know whether their idea and execution will please the brand and be rewarded with a prize, which is why some people view this competitive, one-stage approach of crowdsourcing contests as risky and inefficient.

4.   Crowdsourcing finished content: stage-based contests

One way to direct the crowd's creativity is to break down the production process and to infuse crowdsourcing at different stages, and to organize *stage-based contests*. Creative crowdsourcing platform Tongal, for example, breaks down the production process into three phases, which results in three sub-contests for one video project: an idea contest, a pitch contest, and a production contest. In the first step, the crowd is asked to submit ideas in no more than 140 characters, based on the creative brief provided by the brand. The brand then chooses the best ideas, whose authors get a prize worth several hundred dollars, and the crowd is then solicited again to submit pitches based on these shortlisted ideas. At the end of this second step, the brand scouts these pitches and chooses the ones it prefers, rewarding its authors with another cash prize. The last step of a video project is the actual video contest, where crowd members are asked to produce and submit spots based on the previously rewarded ideas.[13] At the end of this final phase, the brand can choose one or several spots to purchase, acquiring the intellectual property to use it for advertising.

The advantage of this model is that the crowd's creativity is being channeled by the brand, which can decide in which direction the crowd should work by rewarding some ideas rather than others. Another advantage of this mechanism is that the scope of potential participants is broader since it is not restricted to video makers only; someone just with good ideas can participate in the early phases, which is not possible in one-round video contests. 'By breaking creativity into smaller pieces, we allow people in all walks of life to compete', one of Tongal's founders explains (DeJulio, 2012). Recent research has underlined that channeling the crowd's creativity by signaling which ideas are best can also lead to less diverse ideas in the long term (Bayus, 2012), which is an interesting limitation to explore in the advertising area. This model seems to be working well as Tongal-produced advertisements have started making inroads into the landscape of traditionally-produced, successful video ads. In August 2011, a 37-second stop-motion video called 'Duck Tron', produced for Duck Tape via Tongal, went viral by garnering over 2 million views in less than two weeks after release, placing second on the Ad Age Viral Video Chart, the only crowd-sourced video ever to do so. And in 2013, two spots aired on the Super Bowl, for Mennen Speed Stick and Dunder Mifflin, were produced via Tongal, which shows the viability of this emerging model (Elliott, 2012; Heitner, 2013).

It is certainly an interesting hybrid model, where the process uses the distributed creativity of the crowd while leveraging different skill-sets among crowd members. The brand, or the advertising agency that represent the brand's interest, has to invest more time and resources in the intermediate stages, but this investment is rewarded by more control and guidance along the creative process. As some brands hesitate to embrace crowdsourcing because of the risk it represents by potentially harming their brand, Tongal's model constitutes an interesting and innovative alternative to traditional contest-based crowdsourcing.

Now that we have presented the four dominant crowdsourcing models used for the creation of video advertising content, a legitimate question would be to know whether there is a relationship between the use of these different models and a sort of crowdsourcing maturity on the part of the brands, their advertising agencies, the crowdsourcing platforms or even the participants. Are some forms of crowdsourcing more or less desirable than others?

Explaining the Different Crowdsourcing Models

Early forms of crowdsourcing were simple contests, initiated by brands to generate conversations and engagement around their products, and managed with their traditional media and advertising agencies. As we have explained, with the rise of creative crowdsourcing platforms dedicated to the production of branded video content, different models have appeared, and today we see that the four models coexist in the advertising world: idea contests, calls for pitches, simple contests and stage-based contests. Many of the companies included in our study have been using the very same models since their respective foundation. However, other companies have evolved and adopted their crowdsourcing models over time (Table 10.2).

Many creative crowdsourcing platforms have indeed started by using the *simple contest* model to create video content, starting as early as 2006 with eYeka, 2007 with Poptent (called XLNTads at that time) or GeniusRocket, 2009 with Mofilm, and 2010 with Userfarm. While this is still a widely used crowdsourcing model, some of these companies have also adopted other crowdsourcing models to accommodate the needs of their existing clients, namely big companies that run global brands. For example eYeka and Userfarm have started running *idea contests* on their respective platforms, starting as early as 2010 for eYeka and 2012 for Userfarm. In these cases, *idea contests* are being organized on their websites in the very same way as the initially running advertising video contests. Other companies, like Poptent and Mofilm, have launched specific business units to organize *calls for pitches* for their clients. To allow brands to work directly with some of its most talented filmmakers, Mofilm launched Mofilm Pro in

Table 10.2   Evolution of crowdsourcing models by creative crowdsourcing platforms

Platform	Uses. . . (Crowdsourcing model)	For. . . (Type of clients)	Since. . . (Year)
eYeka	Simple contests	Global brands	2006
	Idea contests	Global brands	→ 2010
Poptent	Simple contests	Global brands	2007
	Calls for pitches	Global brands	→ 2012
GeniusRocket	Simple contests	Global brands	2007
	Calls for pitches	Global brands	→ 2010
Mofilm	Simple contests	Global brands	2009
	Calls for pitches	Global brands	→ 2010
Userfarm	Simple contests	Global brands	2010
	Idea contests	Global brands	→ 2012

November 2010,[14] and Poptent launched Poptent Productions in April 2012.[15]

The most radical evolution of the contest-based crowdsourcing model is to change its business model completely, which is what GeniusRocket did by dropping the *simple contest* model to focus on its so-called 'curated crowdsourcing' model, a form of *call for pitches* that we already described above. GeniusRocket's model straddles the line between traditional collaboration found within the traditional advertising agency world, and open call crowdsourcing, to delivering the quality of an agency with the creative breadth that a crowd of talent offers. This particular crowdsourcing model is another rare but highly revelatory example of the evolution of the model when it comes to leveraging crowds to produced video content for brands. Taken together, the above-mentioned evolutions of the traditional *simple contest* model allow crowdsourcing platforms to use the creative power of the crowd, which is at the basis of creative crowdsourcing, and at the same time to lower the risks that the open contest model implies.

CONCLUSION

The purpose of this chapter was to present the growing role that crowdsourcing plays in the production video content used for advertising purposes by brands. Given the difficulty of churning out a steady stream of new and engaging content, crowdsourcing ideas and content is increasingly becoming a new tool in advertisers' toolkits. Marketers are beginning to turn to crowdsourcing in varying degrees, as they seek to have an ongoing dialogue with consumers.

We have seen that the first examples of crowdsourcing were mostly integrated into PR-driven marketing campaigns, some of which are still being run today. But we have also seen that these famous examples do not represent the majority of initiatives, and that a lot of brands use crowdsourcing as a fast, global and cost-effective way to generate video content to be used to advertise their brands online or offline. We have underlined that creative crowdsourcing platforms do not operate in the same way nor do they target the same types of clients. Through a multiple case study methodology, and after presenting the production process of video advertising, we have indeed identified four dominant ways of sourcing video content from the crowd: *idea contests* are being used to get fresh ideas to inspire the makers of advertisements; *calls for pitches* allow small and large organizations to identify talented creative individuals or companies with whom to work; *simple contests* allow organizations to gather video content in a traditional competitive setting; and *stage-based contests* allow clients to have more control throughout the process by being involved at different stages of the process.

We chose to present these four models in this order because they reflect the varying role the crowd plays in the production of video content: *idea contests* only engage the crowd at the early ideation phase, *calls for pitches* engage a selected member of the crowd throughout the production process, *simple contests* task the crowd with accomplishing all stages of the process until submission, and *stage-based contests* do the same by incorporating several moments of interaction points between the initiating brand and the crowd. Our research highlights the diversity of models that brands and agencies can mobilize to engage crowds in the production of original video content for their advertising, and also underlines the growing complexity of the crowdsourcing phenomenon.

We see the use of idea generation and simple contests as the popular ways companies are using crowdsourcing. They start out by engaging and empowering their consumers and encouraging those customers to interact with their brand and to suggest ideas for advertising commercials. It is an opportunity to generate content, fuel viral ads and conduct cost-effective market research. The rise of 'curated crowdsourcing' in the *call for pitches* model and the *stage-based contest* model begins to point to a refinement of the broad definition of sourcing from the crowd. The nascent movement towards precision and gaining control appears to be an evolution of the crowdsourcing model, which urges us to adapt our understanding of the concept beyond the early definitions. This pushes us to question the original, quite narrow definition of crowdsourcing given the innovative forms that have emerged to better accommodate the needs of advertising professionals looking to source creative video content. The diversity of models identified in this chapter reflects the current research trend that aims to identify and classify crowdsourcing models based on the workflow organization or the type of tasks that are being crowd-sourced (Adamczyk et al., 2012; Erickson et al., 2012; Geiger et al., 2011).

After reviewing the literature on crowdsourcing as well as analyzing the different models of web-based crowdsourcing companies, we believe the future of crowdsourcing for the production of video advertising looks bright. We cannot be too sure of the form it will take given changes in technology, but we are certain that companies will continue to remain consumer-centric and thus engage consumers in crowdsourcing initiatives for their authentic point of view. In video production, we specifically see the liberation of experts such as producers or directors and the empowerment of general consumers armed with cameras to become the producer, director and editor of a brand's story. With experts now playing the role of collaborators, we expect to see a rise in creativity resulting in rich video content. As consumers begin to participate and feel more empowered, they will become confident to influence and solve problems with interesting stories that capture their experience with the brand (Jenkins and Deuze, 2008). Curating content and engaging clients in more steps along the way in the video crowdsourcing process is an interesting evolution and one that we recommend to continue to be monitored. The ability to break down each phase of the video production process and to engage consumers while cherry picking the best ideas and talent is an indication of a movement towards professionalism. In some cases this is driven by clients' desire to have high quality video advertising either to run nationally or to feed their social channels. We can assume that clients are seeking to reward their consumers with quality content that is relevant, surprising and delightful.

ACKNOWLEDGEMENTS

The first author would like to acknowledge the Association Nationale Recherche Technologie (ANRT) for CIFRE funding (n°2011/3106). Both authors would also like to acknowledge useful feedback from Mehdi Arfaoui, Madeleine Boisset, Benoit Cappiello, Robert DeFillippi, Catherine De Jong, James DeJulio and John Prpic.

NOTES

1. http://www.johnwinsor.com/my_weblog/2012/11/what-will-advertising-look-like-in-2020.html/.
2. http://www.merriam-webster.com/info/newwords11.htm.
3. The latter has even been widely discussed as a case of 'crowd slapping', which describes the crowd's ability to influence a crowdsourcing initiative in order to harm a brand or a product (Howe, 2008).
4. 2008 Bronze Effie Winner Statement, in the category Entertainment & Sporting Events, http://s3.amazonaws.com/effie_assets/2008/2592/2008_2592_pdf_1.pdf, accessed 28 January, 2013.
5. Sometimes even behind closed doors, as creative crowdsourcing platforms increasingly run contests that are not open to everyone, or in which the brand is not identified, for reasons of confidentiality.
6. http://www.tiki-toki.com/timeline/entry/52997/Crowdsourcing-by-Worlds-Best-Global-Brands, accessed 18 February, 2013.
7. The decision to create a video advertisement is only a minor part of advertising and communication agencies' role. A variety of other services are being provided to transform the brand's objectives into an actionable and effective communication strategy. By focusing on the creation of video content, this chapter leaves broader strategic services aside.
8. Sometimes, depending on the client, the brand, the investment or schedule, the creative ideas either move directly into production or into consumer testing for validation and further refinement.

9. http://en.eyeka.com/projects/6661-Actimel.
10. http://en.eyeka.com/projects/7256-Yogi-Sip.
11. http://blogen.eyeka.com/2012/12/20/yogi-sips-winners-are-here/.
12. Some product sectors are heavily regulated, like the alcohol or pharmaceutical indus-
    tries, which can limit the openness of participation to residents of a given country or
    individuals above a certain age.
13. Tongal also allows 'wildcard submissions' where creators submit videos that are not
    based on previously rewarded ideas. 'Take a creative gamble, and see how it fares against
    the judges' top picks from the previous round,' Tongal explains on its website.
14. http://brand-e.biz/mofilm-crowd-sources-the-pros_10235.html.
15. http://thenextweb.com/media/2012/04/12/crowd-sourced-video-company-poptent-laun
    ches-a-premium-video-production-unit-aimed-at-big-brands/.

REFERENCES

Adamczyk, S., Bullinger, A.C. and Möslein, K.M. (2012). Innovation Contests:
A Review, Classification and Outlook. *Creativity and Innovation Management*,
21(4), 335–60.

Agrawal, A., Lacetera, N. and Lyons, E. (2012). How Do Online Platforms
Flatten Markets for Contract Labor? Toronto, Canada. Retrieved from: http://
andrewkarpie.com/wordpress/wp-content/uploads/2012/06/OLLaborPlat.pdf.

Barley, S.R. and Kunda, G. (2006). Contracting: A New Form of Professional
Practice. *Academy of Management Perspectives*, 20(1), 45–66.

Bayus, B.L. (2012). Crowdsourcing New Product Ideas over Time: An Analysis of
the Dell IdeaStorm Community. *Management Science*, *1909*, 1–19.

Behan, T. (2012). Poptent's Crowdsourcing Model Spotlights Freelance
Creators. *Main Line Today*. Retrieved 7 January, 2013, from: http://www.
mainlinetoday.com/Main-Line-Today/December-2012/Poptents-Crowdsourcing-
Model-Spotlights-Freelance-Creators/index.php?cparticle=1&siarticle=0#art
anc.

Belch, G.A. and Belch, M.A. (2003). Organizing for Advertising and Promotion. In
Advertising and Promotion, 6th edn. New York: McGraw-Hill Companies.

Blattberg, E. (2011). GeniusRocket's Curated Crowdsourcing: The Rise of the
Intelligent Intermediary. *crowdsourcing.org*. Retrieved 19 March, 2013, from:
http://www.crowdsourcing.org/editorial/geniusrockets-curated-crowdsourcing-
the-rise-of-the-intelligent-intermediary/9226.

Boudreau, K.J. and Lakhani, K.R. (2013). Using the Crowd as an Innovation
Partner. *Harvard Business Review*, 91(4), 61–9.

Brabham, D.C. (2008). Crowdsourcing as a Model for Problem Solving: An
Introduction and Cases. *Convergence: The International Journal of Research into
New Media Technologies*, 14(1), 75–90.

Brabham, D.C. (2010). Crowdsourcing: A Model for Leveraging Online
Communities. In A. Delwiche and J. Henderson (eds), *The Routledge Handbook
of Participatory Cultures* (Vol. 85, pp. 2–22). Chapel Hill: University of North
Carolina Press.

Brabham, D.C. (2013). The Origins of Crowdsourcing. *Daren Brabham's Blog*.
Retrieved 19 March, 2013, from: http://dbrabham.wordpress.com/2013/02/23/
the-origins-of-crowdsourcing/.

Dawson, A.L., Hamstra, A.A., Huff, L.S., Gamble, R.G., Howe, W., Kane, I.

and Dellavalle, R.P. (2011). Online Videos to Promote Sun Safety: Results of a Contest. *Dermatology Reports*, 3(1), 17–19.

DeJulio, J. (2012). Tongal: A 21st Century Business Model for Finding Top Talent and Putting them to Work on Something they Love. *Management Innovation eXchange*. Retrieved 10 January, 2013, from: http://www.managementexchange. com/story/tongal-21st-century-business-model-finding-top-talent-and-putting-them-work-something-they-lov.

Dishmann, L. (2011). MOFILM Founder Jeffrey Merrihue on Mining the Crowd for Screen Gems. *FastCompany.com*. Retrieved 19 March, 2013, from: http://www.fastcompany.com/1766599/mofilm-founder-jeffrey-merrihue-mining-crowd-screen-gems.

Elliott, S. (2012). For Super Bowl XLVI, a Bigger Batch of First-Time Advertisers. *NYTimes.com*. Retrieved 19 March, 2013, from: http://www.nytimes. com/2012/01/19/business/media/for-super-bowl-xlvi-more-first-time-advertisers. html.

Erickson, L., Petrick, I., Trauth, E. and Erickson, L.B. (2012). Hanging with the Right Crowd: Matching Crowdsourcing Need to Crowd Characteristics. Proceedings of the 18th Americas Conference on Information Systems (AMCIS), Seattle, WA (pp. 1–9).

Estellés-Arolas, E. and González-Ladrón-de-Guevara, F. (2012). Towards an Integrated Crowdsourcing Definition. *Journal of Information Science*, 38(5), 1–14.

Geiger, D., Schulze, T., Seedorf, S., Nickerson, R. and Schader, M. (2011). Managing the Crowd: Towards a Taxonomy of Crowdsourcing Processes. *Seventeenth Americas Conference on Information Systems* (pp. 1–11). Detroit, Michigan.

Ghani, E., Kerr, W.R. and Stanton, C. (2012). Diasporas and Outsourcing: Evidence from oDesk and India. Cambridge, MA. Retrieved from: http://www. hbs.edu/faculty/Pages/item.aspx?num=43327.

Grabher, G. (2002). The Project Ecology of Advertising: Tasks, Talents and Teams. *Regional Studies*, 36(3), 245–62.

Heitner, D. (2013). What is the Cost of Crowdsourcing Super Bowl Ads? *Forbes*. Retrieved 19 March, 2013, from: http://www.forbes.com/sites/ darrenheitner/2013/01/22/what-is-the-cost-of-crowdsourcing-super-bowl-ads/.

Howe, J. (2006). The Rise of Crowdsourcing. *Wired*. June.

Howe, J. (2008). *Crowdsourcing: Why the Power of the Crowd is Driving the Future of Business*. New York: Crown Business.

Howkins, J. (2004). *The Creative Economy: How People Make Money From Ideas*. Harmondsworth: Penguin Global.

IAB-UK (2012). *2012 H1 Digital Adspend Results*. Retrieved from: http://www. iabuk.net/research/library/2012-h1-digital-adspend-results.

Jenkins, H. and Deuze, M. (2008). Editorial: Convergence Culture. *Convergence: The International Journal of Research into New Media Technologies*, 14(1), 5–12.

Kimani, R. (1996). The Perceived Value of Account Planning in the Development of the Creative Brief For New Business Pitches. In G.B. Wilcox (ed.), *The Proceedings of the 1996 Conference of The America Academy of Advertising* (pp. 252–260). Austin, TX. Retrieved from: http://books.google.fr/books/about/The_Perceived_ Value_of_Account_Planning.html?id=aT_ztgAACAAJ&redir_esc=y.

Kleemann, F., Voss, G.G. and Rieder, K. (2008). Un(der)paid Innovators: The Commercial Utilization of Consumer Work through Crowdsourcing. *Science, Technology & Innovation Studies*, 4(1), 5–26.

Lampel, J., Jha, P.P. and Bhalla, A. (2012). Test-Driving the Future: How Design Competitions are Changing Innovation. *Academy of Management Perspectives*, 26(2), 71–85.

Lawrence, B. and Fournier, S. (2010). Consuming the Consumer-Generated Ad. *Office*.

Malone, T.W. and Laubacher, R.J. (1998). The Dawn of the e-lance Economy. *Harvard Business Review*, 76(5), 144–152. Retrieved from: http://www.ncbi.nlm.nih.gov/pubmed/10185429.

Moskowitz, R. (2006). Are Consumer-Generated Ads Here to Stay? *imediaconnection.com*. Retrieved 19 March, 2013, from: http://www.imediaconnection.com/content/9521.imc.

Moth, D. (2012). How Coca-Cola Uses Co-creation to Crowd-source New Marketing Ideas. *Econsultancy.com*. Retrieved 19 March, 2013, from: http://econsultancy.com/fr/blog/11098-how-coca-cola-uses-co-creation-to-crowd-source-new-marketing-ideas.

Penin, J. and Burger-Helmchen, T. (2011). Crowdsourcing of Inventive Activities: Definition and Limits. *International Journal of Innovation and Sustainable Development*, 5(2/3), 246–63.

Schenk, E. and Guittard, C. (2011). Towards a Characterization of Crowdsourcing Practices. *Journal of Innovation Economics*, 7(1), 1–20.

Stutzmann, C., Paderni, L.S. and Madigan, Corinne, J. (2011). Crowdsourcing Gains Legitimacy For Advertisers. *Forrester Research Report*, Retrieved from: http://www.forrester.com/Crowdsourcing+Gains+Legitimacy+For+Advertisers/fulltext/-/E-RES59512.

Telo, A.R., Sanchez-Navarro, J. and Leibovitz, T. (2012). ¡ ESTA PELÍCULA LA HACEMOS ENTRE TODOS ! Crowdsourcing y Crowd-funding como Prácticas Colaborativas en la Producción Audiovisual Contemporánea. *Icono 14*, 1(10), 25–40.

Torng, C. (2012). Content-Driven Social Marketing: Time to Make the Digital Donuts. *Postano Blog*. Retrieved 19 March, 2013, from: http://www.postano.com/blog/content-driven-social-marketing-time-to-make-the-digital-donuts.

Van Dijck, J. (2009). Users like you? Theorizing Agency in User-generated Content. *Media, Culture & Society*, 31(1), 41–58.

Vranica, S. (2012). Ad-Spending Outlook Dims. *WSJ.com*. Retrieved 19 March, 2013, from: http://online.wsj.com/article/SB10001424127887324020804578151710820996072.html.

Wells, W.D., Burnett, J. and Moriarty, S. (2002). *Advertising: Principles and Practice* (6th edn). Englewood Cliffs, NJ: Prentice Hall.

Wexler, M.N. (2011). Reconfiguring the Sociology of the Crowd: Exploring Crowdsourcing. *International Journal of Sociology and Social Policy*, 31(1/2), 6–20.

Whitla, P. (2009). Crowdsourcing and its Application in Marketing Activities. *Contemporary Management Research*, 5(1), 15–28.

Winter, J. and Hill, A. (2009). The ad space race: Tongal takes off. *Labnotes* (14), 1–4. Retrieved from: http://www.managementlab.org/files/site/publications/labnotes/mlab-labnotes-014.pdf.

Yin, R.K. (2002). *Case Study Research: Design and Methods*, 3rd edn (*Applied Social Research Methods, Vol. 5*). Thousand Oaks, CA: SAGE Publications.

11. Using 'crowd-wisdom strategy' to co-create market value: proof-of-concept from the movie industry

Nadine Escoffier and Bill McKelvey

INTRODUCTION

As of summer 2013, film industry experts expected Disney to lower its spending on 'original' (Chmielewski and Zeitchik, 2013) films after Disney found out that its movie *The Lone Ranger* had no market value. Two years prior to *The Lone Ranger*, Chuck Viane, President of Distribution for Walt Disney Studios, used the word 'scary' to describe the audience's rejection of *Mars Needs Moms* (Barnes, 2011). In general, innovative companies perform better (Kerr, 2010) in a constantly changing global competitive environment. Yet, only 9 percent of America's companies are innovating (Boroush, 2010). Why? New product development is a hit-or-miss bet (the higher the economic value, the higher the risk). Many newly launched products suffer from high failure rates, not because of technical shortcomings but because they simply have no market (Ogawa and Piller, 2006). Moreover, even though managers may have found it difficult to catch the attention of the generation 2.0, the 2.0 generation will not hesitate to go viral with negative word-of-web[1] if a new product is not appealing; sometimes they do this even before the product goes to market. The current studios' risk management strategy is (1) a similar recipe that worked before is reproduced along with (2) an expensive marketing campaign to sell it and (3) bet on strong opening weekends. However, and apart from the loss of creativity and the rise of costs, in order to follow the 'sequel strategy', one needs first to create a successful original movie. And if we add the recent Twitter effect where people critique films quickly, often when they are still sitting in theaters, we argue that current studios' risk management strategy is at best a short-term one. Therefore: how to create a low-risk original movie in the first place?

Ultimately, the audience decides a movie's fate. An added force behind this fact is the digitization of information and communication. So, what if the audience is involved in the process of making a movie? In 1907, Francis Galton was surprised that 'the Crowd' at a county fair accurately guessed the weight of an ox when their individual guesses were averaged. In 1976, Eric Von Hippel observes that most product innovations do not come out of corporate research and development labs but from the people who use the products. Now, more and more companies use '*The Wisdom of Crowds*' (Surowiecki, 2004) (i.e. crowd-wisdom) via crowdsourcing (Howe, 2006) to help them evaluate and generate ideas for their new product before risking high investment, market failure and negative word-of-web. We call this 'crowd-wisdom strategy'. Traditional companies such as BMW use this strategy on specific projects. Some start-ups such as Threadlesss are organized by using this strategy in a continuous way. According to our analysis, based on numerous real case studies using crowd-wisdom via crowdsourcing, we construct a crowd-wisdom strategy business model as a source of constant market value-creation and positive word-of-web. Even though we argue that using crowd-wisdom strategy seems to be the best option so far to reduce market failure, what is the real value of this strategy? Where is the proof-of-concept? From our conceptual model, we localize the 'crowd-wisdom' to a crowd's ability to generate and evaluate ideas. We focus on the latter. In our study, where 500 participants evaluated trailers a few weeks before opening weekend, and after correlating these evaluations with opening weekend receipts and also four weeks later, we provide the proof-of-concept that the Crowd has a high ability to evaluate even a complex new product's market value before it comes to market even better than experts.

THE RISKS OF THE 'SEQUEL STRATEGY' TO REDUCE MARKET FAILURE

Movie production is an appealing industry for studying the risk of new product development because of its high economic value and high performance risk. The average production cost was about $70.8 million per movie when the MPAA stopped tracking the number in 2007.[2] The most expensive movie to date topped $300 million (*Pirates of the Caribbean: At World's End*, production budget only).[3] The average cost of advertising was $35.9 million per movie (about 50 percent of production costs on average) the last time the MPAA reported the figure in 2007.[4] The difference between total average (production and advertising) cost of ~$107 million – believed to have risen since 2007 – compared with the average revenue of 2012 (~$16 million) is staggering.[5] For example, consider one of Disney Animation's movies *Mars Needs Moms* (2011). The production budget of this movie was $150 million with an additional marketing budget estimated at $60 million (Lumenick, 2011) and worldwide revenue of $39 million.[6] 'Scary' is how Chuck Viane, President of Distribution for Walt Disney Studios described the audience's rejection of this film. 'Was it the idea?' (Barnes, 2011).

What is the current strategy to reduce market failure? One way is pursuing franchises based on properties with demonstrated appeal in the marketplace such as sequels, remakes and movies based on properties established in other media such as musicals, books, comics, old TV programs and video games. The popularity of movie sequels best exemplifies this trend, as shown in Figure 11.1.

DreamWorks Animation President, Lewis Coleman, confirmed this trend in January 2007 when he announced:

> What we are really doing is looking for sequels. While sequels are more expensive than the originals, they are less risky and usually more successful. Because of the higher costs involved in luring back the talent, sequels can cost anywhere from $150 million to $170 million, versus $130 million for an original movie (Marr, 2007).

Indeed, out of the 8 sequels mentioned in Figure 11.1 for 2011, only one sequel was less expensive than the original (*Harry Potter and the Deathly Hallows Part 2*). However, we note that the production budget taken in

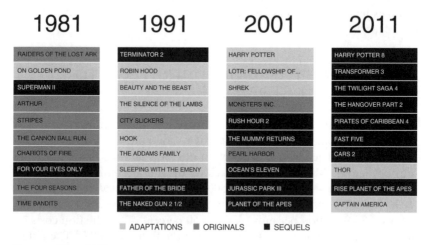

Source: Allen (2012).

Figure 11.1   US gross of the top 10 films shows the popularity of movie sequels over the decades

consideration for *Harry Potter and the Deathly Hallows Part 2* is half of the total that the studios spent on part 1 and 2 combined (\$250 000 000 production budget only). Data do not provide any details per movie.[7] Even though audiences are familiar with the concept, market success for sequels is difficult to predict (Sood and Dreze, 2006). While the US gross of the top 10 films shows the popularity of sequels over the decades, sequels from successful original and even cult movies have gone unnoticed and lost money at the box office (e.g. *Return to Oz*, 1985; *The Rage: Carrie 2*, 1999; *Son of The Mask*, 2005).[8]

Why? Negativity substantially affects consumption and is complicated by the fact that people appear to weight negative and positive information differently. Negative information is more easily recalled, retained longer, and unduly emphasized in decisions (Baumeister et al., 2001; Rozin and Royzman, 2001). Thus, it is not surprising to find that negative buzz affects consumption more significantly than positive buzz – highlighting the disproportionate influence of negative information in consumption decisions (Uzzi et al., 2008). From 1982 to 2013, the average of the 100 biggest drops in box-office receipts from opening to second weekend based on *negative* word-of-mouth was –72.51 percent, whereas the average of the 100 biggest second-weekend increases based on *positive* word-of-mouth was only +43.53 percent.[9, 10] Word-of-mouth, then, appears to be a particularly important driver of a movie's success or failure and the emergence of word-of-web communities, where people share opinions via the Internet, amplifies this effect. Back in 2003 when *Hulk* came out, the studio bowed to incredible pressure from fans and released early footage of the special effects. The plan was to get the fans talking so as to build up positive word-of-mouth. However, the special effects were so bad that the buzz generated went negative (Barnes, 2008). This is a case of what is called 'viral marketing' (Howard, 2005; Terdiman, 2005; Zarrella, 2007) going toxic.

One of the most famous dictums about Hollywood belongs to the screenwriter William Goldman (1983, p. 39): 'Nobody knows anything.' This is the reason why studios spend about 50 percent on average of their production budget to chase the audience. In fact, it seems that the trend among studios is to bet on strong opening weekends supported by mass-media advertising to reduce risk rather than to try to make better original movies so as to protect against negative word-of-web communications that will hurt sales later on. However, box office watchers say Twitter is the latest weapon in an arsenal of smartphones that audiences use to critique films quickly, often when they are still sitting in theaters. 'If people don't like the movie now on Friday it can die by Saturday' said Paul Dergarabedian, President of a box office tracking firm, Hollywood.com (Dobuzinskis, 2009). This phenomenon is well known as the *Twitter effect*.

Thus, it appears that current studios' risk-management strategy – (1) a similar recipe that worked before is reproduced along with (2) an expensive marketing campaign to sell it and (3) bet on strong opening weekends – is at best a short-term one. In the end, not only does the 'sequel strategy' *not* guarantee a market value and a positive word-of-web but also it increases costs and decreases creativity. Finally, in order to create a sequel one needs to create an original appealing movie in the first place. Consequently, the key question is: How to avoid market failure and negative word-of-web while keeping costs low and improve creativity in the movie industry? Or, in other words: How to create a low risk original movie?

USING 'CROWD-WISDOM STRATEGY' BEFORE RISKING HIGH INVESTMENT, MARKET FAILURE AND NEGATIVE WORD-OF-WEB

Listen to the audience? In 1976, Eric Von Hippel observed that most product innovations do not come out of corporate research and development labs but from the people who use the products. Therefore, using James Surowiecki's *The Wisdom of Crowds* to aid new product development is simply a logical next step. Consumers now demand greater levels of personalization in their consumption experience and put businesses under pressure to co-create value with them. Consumers are now:

- seeking and accessing information online, across geographic boundaries;
- providing unsolicited feedback to companies;
- engaging in thematic consumer communities, such as those fostering consumer word-of-web; and
- experimenting or co-creating with other consumers to find their own solutions to problems (Prahalad and Ramaswamy, 2004).

Consumers can now initiate the dialogue and the battle for shaping expectations of 'what's next?'. This requires firms' acceptance of customers as active players instead of a passive audience. 'Business competition used to be a lot like traditional theatre: on stage, the actors had clearly defined roles, and the customers paid for their tickets, sat back, and watched passively. Now, customers have moved out of the audience and onto the stage' (Prahalad and Ramaswamy, 2000, p.79).

Studies confirm the problems of new product commercialization; we see newly launched products suffering from notoriously high failure rates, often reaching 50 percent or more (Ogawa and Piller, 2006). The main culprit is a faulty understanding of customer needs. That is, many new products fail not because of technical shortcomings but because they simply have no market (Ogawa and Piller, 2006). In his book *Hollywood Economics*, Arthur De Vany (2004, p. 72) says: 'The audience makes a movie a hit and no amount of star power or marketing hype can alter that.' In the end, the consumer decides a product's fate. An added force behind this fact is the digitization of information and communication.

So, what if your audience is involved in new product development? In his book, Surowiecki presents numerous case studies and anecdotes to illustrate his argument that the Crowd is better than individuals or even experts at solving problems, fostering innovation, coming to wise decisions, even predicting the future. His opening example relates to a 1907 article in *Nature* (Galton, 1907) where the author is surprised that 'the Crowd' at a county fair accurately guessed the weight of an ox when their individual guesses were averaged. The average was closer to the ox's true butchered weight than the estimates of most crowd members and also closer than any of the separate estimates made by cattle experts.

But not all crowds are wise. According to Surowiecki, independence, decentralization, aggregation, and diversity of opinions are key criteria that separate wise crowds from ineffective ones. In other words, each individual in a crowd has to come from a different background, have at least some relevant knowledge, and maintain independence when offering an opinion; then the average of this diversity of opinions will most often be better than expert ones. This is crowd-wisdom based on ideas evaluation. For example, crowd-wisdom applies to democratic journalism where a group of non-experts determines what news is important and then people outside the group can view the news based on their ranking. The social-news sites Digg and Newsvine both fall into this category; they involve the averaging of opinions. Identically, Google's page-link algorithms involve pages voting for other pages. There are authors behind these pages, so implicitly there are people voting for people or people voting on content.

Alternatively, we have crowd-wisdom where participants are genuinely collaborating. The intelligence that emerges here is different from people providing opinions independently from each other. Instead, people collaborate in ways that sequentially influence and respond to inputs by others such that the outcome differs from the input of any single person. This is crowd-wisdom based on ideas generation. The best example of this phenomenon is the online encyclopedia *Wikipedia*. Millions of people contribute to the collaborative wisdom of Wikipedia, making it one of the most popular information websites on the Internet.[11]

Increasingly, companies use crowd-wisdom via crowdsourcing to help them evaluate and create all kinds of new products before risking high investments, market failure and negative word-of-web. We call it 'crowd-wisdom strategy'. In this context, we define the 'Crowd' as a large group of self-selected participants sharing common interests that represent a broad public community (e.g. potential customers) and we argue that a 'community' is what emerges from the Crowd when it participates more actively on a regular basis and gets information about the preferences/attitudes of other members. Traditional companies (e.g. BMW, Frito-Lay) use this strategy on specific projects. Some start-ups are organized by using this strategy.

Traditional Companies Using 'Crowd-Wisdom Strategy' on Specific Projects

In 2010, the BMW Group launched its Co-creation Lab, which is a virtual meeting place for individuals interested in car-related topics and who are eager to share their ideas and opinions about tomorrow's automotive world with one of the world's leading car manufacturers. BMW's first initiative was the 'BMW Group Idea Contest'[12] (2 March, 2010) in which the Crowd was able to share ideas for innovative mobility services in cities and metropolitan areas of the future. The Crowd was able to discuss and evaluate the ideas of others. In a month and a half, BMW received more than 300 ideas, 2000 comments and 8500 evaluations. Twelve days after the deadline for submissions (14 April, 2010), the BMW Jury selected three winners according to the creativity, topic fit and elaboration of the description. The rewards were a BMW portable Navigation pro for the 1st prize, IPod Touch 32 GB for the 2nd prize and a Mini Messenger Bag for the 3rd prize. At the end of the contest, one of the members of the Jury declared:

> This contest showed once more, how important it is to integrate external sources into the development of new services and innovations. The generated ideas added innovative and valuable input to the topics we are already working on and confirmed us that the overall direction we are following leads into the right direction. We are eager to further pursue the generated ideas and establish fascinating mobility services for tomorrow's world.[13]

Since then, this traditional company uses crowd-wisdom strategy on a regular basis for different type of specific projects (e.g. 'BMW Trunk Idea Contest').[14]

For the 2007 Super Bowl, Frito-Lay launched a contest called 'Crash the Super Bowl'[15] to allow the Crowd to co-create their own Doritos commercial. The Crowd then commented and voted on various commercials. The Jury chose five final ads out of 1065 submissions according to their originality, creativity, adherence to creative assignment, and overall appeal.

The winner of each selected ad received a cash prize of $10 000 and a trip for two to Detroit during the Super Bowl. According to Frito-Lay, the vote was so close that just before the game the company decided to run two of the advertisements rather than just one. Both commercials finished highly in ratings of commercials during this Super Bowl.[16] Frito-Lay re-launched the fan-created commercials for the 2009 Super Bowl with an additional challenge that was that if a consumer-made Doritos commercial could score the number 1 spot on the official USA Today ad meter poll, Frito-Lay would pay the ad's creator a $1 million bonus. Out of 1961 submissions, the five finalists selected received a prize of $25 000 each and a trip for two to the Super Bowl. The best commercial chosen by the jury to run during Super Bowl was the 'Free Doritos' ad.[17] After being ranked by the USA Today's Super Bowl ad meter as best ad of the year,[18] its creator received a $1 million bonus. The company has been using the crowd-wisdom strategy to design its commercial for the Super Bowl ever since. In 2012, using the same strategy, the Doritos ad ranked number 1 again.[19]

Start-Up Organized by Using 'Crowd-Wisdom Strategy' in a Continuous Way

In 2000, Threadless was originally founded as a T-shirts company. In 2013, besides T-shirts, the company produces different type of accessories (e.g. smartphone cases, water bottles, tank tops, bags). This start-up uses crowd-wisdom strategy in an ongoing way. Members of the Crowd upload their designs to the website.[20] If they are not sure that their design is ready or if Threadless declines the submission because the company feels the idea could use more work, members can get community feedback to help them improve their final design. Then new visitors and an ongoing online community score them on a scale of 1 to 5 and leave comments.[21] Each week, the staff reviews the top scoring submissions. Designs are selected based on their overall scores and comments. Each designer selected receives between $250 and $2000 in cash based on what it is printed on and between 3 and 20 percent of royalties based on the number of products sold with the selected design.

Threadless apparels are run in limited batches. When they are sold out, customers can request a reprint. However, reprinting occurs only when there is enough demand. Ultimately, the decision to print or reprint is up to the company. The website releases at least one new design and one reprinted design each day during the week (from Monday to Friday). Threadless has a business model built on the care and feeding of an online community. This is why its employees are focused on getting customers to come back again and again and to bring their friends.

Jake Nickell, one of Threadless's founders, announced in a 2008 *Inc Magazine* article (Chafkin, 2008) that revenue at Threadless was growing 500 percent per year, despite the fact that the company had never advertised, employed no professional designers, used no modeling agency or fashion photographers, had no sales force, and enjoyed no standard retail distribution. As a result, costs are low, margins are above 30 percent, and because the number of prints in each size and gender depends on the scores the designs receive, the comments as well as demographic information, the company has never produced a flop. And last, but not least, at the time of the design submission, the company asks a potential future designer to agree to legal terms and conditions in which the participant releases the copyright of the design and attests that the design is his/her own original work. Now Threadless uses crowd-wisdom strategy for specific projects (e.g. 'My Sound World NPR').[22]

According to our analysis, based on numerous real case studies using crowd-wisdom via crowdsourcing, we construct a business model (see Figure 11.2) for what we call 'the crowd-wisdom strategy.'

THE 'CROWD-WISDOM STRATEGY' BUSINESS MODEL AS A SOURCE OF CONSTANT MARKET VALUE CREATION AND POSITIVE WORD-OF-WEB

'Crowd-wisdom strategy' typically is based on a contest in which the Crowd is usually rewarded in some way. According to the crowd-wisdom processes via crowdsourcing that we have studied (based on crowdsourcing projects online, articles, videos and interviews), designing such a contest comprises seven stages:

1. Market the contest on the Internet by creating an appropriate website. One may quickly learn more details from other existing websites mentioned in this chapter. Alpheus Bingham, the founder of the R&D crowd-wisdom company Innocentive, says that crowd size is a key factor in maximizing the capacities of crowdsourced innovation (he recommends 5000 people for a given contest) (Burge, 2007).
2. Registrations: ask for contact and statistical information (name, email, sex, country. . .) but more importantly make sure all members of the Crowd accept a 'Legal Terms & Conditions' document (rights of use, third party rights. . .).
3. Guidelines: guide your Crowd toward what kind of product design you would like to achieve (general topic, categories. . .).
4. Timeline: define a schedule for the contest (when it starts, deadline for submissions, jury meetings, announcement of winners. . .).

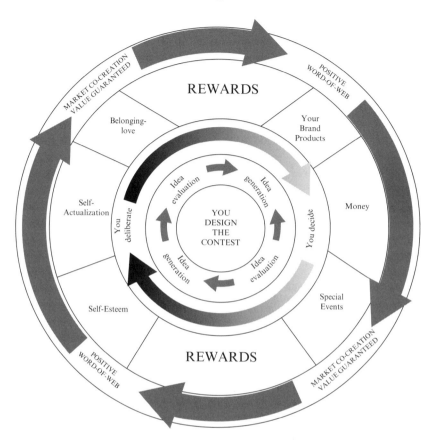

Note: By 'you' we mean the company.

Figure 11.2   The crowd-wisdom strategy's business model: the 'wheel of fortune'

5.   Submissions: provide a toolkit for your Crowd to enter their ideas onto your website (free software, virtual configuration tool, specific platform . . .)
6.   Evaluations: define your criteria (creativity, topic fit, average score from the Crowd, number of 'I'd buy it'. . .). The final decision is yours.
7.   Rewards: choose the number of winners and the type of rewards according to your criteria (your budget, the topic . . .).

Based on your contest-design, an ongoing co-creation process becomes feasible for all concerned.

- First ring: company's co-creation team can play a key role continually stimulating the Crowd to generate and evaluate ideas in a continual way. Data shows that the Crowd appears to be more willing to evaluate than generate ideas (e.g. 'BMW Group Idea Contest;' 8500 evaluations versus 2000 comments).

- Second ring: according to the ongoing timeline and contest-design criteria, the company's co-creation team deliberates and decides what to produce. Companies should not ask the Crowd to get involved in the production phase. Indeed, 'Cambrian House', launched in 2006, attracted about 50 000 members and more than 7000 ideas from The Crowd. The leitmotiv was 'You think it; Crowds test it; Crowds build it; you sell it.' As it turned out, the Crowd was really good at thinking and testing, but less interested at the building component of Cambrian House's model (Howe, 2008).

- Third ring: the Crowd is rewarded for giving ideas that create the best market value before high investment costs become involved. These rewards can be both extrinsic (e.g. your brand products, money, special events. . .) and intrinsic (e.g. belonging-love, self-actualization, self-esteem. . .).

- Outer ring: crowd-wisdom strategy may be used at just about any stage of the value chain and in a continual way. Contests are an important way to motivate the Crowd. If well designed, the results are tremendous. High levels of creativity, significantly shortened new product development process times, high margins due to low costs, brand loyalty, and last but not least, high levels of satisfaction due to the fact that customers get exactly what they want which generates a market co-creation value and a positive word-of-web in a continuous way.

It is important to note that not all examples of crowd-wisdom via crowdsourcing are success stories. In 2007, H.J. Heinz 'invited America to make the next great Heinz Ketchup commercial'. The company spent months and a considerable amount of money promoting the contest. Then they hired an outside promotions firm just to review the flood of submissions, the vast majority of which were deemed offensive, in violation of copyright laws, or simply bad. Furthermore, Heinz was badmouthed on its website forums for being lazy and just angling for cheap labor. Even so, the winning Heinz ads were all clever and effective (Howe, 2008). There is a definite art in using crowd-wisdom strategy for enhancing a product's market value. What unites all successful *crowd-wisdom via crowdsourcing projects* is a helpful interest from the Crowd. It is best to use crowd-wisdom to generate and evaluate ideas *early on* in the co-creation process instead of subsequently hoping that spending millions of marketing dollars to generate a positive word-of-web will improve sales. As a result, to reduce the risk of market failure for a new product before high investment, companies should not use the Crowd simply as marketers but also and more importantly as a readily available co-creation product-design and improvement opportunity.

Even though crowd-wisdom strategy sounds like the best option so far to avoid market failure, what is the real value of this strategy? Where is the proof-of-concept? For our evaluation of crowd-wisdom, we chose one of the most complex, high-risk and expensive products: movies. From our conceptual model, we localize the 'crowd-wisdom' to a Crowd's ability to generate and evaluate ideas. The following study is focused on the latest.

EVIDENCE OF CROWD'S ABILITY FOR IDEA EVALUATION FROM THE MOVIE INDUSTRY

Method

We spent about three years developing a database and signing up online participants by creating all sorts of social media and marketing tools. Our most efficient approach to get people to opt-in was through personal emails (82 percent) followed by word-of-mouth (5.6 percent) and social media (2.8 percent). As a result, a large group of self-selected participants sharing common interests became our Crowd. Because participants knew when they opted in that the experiment would be about movies, we assumed that people had some interest in movies, which represents the common interest and their motivation to participate in our study. The Crowd is not a target audience, which is why no specific justification criteria were asked on the registration page. Before starting this experiment, about 1500 people were willing to participate in our online experiment. Of these 1500 people about 500 evaluated each trailer, allocated as follows: 60 percent female; 40 percent male; 60 percent over 40; 40 percent under 40; 60 percent West Coast USA; 40 percent East Coast USA.

Studio professionals and movie critics represent the Experts. Because of the time spent creating a movie and the huge amount of money at stake, we presume that studio professionals believe they are making a successful movie. But the staggering average loss per movie mentioned earlier suggests that the idea-evaluations of new product concepts from these Experts do not generally reflect market's value. Another category of 'experts' is professional movie critics. Their new movie evaluations are based on actually seeing the entire movie; their evaluations are available online.[23]

We picked trailers based on those available via the Internet, using whatever clues were available, including our own judgment, to create a range from Worst to Best; we were lucky, indeed, to end up with high variance in movie quality. We also opted for different distributors, and different MPAA ratings (these are used in North America to rate a film's thematic and content suitability for certain audiences). We also chose different genres in order to prove that even though some members of a Crowd might prefer horror movies, the wisdom of a sufficiently large sample of a Crowd in general can also assess the value of, for example, a romantic comedy preferred by other members of an audience as well.

Finally, in order to buy a new product the consumers like, this new product needs to be broadly available. Consequently we selected trailers for movies designated for 'wide release', that is, opening in 600+ theaters. For our evidence of movies' market value, we chose box-office gross receipts. Since some movies open in many more than 600 theaters, we use receipts per theater, also available online.[24]

We first designed our survey online where we could include a trailer and explain to our Crowd what to do. Then we asked: 'Based on your evaluation of the trailer, do you think that the movie is going to be: Excellent; Very good; Good; Fair; Poor?'. Participants never saw more than one trailer at any specific point in time. Since each sample of 500 was a random subset of the ~1500 who chose to participate in our online surveys, we tried to maximize the time between each participant's online evaluation so as to assure that each evaluation of a trailer was independent of her/his previous evaluation(s). Furthermore, none of our respondents had information about anyone else's rating. Movies were evaluated based on their trailers and with regard to quality on the 1–5 scale (Poor to Excellent). The evaluations of any particular movie were stopped two weeks before opening weekend. Scores for each trailer were standardized and translated into a 100-point scale. We then correlated the following:

- the Crowd's evaluations with opening weekend receipts per theater;
- the Crowd's evaluations with receipts four weeks after opening weekend per theater;
- the Experts' evaluations with opening weekend receipts per theater;
- the Experts' evaluations with receipts four weeks after opening weekend per theater.

Our independent variables are the Crowd's and Experts' evaluations. Our dependent variable is box office receipts.

Testing the Crowd's Ability for Idea-Evaluation on Opening Weekend

More specifically, our first research question was:

Is the Crowd capable of correctly evaluating opening weekend's market value of a movie before it comes to market – based on viewing its trailer two weeks before its release – better than Experts, who see the actual movie a few days before its release?

Why use trailers? Trailers are the 2½-minute glimpses of future movies. Of the various marketing methods – such as TV spots, posters and trailers – the latter are the most complicated and expensive to produce. The trailer-design process creates mini-stories to attract an audience to a movie. A series of selected shots are usually drawn from the most exciting action or funny parts of the movie. A trailer has to attract the audience in less than 2½ minutes, the maximum length allowed by theaters. Trailers are not just a selection of shots, but very carefully constructed mini-stories that derive their power from key dialogue lines accentuated with strong visual moments and sound effects. Most trailers have a three-act structure similar to a feature-length movie. They start with a beginning (Act 1) that lays out the premise of the story. The middle (Act 2) drives the story further and usually ends with a dramatic climax. Act 3 usually features a strong piece of 'signature music' (either a recognizable song or a powerful, sweeping orchestral piece). This last Act often consists of a visual montage of powerful and emotional moments of the film and may also contain portrayals of key actors if they are famous stars who could help sell the movie. Trailers tell the story of a film in a highly condensed fashion that must have maximum appeal. Thus, a trailer can be seen as a free sample to introduce the new product to consumers while making them want more (or not).

Knowing that the movie producers' dominant strategy is to aim for strong opening weekend box-office results (i.e. Friday evening to Sunday evening), bolstered by strong mass-media advertising, we therefore focused on the primary marketing tool (the trailer) that is created to motivate moviegoers to go and see the movie on opening weekend. Given that:

- opening weekend box-office receipts are presumed by Experts to represent the impact of advertising (the most important item being the trailer);
- the Crowd's evaluation of a movie is based only on the trailer as the primary marketing tool;
- the Experts' evaluations of a movie are based on seeing the entire movie;

- the Crowd is better than individuals or even experts at solving problems, fostering innovation, coming to wise decisions, even predicting the future;

our first hypothesis was:

H1: The correlation between the Crowd's evaluations – based on trailers – and opening weekend receipts will be higher than the correlation between Experts' evaluations – based on movies – and opening weekend receipts.

Testing the Crowd's Ability for Idea-Evaluation Four Weeks After Opening Weekend

Our second research question was:

Is the Crowd capable of correctly evaluating four weeks after opening weekend the market value of a movie before it comes to market – based on viewing its trailer two weeks before its release – better than Experts, who see the actual movie a few days before its release?

Why worry about word-of-mouth/web? As mentioned earlier, negative buzz affects consumption more significantly than positive buzz; that is, negative information has more impact on people's consumption decisions. The word-of-web effect amplifies this effect. One of the latest examples in the movie industry is *Total Recall*'s remake (2012). The movie had an attractive trailer design, high budget, Colin Farrell's stardom and was a remake of the very successful and cult *Total Recall* movie with Arnold Schwarzenegger created in 1990. Nevertheless, this remake is listed as one of the biggest second weekend drops.[25] One could reasonably wonder about, if not challenge, the idea that crowd-wisdom – based on the Crowd seeing only 2½-minute trailers – could efficiently evaluate full-length movies' market value four weeks out into the market. Given that:

- moviegoers had four weeks to see the full-length movie and therefore word-of-web dynamics occurred;
- the Crowd's evaluations are based on seeing 2½-minute trailers more than six weeks earlier;
- Experts' evaluations are based on seeing full-length movies more than four weeks earlier;
- the Crowd is better than individuals or even experts at solving problems, fostering innovation, coming to wise decisions, even predicting the future;

our second hypothesis was:

H2: The correlation between the Crowd's evaluations – based on trailers – and receipts four weeks after opening weekend will be minimal yet higher than the correlation between Experts' evaluations – based on movies – and receipts four weeks after opening weekend.

Results

The first line of Table 11.1 shows a correlation between the Crowd's evaluations and opening weekend receipts of 0.79, which is 36 percent higher than the Experts' correlation (0.58). The second line of Table 11.1 shows a correlation between the Crowd's evaluations and four weeks after opening weekend receipts of 0.74, which is 57 percent higher than the Experts' correlation (0.47). We chose box-office receipts four weeks after opening weekend because they reflect the value stemming from word-of-mouth/web effects (four weeks after opening weekend being the average movie's life in a theater). Given the fact that the Crowd's evaluation of a movie was based only on the trailer as the primary marketing tool, we expected that the Crowd would not see through it and consequently we expected a minimal correlation between the Crowd's evaluation and receipts four weeks after opening weekend. On this account, it is surprising to see that even though the correlation (0.74) is lower than the one based on opening weekend receipts (0.79), it is still highly significant. We can infer that this marketing tool was used by the Crowd as an informative tool rather than a marketing tool, which confirms Elberse and Anand's findings (Elberse and Anand, 2006). As a result, we offer empirical evidence that crowd-wisdom can be used to accurately evaluate the market value of even complex new products based on only marketing information before they actually go to market (i.e. our Crowd's evaluations of movie trailers). Furthermore, we find that the Crowd's evaluation of movie value four weeks after opening weekend (based on judging trailers) is more accurate than the evaluations of movie Experts, who made their evaluations after seeing the actual movie. From

Table 11.1   The Crowd's ability to evaluate products' market value before they come to market compared with Experts' ability

	The Crowd's evaluations (based on trailers)	Experts' evaluations (based on movies)
Opening weekend receipts	0.79	0.58
Four weeks after opening weekend receipts	0.74	0.47

this, we also infer that the Crowd appears to have a better ability to evaluate the word-of-web effect than Experts.

We note that the highest Crowd evaluation was for the Oscar-nominated movie, *The Blind Side*, which was also amongst the top 10 films in terms of domestic box office revenues in 2009[26] (number 21 worldwide[27]) with a second-weekend increase based on positive word-of-mouth of +18 percent.[28] In fact, the success of this movie was so unexpected that some investors were left puzzling over a question that has not often troubled the movie business lately: what went right? (Cieply and Schwartz, 2010). The highest Experts' evaluation was for the movie *Pirate Radio*, which, after its commercial failure at the British box office, was re-edited to trim its running time by twenty minutes, retitled *Pirate Radio* (the original title was *The Boat That Rocked*) and its trailer embellished. Despite this, the US box office was still a market failure (production budget only: $50 million; worldwide revenue: $37 million) with a drop in box-office receipts from opening to second weekend based on negative word-of-mouth of –49.7 percent.[29] We also note that the Crowd and Experts agreed on the worst movie *Transylmania*, also listed as one of the top 5 all-time worst opening-weekend gross receipts for a wide release movie (number 3).[30] Accordingly, the Crowd seems to be equally capable of correctly evaluating market success and market failure whereas our Experts (i.e. movie critics) seem to be better at evaluating the latter. Finally, it is important to note that even though we were not able to compare our worldwide box office results with our domestic box office results (in some instances movies did not go to the foreign market), the correlation between the Crowd's evaluations and worldwide receipts (0.77) is highly significant as well as being even better than Experts' (0.07).

CONCLUSION

Because audience reaction is unpredictable, the movie industry tries to find ways to attract the audience with similar recipes that worked before, or by using new technological trends, and sometimes a combination of both. But in the end, what matters is content. Even with the 3D effect (supposing the movie industry will offer all movies in 3D), audiences will still need an attractive content that will make them laugh, cry and get immersed in the movie – a content audiences will find worth spreading across multiple social media platforms as part of a marketing campaign. But how to make sure that a movie will be appealing to audiences in the first place, not only before spending millions of dollars, but also before moviegoers start to quickly spread negative word-of-web, and by doing so shatter the chance of the movie's success before it gets to market?

Via our theoretical analysis based on real case studies, we conclude that using crowd-wisdom to evaluate and generate ideas before risking high investment, market failure and negative word-of-web – what we call 'crowd-wisdom strategy' – is the best strategy to date. In 2009, when our self-selected participants evaluated each trailer a few weeks before opening weekend, and after correlating these evaluations with opening weekend receipts (0.79 correlation) and four weeks later (0.74 correlation), we provide proof-of-concept that crowd-wisdom pertaining to new-product ideas evaluation is highly valuable – even better than Experts' evaluations. More surprisingly, we find that the Crowd was not fooled by expensive marketing tools (i.e. trailers) and consequently that the idea of using an expensive marketing tool to attract customers early after the release of a non-attractive new product is not an effective strategy.

In 2013, Google confirmed the Crowd's ability for idea evaluation with its 'Quantifying Movie Magic' (Chen and Panaligan, 2013). Although Google's advice is to use crowd-wisdom to adjust marketing campaigns, we can't help but wonder: why spend more money to adjust a marketing campaign in order to sell a non-appealing movie given that the movie industry can use crowd-wisdom to co-create value in the first place? In 2006, because of a few relatively minor changes during post-production based on the use of crowd-wisdom on ideas generation, *Snakes on a Plane*, a B-movie, actually turned a profit even though opinion leaders featured it as a box office disappointment (Waxman, 2006; Rich, 2006). What nobody mentioned, though, is what the movie might have been without the integration of idea-generation from the Crowd.

In 2010, as a first step toward studying the value of the crowd-wisdom strategy during the creation process of a short movie, we find proof-of-concept that after co-creation the market value of the movie is significantly improved. In this study, 700 participants were involved in a 'co-creation process', that is, the Crowd's idea-evaluation and idea-generation pertaining to a short movie coupled with design changes by the creative team. We used crowd-wisdom in two different ways to evaluate the value of each movie-design-element *before* and *after* co-creation. Panel 1 (the biased Crowd) generated new ideas for each movie design element and then evaluated them after the co-creation process. Panel 2 (the unbiased Crowd) only evaluated each movie design element *after* the co-creation process. In this way the Crowd in Panel 2 offers an unbiased evaluation of the Panel 1 Crowd's contribution to the co-creation process (Escoffier and McKelvey, 2011). To conclude, we argue that (1) using crowd-wisdom for idea evaluation to test if companies have an appealing product and, if not, then (2) using crowd-wisdom for idea-generation to help companies improve its market value before high investment is an efficient long-term strategy to create a low-risk original product. In addition, by asking the Crowd to participate in product design, a firm also takes advantage of positive word-of-web since the Crowd becomes an advocate of the product (which is the main argument for using the sequel strategy). However, we strongly suggest that managers genuinely use crowd-wisdom strategy to co-create market value in the first place as opposed to only using the Crowd as marketers.

Even though we offer proof-of-concept that the Crowd is wise when evaluating ideas, David Leonhardt (Washington bureau chief of the *New York Times*) announced in the *New York Times* in 2012 that the Crowd isn't wise when it predicted on 'Intrade', an online real-world-events prediction market, that the Supreme Court will rule Obama's health-care law unconstitutional (Leonhardt, 2012). This same online 'prediction market', where each member of the crowd can trade on real-world events and tap into the wisdom of crowds, was a more reliable guide to the 2006 mid-term election than cable networks. On election night, its odds showed that the Democrats had become the favorites to retake the Senate, while television commentators were still telling viewers it was unlikely.

So what happened? Could it be, as Leonhardt argues, that 'if the circle of people who possess information is small enough – as with the selection of a Vice President or a Pope or a decision by the Supreme Court – the Crowd may not have much wisdom to impart?' Or could it be that in an open-source prediction market people are biased by others' decisions and therefore the Crowd does not reach the correct result (and this is prob-ably the reason why Threadless now hides the number of votes during the evaluation process)? Or could it be that an open-source prediction market generates a signal about a market to customers telling them what is the right choice but when the final decision is not theirs (e.g. a decision by the Supreme Court) the decision maker has no basis and no interest in reflecting the Crowd's wisdom, thereby making the Crowd appear unwise?

The best answer now is that the Crowd, randomly created, is really good at reflecting the interests and preferences of *a crowd*, that is, a large randomly selected population. It cannot be expected to guess what a small group of decision makers are apt to conclude. Crowd-wisdom is, thus, inappropriately applied to most auction markets where a Court, a political group, a sports team, or an un-randomly selected set of people makes a decision.

Additionally in our study, we used a large group of self-selected online participants sharing common interests representing the Crowd, but we can't help but wonder if, by using the same Crowd sample over and over,

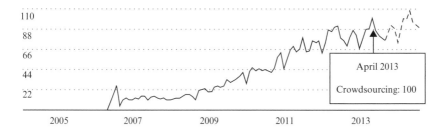

Source: http://www.google.com/trends/.

Figure 11.3   *Web search interest worldwide, 2004–present: crowdsourcing*

would the sample become experts, thinking more and more alike, and therefore lose its wisdom? We argued earlier that a community is what emerges from the Crowd when it participates more actively on a regular basis. By doing so, would the community be less and less representative of the Crowd and therefore biased and less objective? Would the community become more like the Experts and therefore less accurate than the Crowd?

Crowdsourcing is becoming increasingly important in our everyday lives (see Figure 11.3).

As a citizen, we now know that the FBI's Boston field office initiated an unprecedented crowdsourcing manhunt to help the FBI solve the Boston marathon tragedy (Seelye et al., 2013). As a user, what do we do if we want to make sure to have a good time eating in a restaurant (Yelp), reading a book (Amazon), traveling (TripAdvisor), or watching a movie (Netflix)? As a manager, some well-known traditional companies use crowd-wisdom via crowdsourcing to help them create appealing products, for example, BMW, Fiat and Lego. Frito Lay used the Crowd to make the best Super Bowl commercial. We hope that this chapter can be used to: (1) convince the movie industry to use *crowd-wisdom strategy* versus *sequel strategy* to reduce market failure; and (2) to convince academics to contribute future research in what we believe to be a very interesting, promising and value-adding research area. Imagine a new economy where economic agents would go from online-project to online-project according to some personal motivation where he/she can invest, co-create, and get a profit-percentage out of it, and then move to the next project. This kind of online agent becomes a new type of creative shareholder.

Instead of asking after the fact what went wrong, such as in the example of *Mars Needs Moms*, or what went right, such as in the example of *The Blind Side*, why not ask the Crowd in the first place? After all: the best way to predict the future is to co-create it. . .with the Crowd!

NOTES

1. Since most people do not use their mouse any more when using laptops, tablets and smartphones, the authors wanted to update the expression 'word-of-mouse' to either 'word-of-touch' or 'word-of-web'; after a quick crowdsourcing test we ended up choosing 'word-of-web'.
2. MPAA (2007), 'Theatrical Market Statistics'.
3. Boxofficemojo.com (2007), 'Pirates of the Caribbean 3'.
4. MPAA (2007), 'Theatrical Market Statistics'.
5. MPAA (2012), 'Theatrical Market Statistics'.
6. Boxofficemojo.com (2011), 'Mars Needs Moms'.
7. For our data about sequels versus originals: Boxofficemojo.com adjusted for inflation.
8. For our data about sequels: Boxofficemojo.com and Imdbpro.com adjusted for inflation.
9. Boxofficemojo.com (2013), 'Biggest Second Weekend Drops'.
10. Boxofficemojo.com (2013), 'Smallest Second Weekend Drops'.
11. Alexa.com (2013), 'The Top 500 Sites on the Web'.
12. BMW Group (2010), 'Idea Contest'.
13. BMW Group (2010), 'Idea Contest Jury Statements Jörg Reimann'.
14. BMW Group (2013), 'Trunk Idea Contest'.
15. Doritos 'Crash the Super Bowl'.
16. USA Today (2007), 'How all the ads ranked in USA TODAY's Super Bowl Ad Meter'.
17. Santa Barbara Arts TV YouTube Partner Global News (2009), 'Funniest Doritos Commercial Doritos Crystal Ball'.
18. USA Today (2009), '21st Annual Super Bowl Ad Meter Results'.
19. US Today (2012), 'USA TODAY Facebook Super Bowl Ad Meter Scores'.
20. Threadless.com 'Submit a Design'.
21. Comments are visible but the number of votes is hidden during the evaluation process.
22. Threadless.com (2013), 'The NPR Challenge: Sound World'.
23. Metacritic.com.
24. Boxofficemojo.com.
25. Boxofficemojo.com (2013), 'Biggest Second Weekend Drops'.
26. Boxofficemojo.com (2009), 'Total Grosses of all Movies Released'.
27. Boxofficemojo.com (2009), 'Worldwide Grosses'.
28. Boxofficemojo.com (2009), 'November 27–29 Weekend'.
29. Boxofficemojo.com (2009), 'November 20–22 Weekend'.
30. Boxofficemojo.com 'Worst Wide 600+ Openings'.

REFERENCES

Allen, A.S. (2012), 'Has Hollywood lost its way?', *Short of the Week*, available at: http://www.shortoftheweek.com/2012/01/05/has-hollywood-lost-its-way/ (accessed 5 January 2012).
Barnes, B. (2008), 'What's big and green, and desperate to be a hit all over?', *New York Times*, available at: http://www.nytimes.com/2008/04/10/movies/10hulk.html (accessed 10 April 2008).
Barnes, B. (2011), 'Many culprits in fall of a family film', *The New York Times*, available at: http://www.nytimes.com/2011/03/15/business/media/15mars.html (accessed 14 March 2011).
Baumeister, R., E. Bratslavsky, C. Findenauer and K. Vohs (2001), 'Bad is stronger than good', *Review of General Psychology*, **5** (4), 323–70.

Boroush, M. (2010), 'NSF releases new statistics on business innovation', *Science Resources Statistics*, National Science Foundation (NSF) 11–300.

Burge, R. (2007), 'Using crowd power for R&D', *Wired*, available at: http://www.wired.com/techbiz/media/news/2007/07/crowdsourcing_diversity (accessed 13 July 2007).

Chafkin, M. (2008), 'The customer is the company', *Inc. Magazine*, available at: http://www.inc.com/magazine/20080601/the-customer-is-the-company.html (accessed 1 June 2008).

Chen, A. and R. Panaligan (2013), 'Quantifying movie magic with Google search', Google White Paper, Industry Perspectives + User Insights, available at: http://ssl.gstatic.com/think/docs/quantifying-movie-magic_research-studies.pdf (accessed June 2013).

Chmielewski, D.C. and S. Zeitchik (2013), 'After "Lone Ranger", Disney may not be willing to take risks', *Los Angeles Times*, available at: http://articles.latimes.com/2013/jul/09/entertainment/la-et-ct-lone-ranger-20130709 (accessed 9 July 2013).

Cieply, M. and P. Schwartz (2010), '"Blind Side" finds a path to the Oscars by running up the middle', *New York Times*, available at: http://www.nytimes.com/2010/02/06/movies/awardsseason/06blind.html (accessed 5 February 2010).

De Vany, A. (2004), *Hollywood Economics*, New York: Routledge.

Dobuzinskis, A. (2009), 'Movie studios try to harness Twitter effect', *Reuters edition US*, available at: http://www.reuters.com/article/2009/07/17/us-twitter-studios-idUSTRE56G74H20090717 (accessed 17 July 2009).

Elberse, A. and B. Anand (2006), 'Advertising and expectations: The effectiveness of pre-release advertising for motion pictures', *Harvard Business School Working Paper Series*, No. 05–060.

Escoffier, N. and B. McKelvey (2011), 'How Using Crowd-Wisdom Co-creates Value in New Product Development Processes', Working paper, UCLA Anderson School, Los Angeles, CA.

Galton, F. (1907), 'Vox Populi', *Nature*, **75** (1949), 450–51.

Goldman, W. (1983), *Adventures in the Screen Trade*, New York: Warner Books.

Howard, T. (2005), '"Viral" advertising spreads through marketing plans', *USA Today*, available at: http://www.usatoday.com/money/advertising/2005-06-22-viral-usat_x.htm (accessed 22 June 2005).

Howe, J. (2006), 'Crowdsourcing: A definition', *Wired*, available at: http://www.wired.com/wired/archive/14.06/crowds.html (accessed 14 June 2006).

Howe, J. (2008), *Crowdsourcing: Why the Power of the Crowd is driving the Future of Business*, New York: Three Rivers Press.

Kerr, P. (2010), 'Innovative companies perform better, survey shows', *Business Scoop*, available at: http://www.scoop.co.nz/stories/BU1007/S00173/innovative-companies-perform-better-survey-shows.htm (accessed 6 July 2010).

Leonhardt, D. (2012), 'When the crowd isn't wise', *The New York Times*, available at: http://www.nytimes.com/2012/07/08/sunday-review/when-the-crowd-isnt-wise.html (accessed 7 July 2012).

Lumenick, L. (2011), '"Mars needs Moms" a megaton bomb', *New York Post*, available at: http://archive.is/b9lX (accessed 13 March 2011).

Marr, M. (2007), 'DreamWorks reboots for life beyond Shrek', *Wall Street Journal*, available at: http://online.wsj.com/news/articles/SB116952241779384587 (accessed 23 January 2007).

Ogawa, S. and F.T. Piller (2006), 'Reducing the risks of new product development', *Sloan Management Review*, **47** (2), 65–71.

Prahalad, C.K. and V. Ramaswamy (2000), 'Co-opting customer competence', *Harvard Business Review*, **78** (1), 79–87.

Prahalad, C.K. and V. Ramaswamy (2004), *The Future of Competition: Co-Creating Unique Value with Customers*, Boston: Harvard Business School Press.

Rich, J. (2006), 'Oh Sssssnap!' *Entertainment Weekly*, available at: http://archive.is/fQasF (accessed 20 August 2006).

Rozin, P. and E. Royzman (2001), 'Negativity bias, negativity dominance and contagion', *Personality and Social Psychology Review*, **5** (4), 296–320.

Seelye, K., M. Cooper and M. Schmidt (2013), 'F.B.I. posts images of pair suspected in Boston attack', *New York Times*, available at: http://www.nytimes.com/2013/04/19/us/fbi-releases-video-of-boston-bombing-suspects.html (accessed 19 April 2013).

Sood, S. and X. Dreze (2006), 'Brand extensions of experimental goods: Movie sequel evaluations', *Journal of Consumer Research*, **33** (3), 352–60.

Surowiecki, J. (2004), *The Wisdom of Crowds*, New York: Doubleday.

Terdiman, D. (2005), 'Marketers feverish over viral ads', *Wired*, available at: http://www.wired.com/techbiz/media/news/2005/03/66960 (accessed 22 March 2005).

Uzzi, B., S.B. Soderstrom and D. Diermeier (2008), 'Hollywood buzzonomics: From what's said to what's seen', paper presented at the Academy of Management Conference, Anaheim, CA.

Von Hippel, E. (1976), 'The dominant role of users in the scientific instrument innovation process', *Research Policy*, **5** (3), 212–39.

Waxman, S. (2006), 'After hype online, "Snakes on a Plane" is letdown at box office', *New York Times*, available at: http://www.nytimes.com/2006/08/21/movies/21box.html (accessed 21 August 2006).

Zarrella, D. (2007), 'Examples of viral marketing campaigns', *The Social Media Scientist*, available at: http://danzarrella.com/examples-of-viral-marketing-campaigns.html (accessed 4 February 2009).

12. Crowd-sourcing and the evolution of the microstock photography industry: the case of iStockphoto and Getty Images

Robert DeFillippi, Pat Hunt, Colette Dumas and Ken Hung

OVERVIEW OF THEORETICAL ARGUMENT AND DATA SOURCES

Theoretically, this chapter will argue that the changes that have occurred in stock photography constitute a digital disruption of the industry and have transformed its practices for content acquisition, content editing and contributor transaction and relationship management. The primary innovation that will be the focus of our chapter concerns practices associated with crowd-sourcing of content acquisition and content editing. A related theme will be an historical overview of the evolution of business models (including rights management and pricing) and how these have transformed the relationship between content contributors and stock agencies such as Getty Images. The chapter concludes with implications of these transformations for the industry and Getty Images.

Data for this chapter is derived from both primary and secondary sources. A set of interviews with seven members of senior management of Getty Images conducted between February and April 2013 served as a primary data source. The managers interviewed were executives responsible for strategy and business development, product development, contributor relations, creative content and content editing.

INTRODUCTION TO THE STOCK PHOTOGRAPHY INDUSTRY

The industry of photography has been around since the mid-1800s. It can be argued that some forms of stock photography go back to the 1930s, but stock imagery, as we know it today, began to burgeon in the 1970s, with the revamping of the United States Copyright Law and the new popularity of color printing. Also, the advent of Federal Express brought overnight shipping in the United States, which sped up transactions in the industry. By the 1990s, with the advent of the Internet and digital imaging, most photography, as it was previously known, was about to change forever.

The words 'stock photography' refer to the use of pre-produced still or video imagery for use in general publishing. Over the years, a large body of work has been created from many sources to serve the needs of advertisers, book and magazine publishers, marketing needs and public relations use. From billboards to television shows, this type of imagery has served as a basis for illustrating many of the image needs for the industry.

Over the last two decades, central players to this distribution of imagery have been Getty Images, launched with Getty family funds, and Corbis Images, one of the Bill Gates enterprises. The imagery was submitted to these distributors who, in turn, licensed it for use and paid a percentage of revenue back to the creator and copyright holder. Midway through the first decade of the twenty-first century (about 2005), there began a distinction between imagery that was sourced by professional photographers (macrostock) and licensed at higher price points, versus imagery sourced by 'the crowd' (general public) and licensed at lower price points (microstock). Over time, the quality of the crowd-sourced imagery has improved, increasing competitive pressure on traditional professional suppliers who traditionally invested more heavily in pre-production planning, image production and post-production cleaning, keywording and distribution. However, the microstock business model purports to have opened a whole new body of clientele (Vandeberg, 2013).

This chapter examines the impact of digital technology developments and their usage by participants in the microstock photography industry to crowd-source new sources of creative content, new relationships between content suppliers and Getty Images and new online platforms for business and social engagement between content providers and Getty Images.

GETTY IMAGES INTRODUCTION

Getty Images describes itself as a visual content provider and major supplier of creative stock and editorial still and moving image and illustrations, as well as music. It also offers photo services for corporate clients. The company targets four main markets: advertising and graphic design firms; editorial organizations, such as newspapers, magazines and online publishers; corporate communications departments; and film and broadcast producers (Getty Images, 2013).

By 2012, Getty Images employed more than 550 sales staff and 110 full-time staff photographers with offices in 22 countries and delivered over 230 million images per annum directly to its customers located in more than 200 countries. It worked with more than 150000 contracted content contributors, including 300 image partners (Klein, 2012).

DIGITAL TECHNOLOGY DRIVERS OF STOCK PHOTOGRAPHY VALUE CHAIN DISRUPTION AND TRANSFORMATION

Observers of trends in the stock photography industry have identified several important drivers of the transformation in the industry's value chain practices for content creation, acquisition and dissemination (Puscher, 2011). Foremost was the digital revolution in photographic hardware, software and advances in Internet-based communications, connectivity (community) and commerce (e.g. Angus and Thelwall, 2010; Frosh, 2003; Rubinstein and Sluis, 2008). The technology revolution in photographic equipment from analog to professional-quality digital SLR cameras had two important consequences. One was to lower the costs of hardware for taking high quality images. This resulted in a massive increase in the sheer quantity of imagery (iStockphoto, 2013). The second and related effect of advances in digital photography was to lower the skill required to create a quality image.

A second technology revolution was the creation of photo editing digital software that enabled amateur photographers to autonomously create their own collections of imagery for digital display. The third technology revolution was the development of file-sharing software, which, coupled with increasing availability of broadband access to the Internet, enabled the sharing of high-quality, large-size image files. The last trend was enabled by the emergence of online communities based on commonality of interest. Microstock websites such as iStockphoto and social media and storage platforms such as Flickr made it possible for geographically diffuse amateurs to share photographic techniques and gain feedback on photos quickly and easily (Angus and Thelwall, 2010).

Subsequently, the nature of the photography supply chain was transformed. The pre-crowd-sourced and pre-digital microstock value chain had been largely composed of professional photographers with specialized equipment, skills and access to the marketplace through their editors. The emerging crowd-sourced and digital microstock value chain was one in which sources of supply were much more numerous and composed of a mix of professional and amateur photographers who had direct online access to the marketplace through the web posting of their imagery. These transformations in the stock photography industry have been characterized as an example of industry transformation through disruptive innovation (Christensen, 2000, p.xxv). The stock photography industry's value chain structure was to be radically disrupted and transformed in a manner that would create new business opportunities for some players in the industry, for example content aggregators such as Getty Images and Corbis, and micro sites such as iStockphoto (acquired by Getty Images in 2006) and Shutterstock. These transformations and the associated expansion of available imagery would also pose significant business threats to traditional suppliers (professional photographers and other image archives). The stock photography industry discussion to follow elaborates on this history of industry disruption and transformation. We conclude this theoretic overview with a discussion of crowd-sourcing practices and their early implementation by iStockphoto.

EARLY CROWD-SOURCING PRACTICES IN STOCK PHOTOGRAPHY: THE CASE OF iSTOCKPHOTO

Crowd-sourcing is defined as 'the act of a company or institution taking a function once performed by employees and outsourcing it to an undefined (and generally large) network of people in the form of an *open call*' (Howe, 2006). As Howe states, crowd-sourcing is 'an umbrella term for a highly varied group of approaches that share one obvious attribute in common: they all depend on some contribution from the crowd. But the nature of those contributions can differ tremendously' (Howe, 2008, p.280). The technology advances in digital communication and web-based connectivity have made it possible for any organization or individual to broadcast a call for content and to receive this content and assess, select and aggregate that content for subsequent dissemination to prospective users of the content.

An early example of crowd-sourcing in stock photography is the 1998 creation of iStockphoto by Bruce Livingstone, who was trying to market

CD-ROMs of imagery for the traditional stock photographic market. He realized he did not have enough funding to go to market, so he closed the doors and started a website to give away all the images free of charge. He started with a list of people who gave him their emails and personal addresses so they could download, free of charge, the 2000-image collection. About six months later the list was getting very large. Other designers and photographers wanted to share the photographs they were taking and suggested that he start a swapping site. From 2000 to 2001, he invented a credit system where everyone had an account. When someone downloaded an image from an account, that person gained a credit, and when he/she downloaded someone else's images a credit was owed. It was a sharing system, and there was no money involved until 2002, when they could no longer afford the bandwidth bill. 'We started charging a quarter per download and raised the price every year. It took off from there' (Hunt, 2009, p. 2).

In 2002, iStockphoto began selling credits for a high-quality image for under a dollar, and the visual artist (i.e. photographer) who contributed it was paid a royalty. As the volume of inventory increased, and as iStockphoto advertised itself widely, more buyers and contributors came on board. The business model did, in fact, cater to a very price sensitive group of buyers who had not accessed imagery before. The lower prices also began to attract certain buyers who previously had paid higher prices for stock photography.

iStockphoto thus created the template for a new crowd-sourced microstock photography industry segment, with tens of thousands of visual artists contributing their photographs, illustrations and videos to microstock websites such as iStockphoto (owned by Getty Images), Shutterstock and Dreamstime. The basic idea of the microstock photo file-sharing sites was that anyone, anywhere, could join these sites free of charge, find the digital media they needed and sell original content of their own (iStockphoto, 2012).

Howe (2006) claimed that iStockphoto had created a marketplace for amateur photographers to have their work made available to net-savvy buyers accustomed to shopping online for quality at the lowest possible price. Howe (2006) focused on the disruptive impact of the influx of so-called crowd labor of amateurs on the stock imagery prices, which were lowered from perhaps $500 per image for high-end stock imagery to $1.00 per image from crowd-sourced content. Howe's (2008) book on crowd-sourcing examined in more detail the nature of the iStockphoto contributor online community of 50 000 part-time photographers and artists, of whom less than 10 percent earned enough from iStockphoto to live on. The incentives for participation were characterized as originally based on a gift exchange (the so-called credit system).

Howe (2008) also emphasized the important ways in which iStockphoto touched its community by offering free tutorials, discussion forums and other means for community members to improve their photographic craft. Additionally, iStockphoto provided targeted communications to its iStockphoto contributors and solicited their input on specific policy changes the company would periodically consider. Moreover, iStockphoto convened so-called iStockalypses – invitational photo shooting sessions in which iStockphoto (and subsequently Getty Images) would provide attractive venues, professional models and directorial guidance to iStockphoto community members who paid a fee to attend these sessions but who could subsequently earn royalties from their shooting sessions. However, Howe (2008) emphasized that the primary motivation for these photo gatherings was to provide opportunities for online members to meet and learn from each other while practicing their craft. Subsequently, iStockphoto members self-organized their own photo gatherings (minilypses) to expand the opportunities for face-to-face meetings among iStockphoto community members.

Brabham (2008) surveyed the iStockphoto community membership and drew two conclusions: this community was composed primarily of white, married, middle- to upper-class, higher educated, 30-somethings, working in so-called 'white collar' jobs with a high-speed Internet connection in their homes. Moreover, the prospect of earning income was the most frequently listed motive for participating in iStockphoto (90 percent), closely followed by the motives of improving their photographic craft (79 percent), serving as a creative outlet (76 percent) and having fun (72 percent). Brabham concluded that monetary incentives were the dominant driver of iStockphoto member contributions. Brabham reported that about 80 percent of iStockers found their work at iStockphoto to be at least somewhat profitable, and 17.8 percent considered their iStockphoto work extremely profitable.

Zupic (2013) offered an historical interpretation of stock photo community membership incentives in his broader stock photo industry study. This study utilized a Netnography analysis of web discussion forum posts on four major microstock companies (iStockphoto, Shutterstock, Dreamstime and Fotolia) for the period 2005–12 supplemented by 23 in-depth interviews with stock photography industry insiders: microstock photographers, industry analysts, buyers and company employees. Zupic found that the early days of stock photography (i.e. the early days of iStockphoto) attracted photographers for the fun of sharing photos and improving their craft. Non-monetary incentives were vital at the beginning when the microstock business model had no legitimacy among professional photographers and most of the contributors were amateurs. As the model matured, the bulk of sales went to professionals and these professionals came to view microstock photo agencies such as iStockphoto as a legitimate channel for the sale of their stock imagery and a source of professional income.

The following section on the history of the microstock photography industry and Getty Images' role in this industry illustrates the challenging twists and turns in creating viable business models for participants in the emerging microstock photography industry and the opportunities and threats this industry evolution has posed for its participants.

EVOLUTION OF STOCK IMAGERY AND GETTY IMAGES

The stock photography business functioned in a different world in the mid 1990s. This was an era in transition, with the advent of digital technology in the capture of pictures, and the birth of the World Wide Web to be used as a business and marketing tool. Because of business visionaries who saw opportunity in this burgeoning market, the traditional stock agencies began to consolidate from a disparate group of agents, personally representing artists and photographers, to a few large players, such as Visual Communications Group in London and Index Stock Imagery, Getty Images and Corbis Images in the United States (Pickerell, 1996a).

The photographers who supplied visual content to these agents started to experience less personal attention, longer and more complicated contracts, and standardization of their business models. The view into the future showed that, with digitization and the Internet, the costs involved in going to market and access to imagery would go down, along with the pricing to sell the use of the images. The volume of imagery available to the market would go exponentially up.

The transition years of the 1990s saw large amounts of investment capital to foster these changes. New and constantly upgraded computer equipment, the scanning of imagery and the build out of T1 lines (carrying data at high speeds) and bandwidth infrastructure entailed a vast amount of venture capital investment. The time invested in each individual contributor to the supply chain was about to change forever.

One of the major marketing tools for agents and photographers up until this transition had been a variety of printed catalogs. A select number of images would be picked out as potential best sellers. They would be placed in catalogs and sent to the large commercial buyers' list. The first digital products to arrive on the scene were CD-ROM disks, offering from 100 to 1000 images in low resolution for a set CD purchase fee. A number of photographers would receive a percentage of each disk sold, creating the first low cost-per-image return for those photographers. This was the first iteration of the high-volume, low-cost imagery business model that was to portend the future (Pickerell, 1996b).

By 1994, about one sixth of the stock photo sales made in the United States were from photo disks. In the early stages of the development of the clip disk market, as it was called, producers argued that they were seeking new users of stock photography. They said their disks would have little or no impact on the traditional stock photography market. This is the same mantra that was to be heard a decade later with the advent and growth of microstock photography.

In 1995, Getty images launched a subscription service. It was argued then that the images in that service would not compete with their other Royalty Free (RF) offerings (Royalty Free was the new way for pricing digital imagery that demanded no 'rights' tracking and sold by file size). This subscription pricing remained a long-standing threat to suppliers' incomes as pricing models began to experience continued changes (Pickerell, 1996c). So what were the image suppliers really earning in the 1990s? In a 1998 survey conducted by Jim Pickerell of Selling Stock, 35 percent of the respondents to his survey claimed to earn over $70 000 in 1997 (Pickerell, 1998a).

By 1998, the trend in Royalty Free sales was going up. According to Pickerell, 'Royalty free imagery is the fastest growing segment of the stock photo market. I estimate the entire market for stock photography was about $1 billion in 1997 and roughly 10% of that went to purchase royalty free products.' (Pickerell, 1999b). The advent of the RF pricing model caused much controversy at the beginning of the digital age, as the prices for file sizes seemed to be much lower than in the past pricing under the Rights Managed (RM) pricing, and the image usage was not limited to any parameters after the image purchase. In July of 1998, Graphic Design USA reported that 60 percent of creative professionals were using RF imagery (Pickerell, 1998b). This was the era, also, of the beginning of the shrinking of the photojournalism industry. Magazines were firing their staff and cutting budgets, while they used the cheaper new wire images available because of digitization (Pickerell, 1998c).

Jim Pickerell observed in 1998, 'Note the significant amount of stock photos and clip art being bought. It used to be that stock photos were bought for a particular project only. Now beyond that use, whole collections are being bought! Images are now cheap and available enough for the mature, commodity category' (Pickerell, 1998e).

Improved transmission speeds over the Internet would soon eliminate this step. One of the benefits of the digital environment for photographs was the agents' ability to track more data on image sales to feed to the photographers so they could plan their production. Issues gaining in importance for both the agents and the photographers were the quality of keywording to find the digital images, and the proper use of model and property releases for those images.

By 1998, Jonathan Klein, CEO of Getty Images reported: 'The growth (of digital sales) is massive. At this point in time, we have just announced that in the third quarter, 34% of our sales were digital. That is a combination of CD-ROMs and on-line. The pure web commerce now accounts for more than 10% of our total sales, which this year will be about $185 million' (Pickerell, 1998d).

Statistics at the time were showing that between 120 and 150 million users were on the web in 1998, as compared to 57 million in 1994 (Pickerell, 1998e). By 1999, Getty Images was claiming that the stock photo industry was a $4 to $5 billion industry in terms of annual sales (Pickerell, 1999b). By 1999, Getty Images was reporting that 15 percent of their total sales were e-commerce sales (Pickerell, 1999a).

By the year 2000, the field of photography was growing and the average income for photographers, at over $91 000, was sustaining their businesses (Pickerell, 2000a). Their contracts with Getty Images were changing rapidly as Getty worked to integrate the companies they had purchased, including The Image Bank, RPG, The Telegraph Colour Library and VCG. The challenge came with the vast difference between the way the old agencies worked and the focus that Getty Images and Corbis Images visualized for the future. They believed in a business model of 100 percent digital delivery and all sales being e-commerce. There would be little room for analog imagery (film based), and unscanned images would not be viable.

By October of 2001, the stock photo industry in the US was in a recession, exacerbated by the events of September 11th. For Getty Images, e-commerce revenue in the quarter was $51.5 million, or 48 percent of total revenue, up from 35 percent of revenue in the 3rd quarter of 2000. Jonathan Klein reported that about one third of the revenue was represented by Royalty Free image sales. He also said that the company's goal was to eventually have a 50 to 60 percent market share. At this point, the Senior Vice President and Chief Financial Officer, Liz Huebner, stated: 'Prior to September 11th, we had already taken swift and decisive action to meet the economic challenges that we faced, reducing our worldwide staff by more than 300 people and cutting back on expenses throughout the organization.' (Pickerell, 2001).

The other explanation for growth was the introduction of gettyimages. com in October of 2001, with full functionality to purchase online and on account. None of the footage sales were yet to be available on e-commerce, as the bandwidths were not sufficient to deliver them online. Klein praised the migration from 'labor-intensive analog delivery to highly efficient e-commerce and digital delivery' (Pickerell, 2001).

CEO, Jonathan Klein, stated: 'In a sense there is an industry trend of RF becoming more powerful, and more palatable to customers as the quality of the imagery has improved over time. We are not going to buck that industry trend.' He also points out that:

> Getty no longer thinks of having RM or RF customers, or News or Sport imagery customers. Instead the customer groupings they now use are: Creative Professional, Editorial, Corporate, and Soho (Small office, home office) or Credit Card. All four of these categories need different kinds of imagery, different licensing and delivery methods, and often different price points.' (Pickerell, 2003)

By June of 2005, analyst Jim Pickerell made his next global assessment:

> There are basically three major companies in the industry – Getty Images, Corbis and Jupitermedia – with Getty far and away the industry leader. Getty's revenue for 2005 is expected to be in the range of $750 million.[. . .]Two other factors of interest are that the sales of RF discs have been declining relative to single image sales and, based on Getty Images figures, the average price of a single RF image license has risen over 100% since the summer of 2002. (Pickerell, 2005)

By February of 2006 the word was out – Getty Images had purchased iStockphoto for $50 million. iStockphoto's 2005 revenues were estimated to be between $5 and $8 million. At this point iStockphoto's usage fee was $1 per image. This means that they sold a lot more images than Getty's creative department of nearly 1.56 million. It was announced that the company would be allowed to continue to operate as a separate brand. At the beginning, in 2000, the site was created for designers to swap images free of charge. Shortly after, it moved to a credit system of $1 per image in order to afford the bandwidth. This system was called 'micropayment' and it was argued that:

> these price points are necessary to reach certain low end users and that there is little or no crossover between these users and the higher end buyers currently buying RF and RM images. Thus, the theory is that all the revenue generated through these micropayments will be add-on revenue and will not cannibalize in any way the existing market. Pickerell (2006a)

The unique element that iStockphoto brought to Getty Images was the use of social media. Through dialog, and education with sharing and blogs, this business model created new relationships with contributors that were unheard of in the past. The new implication for the advent of microstock at this point in time, was the possible competition that professional photographers would face with the advent of so many amateurs in the business.

Other trends that Getty Images was facing included new platforms such as the web and mobile use. In response to this trend, Getty Images lowered the prices for web use in 2007. They announced a new web-use price of $49 for a 500k 72 dpi file of any image. This was a significant lowering of some prices. It was expressed by Getty that it would capture a portion of the market that might be captured by microstock. Some photographers expressed dissatisfaction with this change. They noticed their revenue going down, their exposure waning, and their contact points with Getty Images getting more remote (Pickerell, 2007a and 2007b).

In mid-2007, Klein noted that Getty Images wanted to become a broad based digital media company. They were expanding into licensing music and growing their stock footage content. Their editorial division was expanding with growth in the sports arena and into the entertainment photography business. Getty Images also introduced another pricing model called Premium Access, which was a customizable subscription service. iStockphoto introduced premium content collections at higher pricing. 'I cannot overstate the importance of innovation to our company and for our industry', states Klein. 'We have driven almost every innovation in the history of this business. Innovation remains key to our leadership in the marketplace and will help us to maintain and expand our lead. Now, 2006 was a good year of innovation, and I expect in 2007 to be significantly stronger' (Pickerell, 2006b). In 2006 Getty Images licensed over 600 000 RM images, and in 2008 iStockphoto licensed 25 million images.

Over this period, many traditional photographers were experiencing lower royalties. This was driven by continued shift toward RF from RM, RM usages moving away from higher priced traditional usages (e.g. print marketing) to lower priced digital usages (e.g. website) and increasing competition from new sources of imagery as crowd-sourced imagery improved. The issue for traditional photographers was the worry that they would no longer be able to cover their production costs.

By the fall of 2008, Getty Images was offering their royalty free (RF) imagery in various brand names and various price points. At the same time, some microstock companies were creating some image collections within their inventory to offer at a higher price point. The complexity for these companies was to determine the right price point and business model for the expanding volumes of imagery (Pickerell, 2008).

By the end of 2011, there were thought to be three main large image distributors left: Getty Images (Getty Images acquired Jupiter Images in 2009), Corbis Images and Alamy.

By the end of 2012, post-pay systems were thought to be a serious business model of the future:

> Payments may be in fractions of a penny per view. Instead of refusing to let your work be seen unless someone is willing to pay a premium price, the new goal will be to post your work in as many places as possible and encourage sharing. Payments would be based on such things as the number of times the image is shared, liked or actually viewed. It is those figures that will determine how much advertisers are willing to pay to have their advertising appear near your photographs. The amount the contributor received would be based on the advertising revenue generated. (Pickerell, 2012)

Aligned to this, by the beginning of 2012, Getty Images was offering an API called Connect that allowed businesses to directly access their search, metadata and download capability. This allowed Getty Images to make its content available in new business models to better align to new potential users of stock imagery (Pickerell, 2013a).

A quote from one of the global distributors in preparation for the 2013 CEPIC conference (European trade organization for picture archives) in Europe went: 'Photography, photographs, photographers are going to be needed within, at least, the next 25 years. I don't believe that motion (video) will ever substitute (fully) still photography. My best guess is that the motion market will grow and coexist with photography at 60/40 market split, 60% still images' (Pickerell, 2013b).

GETTY IMAGES CURRENT PRACTICES

The next section summarizes Getty Images' current sourcing practices, contributor relations and technology platforms for content acquisition and contributor relations. The data in this section is primarily based on interviews with seven members of senior management of Getty Images conducted between February and April 2013.

Getty Images Contributor Sourcing Practices

Getty Images' contributor sourcing practices may be usefully summarized in terms of the following two themes:

1. How does Getty Images source content (use of targeted versus crowd search processes)?

2. How does Getty Images assess creative content offerings and select content for promotion?

Sourcing (crowd and non-crowd) content
Getty Images currently produces none of its creative content in-house (no in-sourcing). Instead, there are four tiers or types of content contributors and Getty's creative suppliers from all tiers number well over 100 000 on a global basis (see Figure 12.1). Getty has exclusive contributors and non-exclusive contributors. 'Non-exclusive contributor' means that the imagery from a provider can be marketed through other distributors that compete with Getty Images. Exclusive contributors offer them imagery that cannot be placed with other distributors. Exclusive contributors receive greater contact and help from Getty Images, as they offer a product that is exclusive to Getty Images.

The first two tiers are non-crowd-based content suppliers. The first level consists of professional photographers, who typically make a living in the world from photography as their primary focus. Their content offerings are utilized in Getty Images' higher-end, higher-priced offerings. These are a group of 10 000 individuals on a worldwide basis.

The second tier consists of image partners. One type of image partner consists of groupings of contributors coming together to aggregate their resources more efficiently, for example Blend Images. A second type of

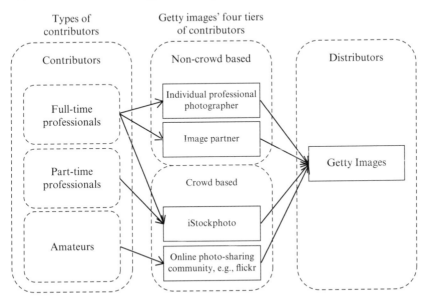

Figure 12.1   Getty Images' supply chain

image partner consists of companies that produce unique content, or the stock content is a by-product of their content production, for example Lonely Planet.

The next two content suppliers represent crowd-based suppliers. The first tier consists of iStockphoto contributors who are a mixed community of full-time professional and part-time professional or non-professional photographers. The fourth and newest tier of content suppliers consists of online photo-sharing communities, such as Flickr, which consists primarily of amateurs.

A key challenge Getty Images faces in managing its array of content suppliers is how much resource and technical service support to provide the contributor in developing its imagery. A general Getty Images policy appears to be to offer the most resource and service support to those content contributors who have exclusive relations with Getty Images. Getty Images invests in identifying photographic talent whose aesthetic style and imagery matches emerging needs in specific market niches. This predisposes Getty Images to seeking sources within its photographic and image partner tiers with proven track records of success in responding to these specialized niches. Another form of resource support is in the assessment and editing of content, which is described below.

Assessing (in-house and crowd editing) content contributions

Getty Images employs an internal team of about 60 individuals for in-source editing for Getty Images but it also engages approximately 250 external editing resources (called inspectors or curators) for crowd-sourced editing of iStockphoto and Flickr imagery. Getty Images utilizes its best internal editor resources for the highest value content imagery that will be premium content made available in high-end collections of imagery. Getty Images applies a more limited amount of internal editing resources and a lot of crowd-sourcing to the other sources of content, particularly its crowd-sourced content. However, some crowd-sourced content is high end. By contrast, the rest of iStockphoto is edited by approximately 120 inspectors, who go through that imagery (interview with Craig Peters). Similarly, Flickr's collections are edited by more than 120 curators composed of Flickr contributors selected and trained by Getty Images editing staff (interview with Andrew Saunders). In the curator model, Getty Images recruits the best Flickr photographers to be curators and Getty Images manages them by communicating what Getty Images is seeking in imagery and relying on the curators to educate others in the Flickr community (interview with Paul Foster). Curating is perceived as a lighter touch (lighter guidance in review and selection) than inspection and Flickr's curators receive less training and guidance from Getty Images than iStockphoto's inspectors.

Contributor Relations Management (Touch) at Getty Images

Getty Images Contributor Relations is summarized as tiered evaluation and support of individual contributors otherwise known as touch issues, and crowd-sourced and targeted relationships. Touch issues involve motivational support, promoting trust and commitment, and providing guidance in navigating changes in the business. Crowd-sourced and targeted relationships involve balancing business needs and creative communities' expectations while managing changes in the business. Using these two themes, we will examine Getty Images' contributor relations, and identify challenges associated with contributor relationship management practices.

Tiered evaluation and motivational support of individual creative content suppliers (touch issues)

Getty Images categorizes content contributors as either non-crowd-based content suppliers or crowd-based suppliers. Non-crowd-based suppliers are either referred to as professional photographers or image partners, and are classified by Getty Images as either exclusive or non-exclusive contributors. Crowd-based suppliers are either iStockphoto or Flickr suppliers. Top contributors are identified as photographers who can provide the creative content that Getty Images needs. Most valued are those whose aesthetic style and imagery matches emerging needs in specific niche markets. This is closely connected to Getty Images' revenue generation potential so earnings for content providers are commensurate with their ability to deliver needed content.

Contracts and agreements are determined through a standard set of parameters established by Getty Images. Touch requires creativity by the Director of Contributor Relations and staff to help contributors produce desired content. Getty Images provides a higher level of support for its consistently active contributors to help them solve problems to get desired creative content. Editors work with contributors with demonstrated potential to produce desired images, and Art Directors help with the photo shoot, casting and wardrobe. The Director of Contributor Relations keeps creative contributors motivated to continue to supply Getty Images with needed content. Given the continuous changes at Getty Images and in the business, maintaining creative content contributors' motivation is challenging, yet key to Getty Images' success as it moves to the new Enterprise Submission Platform.

The democracy that existed between the company and its contributors has changed. While Getty Images still gives weight to contributor concerns, due to the sheer expansion in volume, contributors don't get the same attention once received. To maintain its competitive edge and given non-exclusive relationships, Getty Images cannot reveal to its providers its strategies or clarify the direction it is headed in. Claudia Micare, Director of Contributor Relations, notes: 'When you are talking iStockphoto in the forums, you are talking to the world. Yet they have to keep contributors' faith through "touch". Managing contributor relations shifts to creating a win–win scenario to maintain contributor trust and motivation.'

Micare acknowledges that as Getty Images seeks to better serve its customers by finding more effective ways to create content, the changes they need to make are hardest on their iStockphoto contributors. Contributors have less of a say in how things are done. Photographers often consider themselves to be artists, and business negotiations with Getty Images involve their artwork, bringing an emotional component to interactions in the relationship. That, with the predisposition of the large community to assert their influence over Getty Images, creates a challenging relationship. Micare explains,

> There will always be fees they think should be higher, or royalty percentages they think should be better – higher acceptance rates, relaxed rules around image requirements. There will be sparks or even mini-mutinies to contend with. Bottom line – (we) must be as transparent as possible, we must constantly remind members of the terms they signed. We never attempt to twist arms to bring a contributor over to our point of view. Instead, it is critical that (we) provide as much context as possible, as transparently as possible – making it clear that in the end it is what works for each individual.

Getty Images needs to be flexible unless flexibility conflicts with business objectives. Then they must educate contributors to understand the business context within which they are functioning.

Getty Images communicates with contributors through a contributor website, where they post information, news and a heavily used live forum for discussion. This allows the small team managing contributor relations to stay in touch with their many contributors.

Managing crowd-sourced and targeted relationships

The iStockphoto and Flickr communities are managed through forums and newsletters. iStockphoto started as a group of designers sharing images for their commercial projects, and requires more touch than Flickr, which started as a group of photo enthusiasts wanting to share their photos. To provide the touch needed, Getty Images offers iStockalypses (shooting parties). Participants interact with each other, conduct photo shoots and earn revenue. Socializing and networking, and meeting with Getty Images staff are the most popular parts of the iStockalypses. The Flickr community is more open to online forms of touch.

The iStockphoto and Flickr communities communicate differently because they are more involved with social media. Getty Images' relationship with these crowd-sourced partners has grown from their individual social media entities. At Flickr, Getty Images has a private group where they talk to their contributors. Largely Millennials, born between 1982 and the early 2000s, they are savvy about social media and technology. They came of age when new technology platforms created opportunity for crowd-sourced organizations like iStockphoto and Flickr, allowing Getty Images to use them as content providers. Millennials' expectations come from their experiences in online communities, rather than rules intrinsic to business relationships. They think the community view should dominate Getty Images' fundamental and contractually stated terms.

Contributor questions at Flickr and iStockphoto are grounded in their knowledge of the photography business. Millennials question how Getty Images manages the technology through which they crowd-source. Asserting themselves makes it challenging to manage Getty Images' expectations around technology. Crowd-sourced content providers don't see the big picture that Getty Images sees. Their different perspectives influence content providers' expectations and what they want done differently. Communities carry with them higher expectation of ownership, involvement and transparency. Millennials, accustomed to real-time gratification, expect real-time information on statistics such as the number of times their images have been viewed, and real-time answers to their questions in the forums. Millennials' expectations influence other generations, pushing the business to create real-time tools to manage contributors' needs and expectations. Otherwise, Getty Images runs the risk of becoming competitively disadvantaged in winning contributors.

Contributors' voices must be heard. Getty Images must act on contributor suggestions when possible. Listening takes the form of dialog in the forums, informal surveys – phone calls, conference calls to discuss a new initiative that may be controversial – even a reversed decision if needed. Getty Images must balance business needs and community expectations, as they manage contributor relations to generate value for customers.

Getty Images Technology Platforms for Content Acquisition and Contributor Interactions

Digital technology has greatly extended the need for Getty Images' products. Businesses constantly need content for their digital communications. There are also new markets for images, such as online platforms that enable people to create websites on the fly and websites that provides print-on-demand service. These online uses have shifted the needs of many Getty

Images' customers to lower-resolution and lower-priced imageries but in higher volume and shorter usage time. To meet this fast-growing and diverse demand, it is necessary to reduce the frictions embedded in the traditional transaction process when customers buy images through à la carte licensing.

Getty Images also needs a better way to manage the growing size of its contributors and the new dynamics among them. To meet this increasing demand of a bigger customer base with diverse needs, Getty Images must gather and ingest content from more contributors at a much faster rate. In stock photography, ingestion refers to the act of bringing in content with metadata, such as contributor, location of shot, subject types, to the asset management system. Getty Images' older infrastructure, including ingestion, connection with the supplier platforms, outreach forum and licensing, has to be replaced for Getty Images to invent more new services and access content easier (interviews with Andrew Saunders and Claudia Micare).

Today, most of Getty Images' content sources are isolated. As it reaches to serve different customer bases and grow its contributor pool and diversity, the links between the products and the sources (i.e. contributor types), such as microstock from iStockphoto contributors, are starting to break down. In some cases, traditional stock partners are putting content into iStockphoto, which is a microstock model. This migration increases complexity in relationship management across different sources and can introduce inconsistency in the ingestion process and the relationship management (interview with Erin Sullivan).

To resolve these challenges, Getty Images has introduced a new Enterprise Submission Platform (ESP). This ESP consists of a web interface and Application Programming Interfaces (APIs), which allows Getty Images' content collection to be connected to workflows from the customers and the contributors (interview with Erin Sullivan) so that contents and the associated metadata are passed over from one system to another. The APIs will also automate the ingestion of content into Getty Images' asset management system (interview with Craig Peters and Andy Saunders, and Erin Sullivan). So when an image is submitted, its metadata can be rearranged, translated, or changed automatically before the image is integrated into Getty Images' system.

Getty Images has created the Connect API for its customers to search and download Getty Images' creative and editorial content directly into its publishing process and digital content collections. This enables a seamless integration between Getty Images products and clients' workflow. The Connect API can also allow distributors, such as resellers of imagery and service providers of print-on-demand, to access Getty Images' digital content collections of images and videos in real time.

The Connect API lowers search and transaction efforts for Getty Images' customers. Through integration with its customers' systems, Getty Images' content can be pulled by the customers when it's needed, automatically, free of traditional transactional activities. Thus, Getty Images can reach different kinds of customers with the Connect API and increase the number of relationships where many of the traditional one-to-one transactions are replaced by a subscription or other models. The combination of the Connect API and new pricing models such as the subscription model will greatly simplify the interaction process between Getty Images and its customers (interview with Nick King).

Departing from the traditional multiple product-based web submission portals, the new platform is more unified and robust, with the capability to accommodate the ingestion of a range of content sources for a range of products, thus enabling a more consistent ingestion process. Currently, Getty Images uses portals where contributors upload their content, which is then reviewed, accepted and flowed into Getty Images' system. The expansion of products and partners has resulted in over twenty different submission processes in its editorial systems and about 80 percent of the functionality is the same. ESP will allow most of the submission, selection, review and ingestion activities to take place on Getty Images' system and to consolidate these diverse processes. The overall system architecture also allows flexibility for future potential partners, such as Instagram or Vimeo, to easily integrate their systems with Getty Images' system (interview with Erin Sullivan).

Today, Getty Images uses multiple modes, including forums, Twitter and emails and mail to communicate with its contributors. In the future, applications on mobile devices with the right APIs can push tailored information to specific groups of photographers and communicate the type of content needed in a versatile and timely manner (interview with Erin Sullivan). Thus, Getty Images can quickly and effectively provide creative briefs to appropriate contributors and obtain more coverage, depth or imagery of certain types of stock photography and certain geographic locations. This capability will enable Getty Images to respond to customers' demands on hyper-local content.

Getty Images can provide a range of APIs for different types and different levels of contributors. Some might move between different workflows as they become more engaged or as they become more sophisticated in their work, so they may use a more advanced API that enables them to submit directly and give Getty Images releases. In addition Getty Images can involve people in the workflow that suits them over time. Getty Images can also leverage this platform to identify and recruit contributors for the top end of its business, with much less effort than currently possible. This will allow Getty Images to grow its pool of top-end contributors more quickly with less effort, or to take contributions directly from mobile phones. Overall, the new platform with APIs will enable efficient deployment of creative team resources to support the right kind of touch for different contributors (interview with Erin Sullivan).

ESP will greatly simplify Getty Images' current processes for customer engagement and contributor interactions in terms of access and selection. It will accelerate the ingestion of content that Getty Images brings from existing contributors to existing customers. In the future, ESP will be an open platform with fewer restrictions. This will be important as Getty Images continues to embrace crowd-sourcing for content contributions. The approach of using APIs as interfaces between the external systems (contributors and customers) and Getty Images' asset management system also allows Getty Images to scale up its operation with process automation while maintaining system stability and process flexibility.

IMPLICATIONS OF FINDINGS FOR FUTURE OF STOCK PHOTOGRAPHY INDUSTRY VALUE CHAIN AND CONTENT CONTRIBUTOR AND CONTENT DISTRIBUTOR RELATIONS

As one studies the case of the stock photography industry and the role of technology in its evolution, several interesting questions arise. Does crowd-sourcing provide more opportunities for creative artists to get their work recognized and used? Lowering entry barriers for visual artists would seem to suggest more opportunities, particularly if these artists can offer their services at lower prices and thus attract under-served and more price-sensitive buyers. This would be the optimistic scenario forecast for low-end disruptive innovation offerings as described by Clay Christensen (2000). As illustrated by the case of iStockphoto, initially, the buyers were an under-served and more price-sensitive group who had no access through the traditional channels. These buyers were less concerned about the poor image quality and problematic business transaction model. However, as the volume of imagery grew, and as iStockphoto advertised itself widely, more buyers and contributors came on board. Crowd-sourcing became a valid content distribution channel and started to garner the attention of the high-budget buyers.

On the other hand, as crowd-sourcing matures and becomes a valid distribution channel, does it turn creative content into a commodity, where the economic value shifts from the individual or collective artistic community to the content aggregators who can search, screen, select and classify their collections of the various artistic contributors as their value added services to their customers? Conceptually, crowd-sourcing channels, at least initially, place the burden on buyers to search, screen, select and classify the products. These are parts of the search cost, which was part of the cost that traditional distributors incurred (and charged the buyers). Thus, only buyers who do not mind higher search cost (for example, those who are willing to sift through thousands of photos) will participate. Buyers who cared about search cost will continue to pay higher premiums to traditional distribution channels, which share that higher premium with their contributors. It is possible that higher-end contributors will not observe a lowering in revenue and may even observe revenue increase as new buyers enter the market, even though sales through the crowd-sourcing channels are associated with lower unit prices and smaller margins per image sold.

SUGGESTED AREAS FOR FUTURE RESEARCH INTO STOCK PHOTOGRAPHY INDUSTRY EVOLUTION

Future research needs to be vigilant regarding the appearance of new business models and value propositions that either incumbent firms or new entrepreneurial entrants bring to the microstock photography marketplace. To the extent that these new business models and value propositions are simply incremental improvements on current microstock business models, disruptive innovation theory would predict that the competitive advantage lies with the incumbents in the industry, such as Getty Images and Corbis. These incumbent firms can leverage their superior inventories of content, their established relationships with content-contributing communities and their deep channel ties to the institutional and retail consumers of photographic and video content. Disruptive innovation theory suggests that opportunities for new incumbents to assume dominance in the industry would require them to introduce business models and value propositions that render current models irrelevant. Presently, such models and value propositions have not yet appeared or are in too embryonic a state of development to be assessed for their industry disruptive potential.

Another fundamental industry transformation requiring further research is the changing relationship between content creators and their users. Historically, content distribution agencies such as Getty Images served as a critical lynchpin between the content creators and the end users and these agencies engaged with these communities with varying degrees of hands-on (high touch) forms of guidance and direction in proportion to the nature of the photographic contributor's quality offering and high value contribution. As the scale and scope of available content and content sources increase exponentially, content distribution agencies are transforming themselves into e-commerce platforms where the interactions with their content contributors and customers are largely mediated by portals that provide standard interfaces (APIs) for all parties. The impact of these evolving e-commerce platforms on the value chain relationships between microstock content contributors, distributors and buyers will merit further research.

ACKNOWLEDGEMENTS

The research team thanks the following Getty Images executives for allowing us to interview them for this study: Paul Foster, Senior Director of Creative Content; Nick King, Vice President of Products; Claudia Micare, Senior Manager – Contributor Relations; Craig Peters, Senior Vice President, Business Development, Product and Content; Andrew Saunders, Vice President, Creative Content; and Erin Sullivan, Vice President, Content Development. Lastly, we thank Jonathan Klein, CEO, Getty Images, for supporting our study.

REFERENCES

Angus, E. and Thelwall, M. (2010). Motivations for image publishing and tagging on Flickr. In *Proceedings of the 14th International Conference on Electronic Publishing*, Hanken School of Economics, Helsinki, pp. 189–204.

Brabham, D.C. (2008). Moving the crowd at iStockphoto: The composition of the crowd and motivations for participation in a crowdsourcing application. *First Monday*, 13(6).

Christensen, C.M. (2000). *The Innovator's Dilemma*. Rev. edn. New York: HarperBusiness.

Frosh, P. (2003). Digital technology and stock photography: And God created photoshop. In Larry Gross, John Stuart Katz and Jay Ruby, eds, *Image Ethics in the Digital Age*, Minneapolis: University of Minnesota Press, pp. 183–216.

Getty Images (2013). Investor Relations. Available at: http://corporate.gettyimages.com/source/investors.

Howe, J. (2006). The rise of crowdsourcing. *Wired*, 14.06, June, available at: http://www.wired.com/wired/archive/14.06/crowds.html.

Howe, J. (2008). *Crowdsourcing: Why the Power of the Crowd is Driving the Future of Business*, New York: Crown Business.

Hunt, P. (2009). The meteoric rise of Getty Images, *MacTribe* (print edition), Winter.

iStockphoto (2012). *Buy Stock Photo Credits at iStock*. 23 January 23, *iStock-*

photo, available at: http://www.istockphoto.com/buy-stock-prepaid-credits.php?isource=EN_LO_BUCKET1.

iStockphoto (2013). Pocketography: The democratization of photography.

Klein, J. (2012). We've disrupted our own market, trend, turned competitors into partners and led many innovations within our industry. How culture is everything. *Getty Award Recognition for Global Leadership in Innovation and Collaboration*, 5 November, Center for Innovation and Change Leadership, Suffolk University, Boston, MA.

Pickerell, J. (1996a). Agency consolidations, *Selling Stock*, 15 February, available at: http://www.selling-stock.com.

Pickerell, J. (1996b). Print catalogs vs Digital, *Selling Stock*, 15 February, available at: http://www.selling-stock.com.

Pickerell, J. (1996c). Getty launches subscription service, *Selling Stock*, 15 February, available at: http://www.selling-stock.com.

Pickerell, J. (1998a). 1998 Survey, *Selling Stock*, 6 March, available at: http://www.selling-stock.com.

Pickerell, J. (1998b). Graphic designer use of royalty free, *Selling Stock*, 27 July, available at: http://www.selling-stock.com.

Pickerell, J. (1998c). Myths about an electronic future, *Selling Stock*, 27 July, available at: http://www.selling-stock.com.

Pickerell, J. (1998d). Klein speaks in New York, content in the 21st century, *Selling Stock*, 31 October, available at: http://www.selling-stock.com.

Pickerell, J. (1998e). Net statistics, *Selling Stock*, 10 November, http://www.selling-stock.com.

Pickerell, J. (1999a). Getty Images reports e-commerce success, *Selling Stock*, 24 February, available at: http://www.selling-stock.com.

Pickerell, J. (1999b). Royalty Free and market size, *Selling Stock*, 28 July, available at: http://www.selling-stock.com.

Pickerell, J. (2000a). Stock photographer survey, *Selling Stock*, 9 July, available at: http://www.selling-stock.com.

Pickerell, J. (2001). Stock photography: E-commerce pricing. *Selling Stock*, 4 December, available at: http://www.sellingstock.com.

Pickerell, J. (2003). RF impact on stock revenue, *Selling Stock*, 22 September, available at: http://www.selling-stock.com.

Pickerell, J. (2005). Where's the stock industry headed, *Selling Stock*, 12 June, available at: http://www.selling-stock.com.

Pickerell, J. (2006a). Getty moves to micropayments, *Selling Stock*, 10 February, available at: http://www.selling-stock.com.

Pickerell, J. (2006b). Where is Getty headed in 2007?, *Selling Stock*, 14 November, available at: http://www.selling-stock.com.

Pickerell, J. (2007a). Trends for Getty photographers, *Selling Stock*, 29 March, available at: http://www.selling-stock.com.

Pickerell, J. (2007b). Getty dramatically lowers prices for web use, *Selling Stock*, 27 August, available at: http://www.selling-stock.com.

Pickerell, J. (2008). Is microstock pricing simple?, *Selling Stock*, 28 May, available at: http://www.selling-stock.com.

Pickerell, J. (2012). Do more images result in more revenue, *Selling Stock*, 13 December, available at: http://www.selling-stock.com.

Pickerell, J. (2013a). Getty connect; Minuscule usage fees, *Selling Stock*, 27 March, available at: http://www.selling-stock.com.

Pickerell, J. (2013b). Falling prices; Issue to be discussed at CEPIC, The Cepic Congress in Barcelona, *Selling Stock*, 29 March, available at: http://www.selling-stock.com.
Puscher, F. (2011). Jeff Howe on the rise of crowdsourcing, Blog posted 11 June, *Crowdsourcing.org*, available at: http://www.crowdsourcing.org/editorial/jeff-howe-on-the-rise-of-crowdsourcing/4749.
Rubinstein, D. and Sluis, K. (2008). A life more photographic: Mapping the networked image. *Photographies*, 1(1), 9–28.
Vandeberg, R. (2013). How crowdsourcing advances industries. Available at: http://dailycrowdsource.com/crowdsourcing/crowd-leaders/475-crowd-leader-rob-van denberg-how-crowdsourcing-advances-industries.
Zupic, I. (2013). Social media as enabler of crowdsourcing, forthcoming in Tanya Bondarouk and Miguel Olivas-Lujan (eds) *Social Media and Management* (Advanced Series in Management, Volume 10), Emerald Group Publishing.

13. Users as content creators, aggregators and distributors at Citilab Living Lab

Seppo Leminen, Mika Westerlund, Laia Sánchez and Artur Serra

INTRODUCTION

Media production and consumption are undergoing drastic changes. To investigate the changes in the film, video and photography (FVP) industries and the effects of these changes on content creation, aggregation and distribution in the media industry, this chapter draws on prior research on users as content creators.

The digitalization of production and delivery of content allows the use of media contents in a myriad of different terminals. Media production and consumption are becoming increasingly social, participatory, ubiquitous and multi-channeled. New technologies that enable shared public and interpersonal communication are of significant social, organizational and economic importance. They act as notable change drivers in the media industry and pose major challenges to contemporary media firms. One secret to maintaining a thriving business is to recognize when it needs a fundamental change (Heath and Heath, 2010).

This chapter explores media co-creation with users at a digital lab for citizen innovation. In particular, the chapter describes major changes the FVP media industry is facing and explains the importance of involved users in responding to these changes. In doing so, the chapter aims to answer the following research questions:

- What is media co-creation in living labs?
- What are the roles of users in media co-creation?

This chapter is organized as follows. First, after a brief introduction to the study, we discuss the theoretical foundation of living labs. Then, we depict the research methodology of our study and provide empirical findings on open innovation paradoxes in living labs. Finally, we conclude the study by discussing users as content creators, aggregators and distributors at Citilab Living Lab.

THEORETICAL BACKGROUND

Understanding the customer experience is crucial for businesses and innovation activity. Today's organizations need a constant flow of ideas while competing through emergent technologies and fast new product development (Kao, 1997). Integrating customers into the innovation process to learn from and with them has become a key success factor for companies in all industries (Edvarsson et al., 2010). As few companies can ignore customers' input to their innovation processes, more and more firms are paying attention to users and their views as sources of useful feedback, relevant use experience, important ideas and new information.

Moreover, one of the most important recent trends is the progressive inclusion of consumers in firms' processes where value is co-created (Arvidsson, 2008). Firms involve consumers in the co-production of content, brands, experiences, design, marketing strategies, and even product and service development (Jeppesen and Molin, 2003; Zwick et al., 2008).

Customer involvement is driven by the open innovation model, which is becoming increasingly popular. Open innovation is of interest to many industries today because it provides a promising alternative to the conventional closed innovation development (Chesbrough, 2003; Paulson et al., 2004; Bonaccorsi et al., 2006). The open innovation model is supported by the emergence of social media (e.g. Web 2.0), which has brought many new services to the Internet that are based on content sharing and content-based interaction. Therefore, the Internet has altered the proposition that cooperating and listening to customers can help firms improve their products and services.

One particularly interesting form of open innovation is the living lab, where technology is developed and tested in a physical or virtual real-life context, and customers and users are important informants and co-creators in the tests (Kusiak, 2007). Co-creation helps firms address their customers' latent needs. It reduces market risk in the launch of new products and services and improves return on investment and time to market. However, the role and depth of users' integration in the open innovation model differs from the conventional view.

To co-create value, the firm and its users must reconcile objectives and define the role of and effort required from each party, as well as an equitable division of the returns (Chesbrough, 2003). However, companies still have little experience in open innovation and the literature is silent on what is required to make user innovation models work (Feller and Fitzgerald, 2002). Transforming from an in-house innovator into a user innovator is difficult, and previous studies have predominantly considered a firm's innovation development options as either closed or open, without alternatives between the two (cf. Almirall and Casadesus-Masanell, 2010).

SOCIAL MEDIA AT CITILAB: FROM CITIZEN MEDIA TO MEDIA CITIZEN

Citilab started as a collaborative design project of socio-digital innovation. It was initially proposed to the City of Cornella in 2002 and officially inaugurated in 2007 (Serra, 2001). Citilab literally means citizen laboratory, a new community built to open innovation processes to every citizen and consumer. The model emerged after long experience with telecenters and its goal is universal access and digital literacy. In 2010, Citilab comprised 4500 members and gave out small cards, like the ones used in public libraries, to its members, or 'citilabers'.

Citizens can participate in general activities and have access to telecenter services, including free access to the Internet, basic digital literacy courses, and free attendance at talks and general activities. Digital training and learning are essential for citizens to become citilabers. To become a citilaber, one needs to consider the question written on the back of the citilaber card: 'What do you want to do? If you know, you can do it here by yourself. If you cannot, we can help you.' Citilab has developed many projects[1] and it opened the Social Media Lab[2] in 2009. Since then, the lab has developed a set of user-driven projects. The ideology of the lab is as follows: 'If citizens can have access and learn how to use information and communication technology (ICT) in an innovative way, they can become developers of new media experiences, products, and services based on their own needs and context.'

Citilab has created a new approach. Instead of starting with the media, it placed the citizen at the center of programs. Citilab helps people develop a personal innovation project with the following motto: 'You do not have a boss who tells you all the time what you have to do, and you do not have a professor ordering what you have to learn. Instead, you are on your own, deciding what you want to do and how to do it at Citilab.' The focus has been on new technology in the media sector, and even the recent convergence of media and the Internet in the form of social media has not changed the paradigm. Analog or digital, mass media or networked media, the traditional research program of the media research community has focused on the new communication environment.

Citilab started its activity with citizens after it built the media facility. That is why Citilab talks about users as content creators, aggregators and distributors. Furthermore, Citilab's Social Media Lab has trained people in projects based on user-generated content (UGC). UGC is now widely accepted in media evolution, and current mass media channels are more frequently based on the UGC model established by YouTube, Wikipedia and Twitter, the three most popular Web 2.0 sites in 2012 (http://www.ebizmba.com/articles/web-2.0-websites). Citilab has trained citizens to use the new networked media technologies to develop not only UGC but also user-generated applications and services (UGAS).

METHODOLOGY

Research Design

The research design creates a road map for research objectives, gathered data, chosen methods and results. This study analyzes media co-creation in the Citilab Living Lab. We have applied von Hippel's (2005) proposal on democratizing innovation to organize activities in four living lab cases. First, we proposed social innovation scenarios where amateurs and lead users become producers of new solutions in an uncertain market. Citilab agreed that the new social media field was consistent with this description because the media industry in Spain was facing a lack of investment and it was difficult for the industry to explore new social media specialized contents and formats. On the other hand, media exposure was growing, while communication costs were decreasing and a revolutionary democratization of media production and distribution tools was becoming reality. Therefore, the Social Media Lab (SML) considered that context as an opportunity to deploy open innovation projects with citizens.

SML detected the lack of media coverage for various communities. These communities provided an opportunity to activate involved citizens in deploying that media coverage. Then, it became time to involve them in the project. Citilab used the living lab and design methods for this purpose and the 'Active User Handbook' for Citilab was developed. The book provides a set of techniques to involve citizens during an open innovation project. It summarizes four stages (define, learn, construct, reflect) and a set of methods to achieve empathy, inspiration and co-creation to activate users in innovation projects.

Citilab also used the '3H' methodology, which takes the human body as a metaphor to describe the step-by-step process of a user-driven innovation project. The 3H methodology consists of three major stages: head (understanding the open media innovation ecosystem); heart (building relations and encouraging co-creation with users); and hands on (engaging the participants in co-creation and development activity).

- *Head: understanding the open media innovation ecosystem*
  The aim of this exploratory activity was to identify and map the actors of the innovation community system. This provided protocols and tools to collect and understand the needs and barriers to participation. Once the extent of a research and development problem was detected, it was possible to identify a potential innovation community, as well as proper motivations and circumstances where solutions could be encouraged. The first challenge was to find participants with enough time to become involved in the project.
- *Heart: building relations and encouraging co-creation with users*
  This activity aimed to consolidate the necessary relationships to establish trust and commitment between all involved stakeholders. Following Almirall and Wareham (2008), living labs 'provide structure and governance to user participation in the innovation process'. The crucial challenge involved how users become producers. Colobrans (2010) suggested asking questions about user needs (e.g. what, how and why s/he wants what s/he wants?) and 'taking measures' to adapt the product to user requirements. Using the heart approach, SML contacted participants who were willing to become producers of their own media content (UGC) and ready to distribute and share the created media content with their peers. This content creation was linked with users' own interest areas. We identified the areas that gave us an opportunity to foster UGC production. We learned that to engage users in each living lab community, it was crucial to put them in the center of the design process (UCD)[3] as soon as possible. For us, it was necessary to go beyond just defining user requirements, as our goal was to bring the users into a co-creation process in which they deployed their own solutions.
- *Hands on: engaging participants in co-creation and development activity*
  The final part of this activity included an evaluation based on a client-driven set of indicators. We proposed UGC as the solution for the detected lack of communication reach problems. An overall problem-solving methodology[4] addressed the following questions: how can we shift from customers to prosumers (Toffler, 1980) in the new communication model? How can organizations or firms generate value from user-generated content products and services?

How can participants become able to design and manage a trans-media communication strategy for their content?

The SML employed project-based learning, which was developed at Citilab, as a way to reconcile the learning interests of our users (learning ICT) and the innovation vocation of our institution. In addition, project-based learning was an important tool to engage participants, while learning skills were needed to solve problems that affected participants. This learning was a key motivational asset to engage participants.

'Citizens may innovate' was a vital principle of the project. Therefore, it was important to understand participants' needs and to have the appropriate skills to use the tools needed to develop solutions to meet the indicated needs. It was also essential to provide an adapted training program to encourage UGC production. Therefore, Citilab's staff provided training sessions and held regular project meetings. The internal meetings were as important as the training sessions because participants could share their previous knowledge and skills with the group and it was possible to determine who was ready to perform the required tasks. Once the group became self-organized, it could use the potential of all members. That way, individual UGC production limitations for development were minimized.

Case Studies

In the empirical part of this study, we analyzed content creation, aggregation and distribution through the experiences of four different communities: senior people (Seniorlab); young athletes (Sportic); musicians (Musiclab); and heavy users of video games (Gamecademy) (see Table 13.1). Three of four communities wanted more visibility in their community of interest. Musiclab, Seniorlab and Sportic tackled the lack of media communication among participants about their own activities. On the other hand, Gamecademy took advantage of the potential of the game industry and the lack of professionals in Spain working for that industry.

Young people and seniors are interesting groups to work with because they have a precious resource: time. We searched for a potential steep learning course and observed the experience of young people pointing to fast technological learning and adoption. SML could easily work with the Seniorlab community with a shallow learning curve but with enough time to learn and a lot of knowledge to share. Finally, we searched for impact in terms of publicity. We identified four fields that could provide impact for wide audiences: sports, music, news and video games.

The first participants of SML projects were unexpectedly seniorlabers. The Seniorlab project had already empowered seniorlabers with basic

Table 13.1   Number of participants in media co-creation cases

Project	Number of participants
Seniorlab TV	25
Musiclab	124
Sportic	12
Gamecadamy	38

ICT skills, allowing them to become familiar with the Citilab action research approach and willing to learn how to use media for their own interest. Afterward, Citilab agreed with the Fontsanta Fatjó Futbol Club to create a group of young athletes to become its media team. Thus, the Sportic project was born. Then, with help from the SML staff, a couple of professional musicians started the Musiclab project: its Artistic Open Community consisted of professionals, amateurs and local music schools. Finally, Gamecademy involved 38 youngsters who wanted to learn how to develop their own video games.

Those four innovation communities configured the Seniorlab, Musiclab, Sportic and Gamecademy. They were the four experimental media projects that Citilab's Social Media Laboratory developed from 2008 to 2012 to help in understanding the new user-driven model.

Seniorlab (2008): seniors produce their own media content
SeniorlabTV explored opportunities for television media development by seniors. This UGC project was developed under the umbrella of the Seniorlab project that started as an initiative by Citilab, the i2CAT Foundation, the University of Barcelona and the Senior University. Seniorlab's initial hypothesis was that 'senior people can contribute to design in innovative ways and build a knowledge society by contributing to its experience and its memory as a capital asset.' To bring that idea into practice, the Seniorlab explored the senior profiles, their needs and social attitudes toward the senior-age community (see Figure 13.1).

During the innovation stage, seniors were competent in the innovation that affected their problems directly. During its third stage, the group presented projects and new proposals, and the Seniorlab community was consolidated on site and online (http://citilabpro.eu/seniorlab). At this moment, seniorlabers were able to develop new projects under the tutor's supervision. The SeniorlabTV new media literacy project started as a new iteration of innovative projects for Seniorlab. Therefore, the Social Media Laboratory and Seniorlab teams joined forces to develop the SeniorlabTV project with an active group of seniorlabers. The SeniorlabTV aimed to

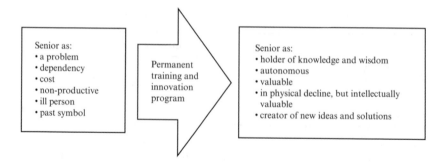

Figure 13.1   Shift of senior people contribution

empower seniorlabers in the use of new media technologies; they then became media producers and managers of their own WebTV shows. SeniorlabTV started after the Seniorlab community had already been consolidated.

Media empowerment was a motivational asset to engage seniorlabers and to give seniors voice and decision power. Seniorlabers decided what they wanted to do, and which format and content they wanted to use, and the staff were with them just to facilitate their empowerment. The key for development of the UGC was that the senior participants brought their common knowledge of the media field. The co-design process took the shape of a WebTV debate show. Seniors were interested in expressing their opinion about the news, and they were critical of the sensationalism and non-civic form of many debates on contemporary television.

An analysis of seniorlabers' preferences and skills in terms of task development revealed two main groups: responsible technicians and content. Then the staff facilitated an adapted learning program. By participating in various activities, seniorlabers learned the new technology, media tools and procedures they needed to become capable of producing their own WebTV shows. The technical team worked at Citilab's studios. The Seniorlab participants who belonged to the technical group learned how to use streaming software, how to use cameras, and how to set up the TV studio to produce their live SeniorlabDebateShow. Thus, members of this group recorded the programs produced on the set and produced other audiovisual products for the Seniorlab.

The other team was in charge of content creation. Team members dedicated their working sessions to learning the scripting techniques required to design quality programs. They also learned how to face speaking in front of a camera to play the role of conductor or interviewee.

Once this first stage was complete, the group was organized to choose a relevant issue from the news and to gather information about it. Finally both teams met in the studio and performed their debate on the set. The show was broadcast live on the Seniorlab WebTV channel. After the first debate, 14 more shows were developed, including all the involved tasks.

Musiclab (2009): musicians develop their own applications and services
In 1999, Napster changed the music industry, and since then sharing has had a huge impact in audiovisual terms. The millennial generation has grown up with Internet music, first downloading, then playing on YouTube, and finally being willing to compose. However, training goals in the use of technology to co-create music are lagging behind.

In 2009, SML joined forces with two musicians to tackle how young people can learn music. Typically, local professors are not professional musicians and usually professional musicians do not teach in local music schools. As a consequence, schools' music programs have high levels of student dropout. Therefore, SML took advantage of this opportunity to use new media in the development of a new solution.

Citilab's SML staff provided the media equipment and media know-how, i2cat's IGLOR team members contributed with their media network expertise, and Sergio Ramos and Santi Sánchez, two local musicians, became the leaders of this research project and developed the training program. By joining forces and expertise, it was possible to deploy an innovative solution.

A professional master class made it possible for the project to become more sustainable, where costs and learning were shared among different music schools. This professional training targeting the new creative youth was necessary to enhance the students' music skills during two pilots (2009–10 and 2010–11). Musiclab fostered innovation and musical experimentation by developing creative tools, new formats of cultural content, and participatory networks for sharing knowledge while also exploring different online and interactive learning contexts.

Development: live online musical training   The Musiclab methodology was tested in different experimental media training formats. To enhance the live online educational sessions, Citilab connected its studio with local music schools, where musical guests provided exercises and interacted with students. This learning format allowed participants to stream and record performances. It was possible to show different authors' musical works from a pedagogical point of view and to highlight new talent. It was also necessary to provide a multicam set to provide better perspectives on the performance and the learning resources used by the session's conductor. Before using video streaming or video conferencing in educational sessions, a technical scheme for broadcasting and transmission technologies was defined to guarantee the quality and flow of interactions. The conditions of the session stage depend on complex elements, such as 'chroma key', or mobile cameras used for the purpose, and an experimental one-day Musiclab community session took place in early 2011.

Another experimental format was 'innovative live online experiences', in which the Cornellà session in Spain and Korea was connected. This was the first internationally successful experiment where technology and the passion for music were keys to introduce two musical styles: the traditional Mediterranean rhythm and the Pansori (traditional Korean music). This pioneer experience, propelled by Musiclab and Fundació i2CAT, was a success despite technical difficulties regarding the delicate synchronization and over 10 000 miles in distance.

The team members faced the challenge that musical interpretation on the Internet brings. The session sorted out the difficulty of synchronizing the signal of several musicians while playing a musical piece together from different places. The main challenge was the 'delay effect' caused by the asynchrony in the bit streams of image and audio when traveling through the Internet.

An interactive and distributed live performance activity was developed to allow users (i.e. musicians) to create music in real time. Musiclab established a set and its operative protocols, and a distributed co-creative activity was developed in coordination; in addition, conducting the event was key in both locations' sets and scenarios. Each scenario functioned as a transmitter and receiver simultaneously, and the audiovisual signals traveled from center to center sequentially. For the audience, the result was the experience of attending a concert that took place in a concurrent and distributed way. The Musiclab tested this format for live concerts after the Cornella–Korea experience as well. The team played at the Citilab studio with a group playing live at the Altaveu Festival.

Each performance was recorded and the final scenario contained the complete contribution. After the live online session, all the content became on-demand educational content available on the Musiclab's YouTube channel, which contains 12 interactive master classes (reaching 124 participants and providing 5 distributed performances in real time). Finally, 12 high-quality learning contents were produced and can be consulted in the Musiclab YouTube playlist at the Citilab's YouTube channel.

Sportic (2009): football players and media editors

Football is a local passion and 'La Liga' clubs like Barcelona FC ('El Barça') are popular worldwide. Although they appear constantly in the media, smaller sports clubs rarely do so.

A small club had difficulty in communicating with its fans until the emergence of social media such as Facebook, Twitter, blogs and Internet TV, which is a new web application environment that provides a more horizontal 'social' dimension to media. This allowed SML to focus efforts on fostering UGC creation and not on technological issues.

A young sportsman, like most of the youth today, uses predominantly new technologies. For these young people, the Internet is a space of autonomy for promotion, but users need proper guidance. Sportic's proposition was to provide a creative space in which players could make their sportive activity visible and have an opportunity to lead an activity in a responsible and professional manner, being useful for the club and the community.

Citilab offered local sports clubs the chance to produce streaming video of their own matches. The club empowered its own media team to design and produce the communication strategy, which was developed by the club and its young athletes.

Development and empowering the Fontsanta Fatjo Sportive Media Team   The SML team launched a new media literacy program to empower a media team composed of 12 young athletes (12–16 years old) from the local club to produce their own new media content. Sportic's co-design process started with conversations with coaches and the young athletes. The idea of the experiment was explained to them and their opinions and interests were incorporated before developing the experiment. During the process, it became clear that the club's players and administrative staff had fewer digital competencies than the young digital natives. Amateurs, fans and communities of practice (Wenger, 2000) had precious knowledge of the subjects that gave them an advantage in their ability to find innovative solutions to their own problems.

The young athletes were experts in their sport, as well as in the media that cover it. They knew more about their own football league than any 'La Liga' journalist would know. They were also better positioned to talk to their own fans and followers (mostly friends and relatives); however, young athletes need knowledge to use the available media tools in a professional manner. Co-design processes offered learning-by-doing digital and media training, which was adapted for the young athletes' group to design and develop the CD Fontsanta Fatjó communication strategy. The training covered activities such as planning, production, post-production, and sharing all the content related to young athletes' sports activity by using the new social media platforms. From this training, the club acquired a new collaborative audiovisual environment, Fontsanta-Fatjo TV. Once the new collaborative audiovisual environment was set up, the training helped them produce, upload and manage their videos.

The young athletes' group conducted many training sessions as well as team presentations. Parallel to the offline production, they were also trained to conduct live streaming. All releases of their matches were available from 2009 to 2011 to view on demand free of charge. The SML staff and the media team also explored the different themes and wireframes for the FontsantaFatjoTV website and the team chose those they considered most suitable. After that, the website was launched and users learned how to manage publishing content.

Sportic trained and empowered the CD Fontsanta Fatjó media team to become WebTV channel producers and managers. The media team produced 12 team presentations and live streamed 15 matches on their own WebTV channel. They also learned to use social media platforms (Facebook and Twitter). Unfortunately, the facilities of the club were being renovated and the club could not provide the necessary technical conditions to stabilize the streaming of the matches, which influenced the lack of adoption of the innovation. The club was not able to consolidate all the positive effects of the media team and its results. However, it currently uses both Facebook and Twitter to share its activities with its audience.

Gamecademy: from a hobby to a profession in the new game industry[5]

'Turn your passion into your profession' is the central idea of Citilab's innovative practices. The video game industry is a growth industry that will play a significant role in media industries of the future. Although Spain is one of the world's largest video game consumer markets, its production is still marginal; therefore, skilled professionals are needed to grow these businesses and create new ones. The video game industry paradigm is challenged by changes in development and distribution models.

Probably the largest app store, the Apple store, has 400 million active devices that are used to buy games with credit cards. This means a huge market of potential buyers. The Android market and the new Google Play are also very important. Similar operational models include the Google Chrome store and the Windows Phone store, and the number of players is constantly growing. Meanwhile, youth unemployment is growing. Therefore, it is important to focus on how to change the frustrating 'looking-for-a-job'[6] activity into an entrepreneurial attitude of 'invent your own job'. Therefore, a formative course was developed for local unemployed youth to enhance their work opportunities via their real passion for video games. The course was hosted by Citilab and a three-dimensional (3D) environment and video game company.[7]

The Gamecademy course provided its participants with the knowledge and skills to create their own video game from scratch. The training covered programming, game design, virtual reality, 3D modeling, and graphics and multimedia, that is, all the techniques needed to create video games. Gamecademy participants developed their video games into a multiplatform environment for different devices, distributed through online stores. The video game course achieved and passed its first objectives by tutoring participants' own projects. Gamecademy participants, approximately 50 youngsters, developed 29 video games, which can be published on PC, Mac, Web, iOS and/or Android platforms.

The video game course achieved results that have been configured as an online training platform providing more than 300 video tutorials: the platform is currently operative.

CONCLUSION

The four Citilab projects discussed in the chapter have contributed to changes in the standard communication model by focusing on media consumers as engaged active users, designers of transmedia strategies, and producers of valuable content and media experiences rather than passive spectators. Users are becoming skilled in the available Web 2.0 social media and related networking capabilities (see Figure 13.2).

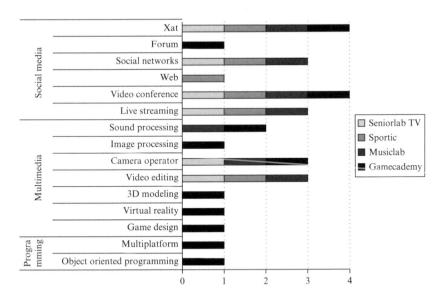

Figure 13.2   Web 2.0 social media and related networking capabilities in the cases

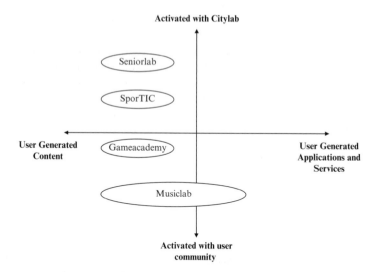

Figure 13.3   User-generated content and user-generated applications and services

In particular, the four projects demonstrate how to open the culture of innovation to the general public by focusing on user-generated content and user-generated applications and services (see Figure 13.3).

Even though the Sportic pilot was successful, more social pressure and institutional commitment are needed to consolidate new practices within external communities. Digitally connected sports facilities are a must for the adoption of this new communication practice. The technology is available and the passion for sports is an engagement motor to involve young people to collaborate with their club; however, this is not sufficient. The sportsman reporters were also coaches of younger teams, so it was difficult for them to sustain their media work during the time. Club involvement, authority and appreciation of the media team's task are important to sustain their commitment.

Seniorlabers want to be part of the public sphere and use new media tools, and the new digital culture allows them to do so. Co-design was a success factor, as seniors acquired thorough knowledge of the media structure and content. They have different and complementary knowledge ranging from general information to entertainment. Furthermore, they have clear ideas on what they like in media content (see Figure 13.4). Respect and the possibility of offering pluralistic voices are very important to them. The golden rule is that seniors learn how to become digital and media-autonomous at their own pace.

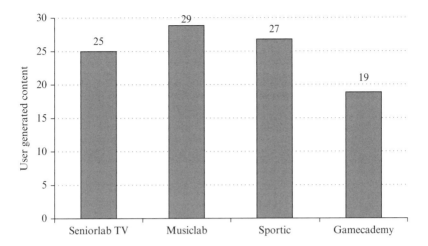

Figure 13.4   User-generated content in cases

Musiclab experiments have consolidated the Musiclab team as pioneers in the creation, research and production of new cultural formats and offered a stabilized methodology for live online musical experiences. Musiclab has developed experiences that sustain its hypothesis, but further work and thorough transformations are needed to consolidate these achievements in the musical formative institutions and associations. The development of these new formative and co-creative practices opens up new possibilities for sharing knowledge and creating value between musicians and society.

Music and technology put together allow the enhancing of new communication practices between cultures, with the objectives of generating participatory networks and cultural interaction among different musical languages. However, more community work, new ways of acting and playing by making use of new technologies, and adoption of the practices of digital culture are necessary in the music field. Training for these new experiences has been incorporated and the Musiclab methodology has been standardized.

With video game learning experiences, it is now possible for a youngster to become a video game developer – without previous technical knowledge – after approximately one year of focused training. This represents a new opportunity that changes the logic of production because previously access to development tools was fairly exclusive and once a game was developed it was necessary to pay license fees of several thousand dollars. Those licenses were tied to the approval of the company. However, today, the Android store is free, and the Apple store costs $99 per year, which allows new developers to distribute as many games as they can create and to maintain access to an enormous market.

This transformation of online stores represents a paradigm shift in that young developers can distribute their games and, if they are successful, form their own companies instead of waiting to be hired by an established company in the industry. To convert these experiences into a business model, Citilab needs to develop new learning experiences on the techniques of market positioning and promotion. Indeed, very important areas of video game industry operations remain to be explored.

SUMMARY OF FINDINGS

People can become media citizens if they find an appropriate innovation environment that favors their involvement as generators of content and technology. In contrast, people can be passive consumers of mass media content and/or active co-designers of user-generated content, applications and services if such an innovation environment is not available to them. Methodologies consuming resources, such as live streaming and interactive actions, have significant potential in user-generated content and user-generated applications and services, while the old way of media production is costly in terms of time for post-production.

Co-design is a key factor of success and it is important to establish methodologies and protocols to enable user-driven activity. Cultural and sports facilities do not have the technical infrastructures to provide live streaming and interactive live online experiences, even when these infrastructures are basic. Training linked to a specific goal is a motivational motor. 'Turn your passion into your profession' is a motivational idea that arose from the Social Media Lab's past innovative practices. This has been the key for successful citizen engagement in innovation projects at Citilab. Sports clubs and cultural institutions start to care about digital life, but it takes effort to change their vertical control-oriented mentalities toward a more horizontal digital culture. More actions are needed to sustain those practices within these communities.

Closing our analysis, we can summarize that citizen use of media is changing fast. This is an unstoppable change process that is transforming many aspects of media production, distribution and consumption. Beyond that, citizens' activity on the Internet has changed the understanding of it not only as a new medium but also as a new space for doing and sharing. The knowledge society must enable a new territory and a new culture. Transformations have to be accompanied by policies that provide countries with new universal social systems to provide guidance in building a competitive Europe that has a clear understanding of this new logic. The power of the digital culture is going to force media stakeholders to adapt its practices and operators and this is radically transforming the media context of production, from its technological aspects to its aesthetics.

In this battlefield of progress, media conglomerates and operators have lost the total domination of their audiences, and now they need to learn how to interact with new kinds of actors: communities of fans who are able to articulate a collective intelligence as a new productive force. Social networks, utilization of mobile and social media, and the capacity to become multimedia producers are the tools that change the system.

Future Research Areas and Limitations

Every study has its limitations. Our multiple case study analysis is limited to a restricted time period in one living lab in Spain. This study proposes that passion is a key for successful engagement, and transformation into digital culture enables a greater user engagement in living labs. This is consistent with Leminen et al. (2012), who argued that passion is one of the most crucial elements affecting the outcome of innovation in living labs. It is vital to further analyze versatile forms and types of co-creative situations that support greater user engagement. According to Leminen et al. (2014) different user roles represent different degrees of creativity. In particular, types of co-creative actors, different and multiple actors' roles in co-creating, passion for innovation, and the degree of technology support deserve closer attention in future research facilitating successful implementation of living lab design.

NOTES

1. Mapa.
2. http://www.youtube.com/watch?v=IgGD8pWFX-c.
3. Lubsen, A. (2010). Citilab Little Handbook, available at: http://issuu.com/astridlubsen/docs/2010_06_06_citilab_little_handbook_versi_n_digital.
4. Definition of the problem to solve, research on the field, ideation, prototype, choose, implement, learn.
5. http://www.citilabpro.eu/cursvideojocs/esp/index.html.
6. http://www.citilabpro.eu/cursvideojocs/esp/index.html.
7. www.tetravol.com.

REFERENCES

Almirall, E. and Casadesus-Masanell, R. (2010), 'Open versus closed innovation: A model of discovery and divergence', *Academy of Management Review*, 35(1), 27–47.

Almirall, E. and Wareham, J. (2008), 'Living labs and open innovation: Roles and applicability', *The Electronic Journal for Virtual Organizations and Networks*, 10, 21–6.

Arvidsson, A. (2008), 'The ethical economy of customer coproduction', *Journal of Macromarketing*, 28(4), 326–38.

Bonaccorsi, A., Giannangeli, S. and Rossi, C. (2006), 'Entry strategies under competing standards: Hybrid business models in the open source software industry', *Management Science*, 53(7), 1085–98.

Chesbrough, H. (2003), 'The era of open innovation', *MIT Sloan Management Review*, 44(3), 35–41.

Colobrans, J. (2010), 'A little more about understanding living labs', European Living Labs Summer School Collaborative Innovation through Living Labs, 25–27 August, Cité des Sciences, Paris, France. Retrieved from: http://www.ictusagelab.fr/ecoleLL/sites/default/files/Colobrans_Summer%20school%202010_Understanding%20living%20labs_en_1.pdf.

Edvarsson, B., Gustafsson, A., Kristensson, P. and Witell, L. (2010), 'Service innovation and customer co-development', in Maglio, P.P., Kielieszewski, C.A. and Spohrer, J.C. (eds), *Handbook of Service Science – Service Science: Research and Innovations in the Service Economy*, New York: Springer, pp. 561–77.

Feller, J. and Fitzgerald, B. (2002), *Understanding Open Source Software Development*, London: Addison-Wesley.

Heath, C. and Heath, D. (2010), *Switch: How to Change Things When Change Is Hard*, New York: Broadway Books.

Jeppesen, L.B. and Molin, M.J. (2003), 'Consumers as co-developers: Learning and innovation outside the firm', *Technology Analysis and Strategic Management*, 15(3), 363–83.

Kao, J. (1997), *Jamming: The Art and Discipline of Corporate Creativity*, New York: HarperCollins Publishers.

Kusiak, A. (2007), 'Innovation: the living laboratory perspective', *Computer-Aided Design and Applications*, 4(6), 863–76.

Leminen, S., Westerlund, M. and Nyström, A.G. (2014a), 'On becoming creative consumers – User roles in living labs networks', *Int. J. Technology Marketing*, 9(1), 33–52.

Leminen, S., Westerlund, M. and Kortelainen, M. (2012), 'A recipe for innovation through Living Lab networks', paper presented at the XXIII ISPIM Conference, Barcelona, Spain, 17–20 June.

Paulson, J.W., Succi, G. and Eberlein, A. (2004), 'An empirical study of open-source and closed-source software products', *IEEE Transactions on Software Engineering*, 30(4), 246–56.

Serra, A. (2001), 'Proposta del Centre-Museu-Taller', C@t Cataluny@Internet, Un forum per a la societal del coneixement a Catalunya, 12 September, in Catalan.

Toffler, A. (1980), *The Third Wave: The Classic Study of Tomorrow*, New York: Bantam Press.

von Hippel, E. (2005), *Democratizing Innovation*, Cambridge, MA: The MIT Press.
Wenger, E. (2000), 'Communities of practice and social learning systems',
   Organization, 7(2), 225–46.
Zwick, D., Bonsu, S.K. and Darmody, A. (2008), 'Putting consumers to work:
   "co-creation" and the new marketing govern-mentality', *Journal of Consumer
   Culture*, 8(2), 163–96.

Index